Colorado's
Best Wildflower Hikes
VOLUME 2: The High Country

TEXT BY
PAMELA IRWIN

PHOTOGRAPHY BY
DAVID IRWIN

WESTCLIFFE PUBLISHERS

Dedication

To Those Who Quest

To our grandchildren

in hopes they will

quest for beauty

throughout their lives.

એ૭

A SPECIAL TRIBUTE TO MOTHER NATURE

Beckwith Pass

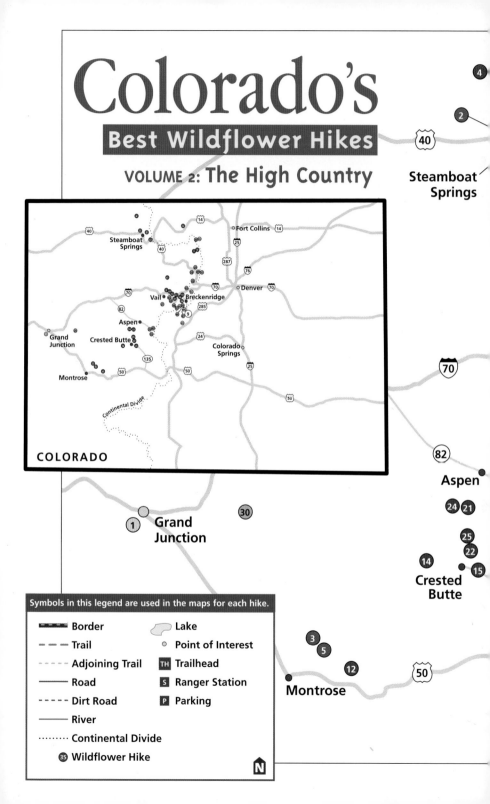

Colorado's
Best Wildflower Hikes
VOLUME 2: The High Country

COLORADO

Symbols in this legend are used in the maps for each hike.

- ▬▬▬ Border
- – – – Trail
- – – – – Adjoining Trail
- —— Road
- - - - - Dirt Road
- —— River
- ·········· Continental Divide
- 35 Wildflower Hike
- Lake
- ○ Point of Interest
- TH Trailhead
- S Ranger Station
- P Parking

N

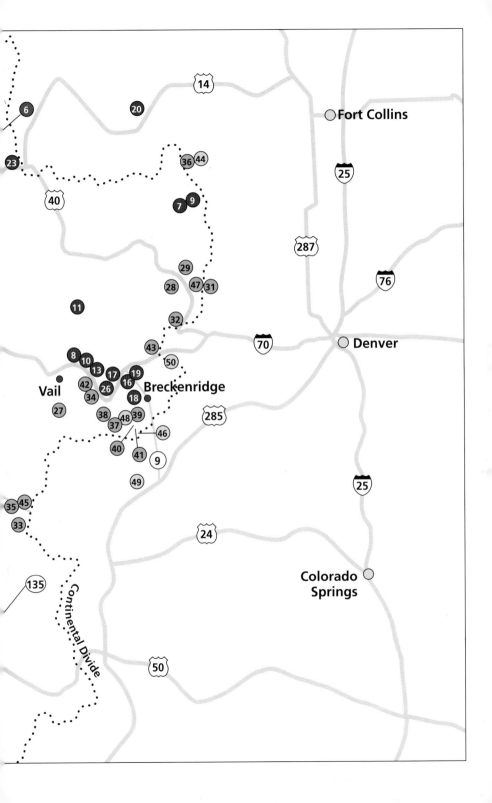

Table of Contents

Wildflower Profiles
(arranged alphabetically)

Introduction

Residents and visitors of Colorado are drawn to the state's backbone—the Rocky Mountains. Colorado embraces about three-quarters of all the land in the continental U.S. above 10,000 feet. Additionally, about forty-percent of Colorado's 104,247 square miles are comprised of public lands, offering a lot of room for roaming. The land above treeline houses approximately 300 different species of blooming plants, and over 2,300 different plants bloom within the life zones of the Centennial State.

Enthusiasm for things floral is widespread here, where wildflowers leap from the soil as soon as the snow melts and persist until, once again, the earth rests under snow. It was natural that a high-country sequel to *Colorado's Best Wildflower Hikes: The Front Range* should follow so quickly.

This volume, *Colorado's Best Wildflower Hikes Volume 2: The High Country,* covers both the high country and the western slope. All 50 hikes are designed for day destinations, and most suit all hiking abilities (although some are more appropriate for the moderately experienced hiker). The rating is a general guide only, based on steepness, elevation, ruggedness, and length of an individual trail.

While nearly all trails in Colorado have wildflowers along them, some are far more endowed than others. It is the purpose of this book to offer wildflower aficionados, or those who might someday be, choices. Some trails are highly floristic, containing a large number of different species; others are marvelously florescent in color and bloom. In this volume, nine hikes qualify for "century" status, which means that there are one hundred or more wild-flower species along the trail during the peak bloom period.

This guidebook offers maps and directions on how to experience both the full bloom season and peak bloom of each trail, as well as full-color photographs of each specific area. For those who wish to delve deeper into the realm of flora, there are "Wildflower Profile" sidebars accompanied by detailed photos, along with the Latin name.

A jaunt during peak season bloom will be gratifying and even astonish-ing. Coupled with inspiring scenery, the experience of Colorado's wildflowers represents the best of the state's natural beauty. As in the first volume, trails are arranged according to elevation to help you know where to take early-season treks and where to head as the snow recedes. Trails are listed according to life

Missouri Lakes

zone—but remember, nature doesn't always follow the life zone boundaries we set. Some plants grow in environments that prove an astonishing ability to adapt.

Colorado life zones and their approximate elevation ranges:

PLAINS: up to 6,000 feet
FOOTHILLS: 6,000 to 8,000 feet
MONTANE: 8,000 to 10,000 feet
SUBALPINE: 10,000 to 11,500 feet
ALPINE: 11,500 feet and above

Generally, plants in the lower elevations bloom earlier than those in the higher areas. Environmental factors that affect bloom season include slope, pockets of relative warmth, snowpack, and weather, especially drought, wind, heat, and cold. Lifespans of different flowers also vary tremendously. Flowers are fickle—a fact that challenges and inspires wildflower enthusiasts. Expect the unexpected.

High-country travel requires thoughtful and careful preparation. Books abound on the basics of high-country hiking—briefly stated, be sure to carry sufficient water, maps, a compass, and a whistle. Wear weatherproof outerwear, sturdy boots, and a hat to block the sun. Don't forget sunscreen, and be prepared for sudden changes in the weather. When above treeline, always be on the lookout for afternoon thunderstorms, which can build quickly.

That said, stow your gear in a pack along with your *Colorado's Best Wildflower Hikes* guides and come experience the wonderful world of wildflower viewing. What better way to spend a day than an adventure into the high country to see Colorado's most alluring wildflowers? Walking these pathways is a marvelous way to not only discover but help protect our valuable flora. As we learn more about our beautiful natural environment, we help others to do so as well.

— PAM IRWIN

We conserve what we love
We love what we know
We know what we are taught.
— Baba Dioum, Senegal

Mohawk Lake area

*Wildflower
Hike*

1

No Thoroughfare Canyon
(Colorado National Monument)

Wildflower alert: June begins with colorful cacti ranging from yellow, red, and peach to rich magenta.

Watch for colorful collared lizards along this trail that follows dramatic sandstone cliffs.

SOME OF COLORADO'S most spectacular colors can be found in the amazing land of carved sandstone just outside of Grand Junction. Colorado National Monument is a shining example of fantastically-sculpted, colossal geology, full of color, texture, shape, and the diversity of wildflowers that dwell there.

Just inside the Grand Junction or east entrance of Colorado National Monument is an easy hike from the north trailhead which offers dramatic

Trail Rating	easy
Trail Length	3.0 miles out and back
Location	Colorado National Monument/Grand Junction
Elevation	5,000 to 5,100 feet
Bloom Season	late May to early June
Peak Bloom	first of June
Directions	From I-70, follow signs through Grand Junction to the east entrance of Colorado National Monument (approximately 4 miles to the entrance on Monument Road). Fee required.

springtime blooms of cacti. No Thoroughfare Canyon travels a mile or so up a generally level drainage leading to a pour-over pool, and beyond to a 100-foot-high intermittent waterfall. Brilliantly-hued collared lizards—also in their springtime prime—scamper in the sand along the way. Less attractive but more prevalent are the biting gnats or "no-see-ums" often near the trailhead. The trick is to keep moving or use insect repellent.

Parking is adequate at the trailhead. Check the visitor center for more information about the area.

Typically, the first week of June in a normal year—Colorado weather is a bit capricious—marches out brilliant cactus flowers on the No Thoroughfare Canyon Trail. The trail itself putters along, sometimes defined and other times only a trace. But following the creek bed, whether dry or trickling, is not a problem.

Broad as it leaves the south end of the parking area, the trail immediately encounters **golden aster**. In the same area, numerous yellow-gold **cream tips** display ray-less heads and protruding disk florets. This particular species is a Western Slope resident.

At the right time in the bloom season, technicolor cacti begin not far from the trailhead. The huge blossoms of **prickly pear cactus**, silky and hot magenta, advertise their availability to pollinators. Myriad pollen-covered stamens, all nestled deep in the silky petals, are tactile reactive—if you stop to tickle their bases, they bend inward like the tentacles of a sea anemone in a tide pool.

Nearby, New Mexican **prickly pear cactus**, this one sporting long brown-tipped spines and satiny yellow blooms, competes for passing pollinators.

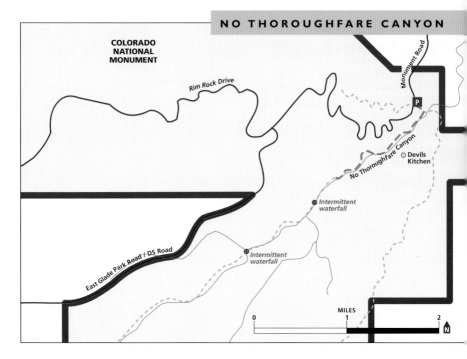

NO THOROUGHFARE CANYON

COLORADO NATIONAL MONUMENT

Rim Rock Drive

Monument Road

P

No Thoroughfare Canyon

Devils Kitchen

Intermittent waterfall

East Glade Park Road / DS Road

Intermittent waterfall

MILES
0   1   2

N

Though individual flowers are not long-lasting, numerous buds opening in sequence make fertilization more likely. The resulting reddish-purple fruits (edible and tasty but tricky to eat) are called tunas.

In the same vicinity, little tufted clumps of **Easter daisy** or **Townsendia**, virtually covered with white open-faced flowers, cling to the arid earth. **Puccoon's** yellow trumpets and a small **gaillardia** or **blanketflower** appear sporadically. A very early-blooming **blue penstemon** adds an unexpectedly cool color to the scene.

A visit when cacti are flowering makes slow going for wildflower lovers. The wide trail descends easily, passing more of the spiny plants' glorious blossoms, with colors from shell pink to blistering magenta, green-tinged yellow to almost apricot. Utah juniper dot the desert-like landscape. Behind these drought-resistant trees rise the colorfully banded formations of Colorado National Monument.

You'll pass the point where the Old Gordon Trail veers off to the left from No Thoroughfare Trail and then continue through sagebrush and **three-leaf sumac** bushes as the ground becomes sandy underfoot. Take note that sagebrush can harbor ticks, especially in early spring. Beautifully sculpted by wind and water, the sandstone, when in a decomposed state, makes a fine soil for **white evening primrose** and **copper mallow**, both with deeply cut leaves. The dark peach-blush color of the mallow petals match some of the bands in the slickrock beyond.

Off to the left is the gaping mouth of Devil's Kitchen, ready to swallow any hikers that venture up that spur. No Thoroughfare heads up a dry creek bed through more **white evening primroses**. Wilted blooms are an aging pink.

Fresh and brilliant scarcely begins to describe the incandescent scarlet chalices of **claret cup cactus**. Less notable in color is yellow **bladderpod**, the compact racemes rising from tidy gray rosettes. Each 4-petaled cruciform flower matures into inflated double pods, which explains the common name.

While hiking up the canyon on a trail that is sometimes hard to discern, watch for the yellow-headed collared lizard. Spring is mating season, and this reptile with its signature black neck stripes pumps up its yellow, orange, green, and turquoise pigments. Coloration varies with the individual animal, even to robin's egg blue and touches of red.

Walking in the stony-wash amidst stick-like Mormon tea allows sightings of **golden aster**, **cream tips**, and an occasional **penstemon**. With battlements of stone rising in the distance, **tufted evening primrose** unfolds its wide, white flowers as the day is done. Also in white, note the wonderfully fragrant starry flowers of **carpet phlox**.

Just up the way, nestled by a stream bed boulder, a spiny clump of spellbinding **claret cup cactus** sings its pollination song. Within yards of this scarlet beauty, quiet gray mats of **cushion buckwheat** send up bare stems topped with ivory-umbelled heads. It may have been called **silver plant** because of its platinum leaves, but it was the belief of early miners that **cushion buckwheat** was an indicator of silver ore. Like many buckwheats, these change to a warmer, darker shade with maturity.

PRICKLY PEAR CACTUS
Opuntia phaeacantha

There are a number of prickly pear species in Colorado National Monument. This one, with brown-tipped long spines (up to 2.5 inches) carries common names, such as purple-fruited or New Mexican prickly pear. Its three-inch silky flowers tend to be yellow and when pollinated become plump fruits that ripen a rosy-purple. The large, green pads modify to a bluish-green, often suffused with a bit of purple, in winter. The species Latin *phaeacantha* means brown-spined.

As the stream bed narrows, on-again, off-again water may start seeping at this time of year. On the banks, look for **wild rose** in perfect pink and **orchid** or **one-sided penstemon**, with tubes of a particularly luminous lilac.

The waterway trickles between rising walls of dark rough outcrops and the trail picks up the character of the rock as it rises up a small embankment. Ancient and twisted, Utah junipers find a root-hold on slopes where bird song and butterflies add to hikers' enjoyment.

Again, sand appears underfoot in the vicinity of early blooming **locoweed**, its furry pods now in evidence. As the trail winds past more beacons of magenta **prickly pear**, note the plant's spines and waxy green pads: survival insurance.

To the south, a side canyon materializes and No Thoroughfare Canyon continues, passing **scarlet gilia**, **blanket flower**, and at a sandy cut bank, rosy-purple **northern sweetvetch**. Another common name, **chainpod**, makes perfect sense upon examining the linkage of the seedpods.

PRICKLY PEAR
Opuntia species

The genus *Opuntia* is a notorious hybridizer. While this plain-spined prickly pear cactus often has yellow flowers, it is those with vivid magenta blossoms that are showstoppers.

At a stride-wide creek crossing, detour left to the base of a crumbling sandstone wall and search for fire engine red **desert paintbrush**, very compact compared to **narrowleaf paintbrush**. Fond of sandy places, this latter plant adds bits of scarlet bract and chartreuse flower along the creek.

Continuing up a rocky segment next to the now-flowing creek, the trail becomes more tenuous. Narrowing further, the canyon's inner bastions are quite rugged. Beyond these crude outcroppings are glimpses of the higher, smooth sandstone escarpments.

As you wend up the canyon, listen for the sound of falling water—in season. A pool with winsome falls spilling off a shelf of eon-smoothed sandstone awaits discovery. This is a good place to stop under a cottonwood tree and watch water in motion. The olive green, algae-rich pool supports a mob of tadpoles and you might catch a glimpse of a green-as-grass adult frog.

While this is the turnaround point for this book's description, the trail climbs sharply above the tranquil pool to access another waterfall (in season) that has a drop of 100 feet.

This first mile or so of No Thoroughfare Canyon is a sight to behold when the cacti are in bloom. The charming waterfall at the turnaround point makes the trail very appealing, as do the rainbow-hued collared lizards. Walking here early in the season offers great rewards without much effort.

CLARET CUP CACTUS
Echinocereus triglochidiatus

Far less common than the prickly pear, showy claret cup cactus is considered endangered. Other names are king's cup, strawberry, and mound cactus. Spiny clumps, often growing in mounds by rocks, produce 2 1/2 inch goblet-shaped scarlet flowers lasting but 2 or 3 days. The green stems produce areoles, along vertical ribs, with a central spine surrounded by shorter ones. The short common name makes up for the long Latin nomenclature. The prickly nature of claret cup is taken from the Greek *echinos,* meaning "hedgehog."

Mad Creek/Red Dirt

Wildflower Alert: This delightful path is an early-blooming "century" trail in the foothills zone.

This meandering trail offers a pleasant early-season jaunt into a beautiful canyon just outside of Steamboat Springs.

ONE OF THE EARLY SEASON TRAILS out of Steamboat Springs also happens to be a "century" wildflower hike. Approximately 100 species may be spotted along Mad Creek Loop. Add to that achievement, habitat diversity, pleasant scenery, and an easygoing route, and the loop is a great way to kick off the wildflower hiking season.

The Mad Creek/Swamp Park segment of the loop angles up an exposed hillside before reaching more verdant locales, where it takes a left and climbs

Trail Rating	easy to moderate (includes 1.2 miles along the shoulder of blacktopped Elk River Road)
Trail Length	3.4 mile loop
Location	Steamboat Springs
Elevation	6,740 to 7,640 feet
Bloom Season	June to August
Peak Bloom	mid-June to mid-July
Directions	Take US 40 west from Steamboat Springs for approximately 2 miles. Turn right onto County Road 129. Then take Elk River Road for 5.7 miles to trailhead on the right.

up to connect with Red Dirt Trail. Descending along a cool north slope before wrapping around to a south exposure once more, the loop drops to a trailhead adjacent to Elk River Road. From there, it is 1.2 miles of shoulder-walking alongside pavement.

Parking at the Mad Creek trailhead is generous within a fenced enclosure.

A trailhead kiosk notes that the trail heads up Forest Service Trail 1100 and to Mad Creek Guard Station at Swamp Park.

The trail slants up through **wild rose**, **sticky geranium**, and **chokecherry**. Imported **clovers,** exuding sweetness to attract butterflies, are often seen. Banks of bare soil provide a niche for hundreds of showy **tufted evening primroses** illuminated by immense, white-notched petals and wonderful fragrance. Morning is the best time to catch the exhibition. Nearby **Rocky Mountain penstemon** sends up intense blue-purple wands of tubular flowers.

Mad Creek continues to roar as the canyon narrows. **Dogbane** grows near a jutting outcrop. High above the creek, the leveling road-wide track comes into the Douglas fir community where **false Solomon's seal** basks in the shade. After a slight rise you'll see the eye-catching combination of vibrant pink **sticky geranium** and clear golden-yellow **heartleaf arnica**. Softer in color and just up the way are **antelope brush** and **dusty maiden**.

The roadbed balances on a dry-stack stone wall clinging to a steep slope, high above rushing water. In the open, **creamy buckwheat** accompanies pink **tiny trumpets** and tall **lavender fleabane**. On this warm south-facing slope, Douglas fir shade welcomes again. Look for the glossy leaves of **mountain balm** close at hand. Clouds of creamy flowers give it another name: **snowbrush**.

Scrub oak oversees the forming fruit of **serviceberry** as the trail resumes its open character and curves up to find **lupine** and **scorpion weed**. Where a mountain appears in the background, be on the spy for **giant hyssop**, a tall mint with dusky-pink conical heads. Clumps of **mule's ears**, with sunflower heads and unmistakable leaves shaped like the ears of its namesake, grow in the vicinity. Similar in flower, but very different in stature, **aspen sunflowers** stand tall and straight by the trail.

Quaking aspens signal an old log building up ahead. Almost flat now, the pathway travels through a moist spot anchored by a buck-and-rail fence. The right side nurtures **mule's ears**, **geranium**, and **wild onion**. On the left, a seep conceals long-stemmed **woodland star**, each flower a small white flare. This winsome member of the saxifrage family and **beauty cinquefoil** lead up to a gate.

Upland Yellow Violet
Viola praemorsa subspecies major

Also called canary violet, these fetching flowers are as pure a yellow as the proverbial feathered singer. Lacking the purplish-tinge on the petal reverses that mark many yellow violet species, upland violet bears dark nectar guides in its throat. It is typically found in mesic areas (places of balanced light and soil moisture). All violets are edible; in fact, they are good sources of vitamins A and C.

Yellow cousins include Nuttall's or yellow prairie violet *Viola nuttallii* and goosefoot violet *Viola purpurea*. Both tend to display purplish petal reverses. A blue cousin, mountain blue or hooked violet *Viola adunca*, is also found in the region.

Past the gate, the murmuring river, content now in its golden-granite bed, is left behind in a sagebrush flat. The trail is sprinkled with more **wild onion** (bulblets replace some of the flowers, enhancing reproduction) and towering behind it, **false hellebore**.

A sign indicates a turn to the left to continue the loop on Saddle Trail 1140. Following the change of direction, check for more **woodland stars** in the protection of **mountain snowberry** bushes. The quaking aspen understory yields thick grasses punctuated by **lupine** and an occasional **camissonia**. This member of the evening primrose clan nestles smooth-leaved rosettes deep in the grasses: its 4-petaled yellow flowers lie tucked within the rosette as if they fell into it rather than grew from it.

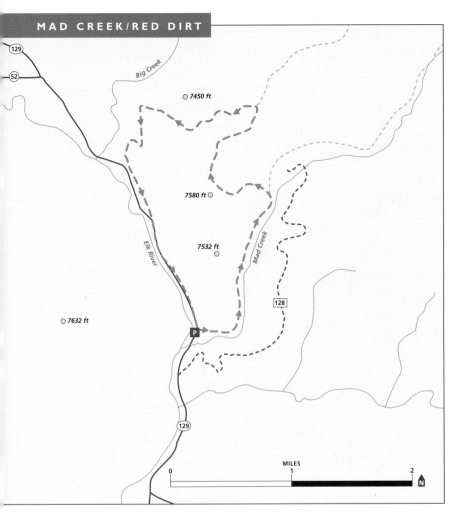

MAD CREEK/RED DIRT

129
52

Big Creek

○ 7450 ft

7580 ft ○

Elk River

7532 ft
○

Mad Creek

128

○ 7632 ft

P

129

MILES
0   1   2
N

Ascending gently, Saddle Trail unveils tall **western valerian**—its tiny white flowers with their expressive stamens bloom early. **Lupine** and **geranium** are particularly intense in pigment among stunted aspens.

The trail, at times a bit damp and other times thistle-bound, follows a wide-slash cut through the woods. Seeps are good places to watch "puddling" butterflies taking advantage of moisture and minerals. In the mud, elk tracks may be evident. Like thistles, alien **hound's tongue**, its port-wine flowers reminiscent of forget-me-nots, favors disturbed soil.

You'll need to trek single-file through the jungle-like undergrowth tangled with **white peavine**. Bracken fern tries to hide huge slash piles. A wide view of the landscape up the Mad Creek Valley and over to Rocky Peak opens in scrub oak.

A number of marked stakes on the trail lead back into aspen as the trail rises, levels, then descends. Here, lovely **blue columbine** is a welcome sight. With down-sized foliage similar to the columbine's, **meadow rue** or **false columbine** grows along the path for comparison. **Meadow rue** lacks showy flowers.

With eyes full of lush vegetation highlighted by **tall chiming bells**, **blue columbine**, and **white geranium**, the hiker approaches a trail junction. The loop turns left on Red Dirt Trail 1171. On a north slope now, the trail descends briefly into conifer forest before dappled aspen shadows pamper heavenly scented **wild rose**. At this point, watch for the clear yellow blooms of **upland** or **canary violet**.

Leaving the conifers behind, the lavender spheres of **ballhead waterleaf** may appear. Look also for **western blue clematis** with its graceful splayed bells and later in the season, plumed seedheads. Damp sites may turn up **cow parsnip**, **larkspur**, **valerian**, and more **tall chiming bells**. In the distance rises a majestic peak. A drier habitat supports **sugarbowls**, **mule's ears**, and **hound's tongue**.

As you head down down the trail, Elk River Valley comes into view. The trail then drops to a small meadow at the bottom of a hill, setting the scene for the downstream sighting of exquisite **shooting stars**, **wild onion**, and **homely buttercup** growing near a tiny rivulet. This beguiling cornucopia of color offers a visual feast before evergreens take over.

In the deep shade, search on the upper side of the trail for the white-veined leaves of **rattlesnake**

GIANT HYSSOP
Agastache urticifolia

Anywhere from one- to four-feet tall, this member of the mint family may also be known as nettleleaf horsemint or nettle-leaved giant hyssop. Each mauve terminal floral spike pops out pale flowers amid colorful bracts. Fragrant giant hyssop colonizes itself by its creeping roots and is much beloved by bees. Native Americans ate the seeds both raw and roasted, brewing the leaves for tea which tastes like anise. Cousins include the beebalm *Monarda fistulosa v. menthifolia* and white Monarda *Monarda pecinata*.

plantain orchid. Its racemes of flowers are not particularly showy, but it is one of the few orchids that like drier forest conditions. Preferring a tad more moisture is the pretty pink **Calypso orchid**, which is worth watching for. Early-season hikers along here might expect **glacier lilies** and **pasque-flowers** in bloom.

A muddy patch, where **thimbleberry** flanks the trail, begins an undulating section where the **wild rose** is exceptionally deep-pink and the **blue columbine** exceptionally large. Scrub oak and river-valley vistas welcome hikers back to a south exposure.

The trail drops at a steeper gradient now, passing two members of the sunflower family, **arrowleaf balsamroot** with its felted gray-green, heart-shaped leaves, and **mule's ears** with its shiny-green lance-shaped ones. Also find **long-leaved phlox** and **narrow-leaved paintbrush**. The trail turns to red dirt as it pulls even with Elk River Road. 1.2 miles of walking south on the shoulder of this paved road returns hikers to the Mad Creek trailhead parking area.

With names like Mad Creek, Swamp Park, Saddle, and Red Dirt, it comes as no surprise how diverse this loop trail is. And the "century" designation reflects the floristic scene. This interesting loop should be high up on a late spring or an early summer list for wildflower aficionados in the Steamboat Springs area.

Wildflower Hike

3

North Vista
(Black Canyon of the Gunnison National Monument)

Wildflower Alert: Wildflower gardens pave the way to a stunning viewpoint looking 2,000 feet into the Black Canyon of the Gunnison.

Aptly named Exclamation Point is your goal on this not-too-strenuous jeweled path.

Trail Rating	easy
Trail Length	3.0 miles out and back
Location	Black Canyon of the Gunnison National Monument North Rim/Crawford/Delta
Elevation	7,680 to 7,702 feet
Bloom Season	late May through July
Peak Bloom	June
Directions	Take State Route 92 east for approximately 20 miles. From Delta to Hotchkiss, bear right to continue on 92 for another 11 miles to Crawford. Go south to Crawford Lake State Park (passing the lake). Turn right onto North Rim Road. Follow the signs to Black Canyon of the Gunnison National Monument. Turn right at the rim junction to the North Rim ranger station. Park there for the trailhead.

IT HAS TAKEN TWO MILLION YEARS of relentless toil for the Gunnison River to carve some 2,000 vertical feet of resistant schist and gneiss. The awesome result is the Black Canyon of the Gunnison. Twelve miles of this naturally-sculpted gorge were designated a national monument in 1933. While the south rim is the most popular destination, a visit to the north rim offers more solitude. The first week of June is a great time to experience this along North Vista Trail.

The trail follows the rim a fair distance from the chasm's edge along the one-and-a-half-mile jaunt out to aptly named Exclamation Point. Once there, the overlook allows an unfettered heart-stopping view almost 2,000 feet down to the roaring Gunnison River, bound by an incredibly rugged dark gorge. This easy trek is characterized by approximately four-dozen varieties of wildflowers.

Adequate parking is located in front of the ranger cottage near the signed trailhead.

West of the ranger cottage, the trailhead leads immediately through a dozen different kinds of wildflowers such as **arrowleaf balsamroot**, **longleaf phlox**, **milkvetch**, and **scarlet gilia**, sometimes referred to imaginatively as **skyrocket**. Festooned with fresh-white petaled blossoms centered with 20 enthusiastic stamens, **serviceberry** bushes reach over eight feet high. **Lupine** and **chiming bells** grow all around.

While drifting down a few gentle steps through scrub oak, the trail encounters **white peavine** and continues into an area of silvery sagebrush, where yellow **wallflower** and white **milkvetch**

LONGLEAF PHLOX
Phlox longifolia

Generally found in xeric (requiring only a small amount of moisture) habitats, perky longleaf phlox, like other phloxes, is sweet-smelling. Five bright pink, flared petals (sometimes white or lavender) fuse into a tube centered by an "eye." In Greek, *phlox* means "flame," and *longifolia* means "long-leaved," making the Latin scientific name coherent for the layman. Cousins are Rocky Mountain phlox *Phlox multiflora,* found at lower elevations, and alpine phlox *Phlox condensata,* which is a tundra star.

Native Americans made medicinal tea from phlox to treat anemia. Livestock and wildlife forage on longleaf phlox.

are accented by rich red **desert paintbrush**. A low-growing, refined **fleabane daisy** or *erigeron* with cool pink buds leads up to a mesh gate and into a garden of **arrowleaf balsamroot**, **early larkspur**, and an abundance of **lupine**. **Longleaf phlox**, in soft pink, adds cheerful touches.

Following scrub oak, the trail continues into the next "garden," loaded with the knockout combination of purple **lupine** and **larkspur**, red **gilia** and **paintbrush**, tempered by gray-green sage and an occasional piñon pine. With all this beauty at your feet, look up and to the west to a stone tapestry. This is the famed Painted Wall, the highest cliff in Colorado at 2,200-plus feet. Lit by early morning light, the sheer wall with its signature intrusions of contrasting stone is a photographer's delight. Evening light, on the other hand, is best on the graduated series of channeled spires that can be seen to the east.

Continuing on, dwarf **yucca** claims some barren earth surrounded by **mountain mahogany**. Ponderosa pines start showing up and under them, **Fendler senecio**. **Mountain mahogany** dominates the next trail decline before scrub oak takes over. Here, as well as under neighboring ponderosa trees, watch for a mustard family member of medium-height—**thelypody**, with wraparound leaves and rosy-lilac flowers. A funny name to contemplate, it is derived from the Greek *thelys* meaning "woman" and *podium* meaning "foot." In the same area, look for yellow **bladderpod**, another member of the mustard clan. A family trait is four petals configured in a cross shape.

The voice of the Gunnison River can be heard laboring to carve the chasm deeper through the Black Canyon off to the left. Coming into a "P-J" (piñon-juniper) community, more **thelypody** stands out. Later in the season, **actinea** and **penstemon** bloom here.

The trail steps down on well-placed stones and then wanders through oak. A sign marked "overlook" indicates a left turn to reach Exclamation Point. Along the way, rocky ground manages to support low clumps of **actinea**, sometimes called **perky Sue**, a bright bit of saucy gold in the quiet forest. Scattered here and there are the red lights of **desert paintbrush**.

Remaining on the trail is extremely important because cryptogramic soil forms the heaved-appearing, black-encrusted dirt. Cryptogramic soil, essential to the ecosystem and incredibly slow at repairing any scars created by uninformed feet, is to be treated with respect.

At the head of a drainage, the trail crosses mudstone or siltstone before traveling over lichen-covered slickrock. On the left, two pieces of orange sandstone frame yet another glimpse into the mysterious gorge, deep, dark, and beautifully sinister.

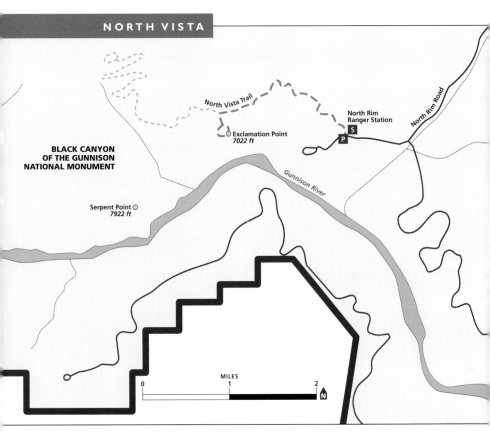

BLACK CANYON
OF THE GUNNISON
NATIONAL MONUMENT

North Vista Trail

Exclamation Point
7022 ft

North Rim
Ranger Station

S

P

North Rim Road

Gunnison River

Serpent Point
7922 ft

MILES

0   1   2

N

Another passage through **serviceberry** and scrub oak is lined with
arrowhead balsamroot, a long-used, multi-use food source of Native Americans.

The path becomes increasingly rocky as it approaches Exclamation Point.
Rugged chunks of rock sit on the edge of a sheer precipice that can be described
only as awesome. Nearly 2,000 feet below, squeezing between towering walls,
the green Gunnison River thunders westward down one of the sharpest river
gradients in the country. Jade rapids race downriver, dropping 180 feet in just
1/2 mile. This is not a place for rambunctious kids or folks prone to vertigo.

Just before you reach the point, if the time of year is right, the
sensational scarlet goblets of **claret cup cactus** may divert your attention
from the intriguing maw of Black Canyon.

The mystique of deep, dark Black Canyon of the Gunnison is never
more apparent than when standing on the north rim at Exclamation Point.
Add flowery passages and solitude, and you have the makings of one grand
trek. North Vista Trail to Exclamation Point is a prize winner.

Wildflower Hike
4

Tombstone Nature Loop
(Steamboat Lake State Park)

Wildflower Alert: This hike features a gentle loop trail with fairyslippers and phlox in early summer.

A pretty view of Steamboat Lake rewards the hiker on this gentle loop.

Trail Rating	easy
Trail Length	0.75 mile loop
Location	Steamboat Springs
Elevation	8,000 to 8,140 feet
Bloom Season	June to August
Peak Bloom	mid-June to mid-July
Directions	Take US 40 west from Steamboat Springs for approximately 2 miles. Turn right onto County Road 129. Take Elk River Road to Steamboat Lake State Park. Turn left at the visitor center to the Placer Cove Picnic Area trailhead. Be prepared to pay a fee.

SCENIC STEAMBOAT LAKE occupies 1,053 acres of broad valley in the shadows of Hahns Peak and Sand Mountain. Volcanic Hahns Peak, at 10,839 feet, was the locale of early mining activity for silver and gold. On the north boundary of Steamboat Lake State Park, the little town of Hahns Peak Village was founded in the 1870s. The expansive setting of the 1,550-acre state park showcases a great little loop called Tombstone Nature Trail on the north shore of the shimmering man-made lake.

Wrapping around a water-view hillock, the trail provides grand vistas, convenient benches, and about four-dozen wildflower species, including the exquisite Calypso orchid in mid-to-late June. The loop wanders through the forest, passing openings to arrive above the lake. A short spur leads to a tombstone. The main trail remains level, exposing more views of the water and distant landscape, before drifting down to a damp area and returning to the trailhead.

The trailhead parking area is shared by picnickers.

Begin exploring Steamboat Lake State Park at the handsome log visitor center, which is a great source of information. A brochure, with numbers corresponding to those along the nature trail, is available. The loop is best hiked clockwise, starting to the left.

Evergreens watch over the small meadow at the start of Tombstone Nature Trail loop where **homely buttercup** asks for a glance before fancier flowers show up. They arrive as **dwarf chiming bells** in blue, **shrubby cinquefoil** in yellow, and **sticky geranium** in pink.

At a post marked #2, a glorious view of shapely Hahns Peak frames the attractive visitor center. Plucky white-colored **mountain** or **wild candytuft** dot the meadow on the left, while on the right, sheltered by conifers, the charming **Calypso** or **fairyslipper orchid** puts in a pink appearance here and there.

The trail weaves past fallen logs where **prickly mountain currant** or **gooseberry** thrives. Its scallop-lobed, dusty salmon flowers show well, though the ensuing fruits are not very palatable. Nearby, **twinberry** droops pairs of soft gold tubes which develop into side-by-side black berries cupped by bright red bracts. These inky fruits are inedible.

The pathway rises a bit. Almost concealed by fast-growing grasses, **ball-head waterleaf** presents spheres of lilac trumpets tucked deep in its foliage, each trumpet fanning a shower of stamens.

Straight and slender lodgepole pines shelter an occasional dainty white burst of **woodland star**. Watch on the left for these members of the saxifrage family. Quaking aspens add a woodland facet to the landscape, and **white peavine**, some pink-tinged, wanders happily among them. Watch for **mountain blue** or **hooked** as well as **upland** or **canary violet** in clear yellow.

Reentering the woods, keep an eye out for the ephemeral but striking **Calypso orchid**. Near signpost #4, **lupine** frames a bench and **serviceberry** blooms on the slope down to the lake. The white blossoms will mature into blue-black fruits that are quite tasty. Native Americans taught incoming mountainmen how to make nutritious, long-lasting pemmican using the berries. The fruit was easy to come by; the bear fat that bound the concoction was more difficult.

A spur marked "Wheeler Tombstone" takes off to the right, and aspens shade the memorial commemorating a brother and sister whose parents homesteaded on 243 acres now covered by Steamboat Lake.

Back on the main trail, the path becomes a bit rocky. Descending now among evergreens, roots cross the path as it heads out to a point, accompanied by **tall pussytoes** and cool yellow **western paintbrush**. Out under open skies, the ground is spangled by the stars of **cushion phlox**. The lake dances in the summer sun, and beyond it rises 10,847-foot Sand Mountain. Previously called White Head Peak due to white quartzite deposits, Sand Mountain was mined by Utes for projectile points and tools.

CALYPSO ORCHID
Calypso bulbosa

Perhaps the name fairyslipper best describes the perfect Calypso orchid, although Venus' slipper sounds equally alluring. The overall loveliness of this orchid is delightful, but close up, Venus has a yellow mustache and purple freckles on her scooped petal lip. Bright pink sepals and petals arrange themselves into a gently scented blossom that defies written description. This precious beauty sits singly atop a fleshy four- to eight-inch stem, with a round leaf at the base.

The Calypso is endangered and deserves protection. Rarely does one of its many thousand minuscule seeds contained in a single mature capsule come to fruition. Easily damaged, often fatally, the plant is dependent on specific soil fungi. Spotting one is like seeing a living jewel. *Calypso*, meaning "concealment" in Greek, relates to the orchid's favorite habitat in damp, conifer shade.

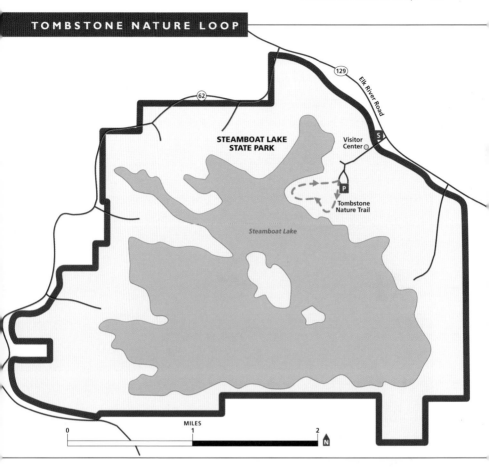

Leaving the main body of water, the trail, via log steps, descends toward Placer Cove. Covered by water now, the area once yielded a surface vein of gold ore which miners quickly extracted. Today, gold is found in the coin-sized blossoms sprinkled on **shrubby cinquefoil** here.

The trail flattens in view of the Placer Cove arm of the lake, revealing brilliant blue **dwarf chiming bells**, white **wild candytuft**, and **western valerian**.

Logs step the trail down to lake level. Footing is a little squishy through an area where **bistort** waves its long-blooming white head. The loop finishes with a flourish of starry **phlox** before evergreens return you to the trailhead.

Tombstone Nature Trail adds up to a delightful walk with scenic lake views and a variety of sweet wildflowers. Early morning and late evening puts the hike in its best light. Birdsong, spring-voiced frogs, and the possible sighting of a great blue heron sailing overhead are visitor bonuses.

Oak Flat Loop
*(Black Canyon of the Gunnison
National Monument)*

Wildflower Alert: Wildflowers collect along an intimate
look into the awesome Black Canyon of the Gunnison.

*This trail takes you through brightly colored hillsides
shadowed by dramatic cliffs.*

Trail Rating	moderate
Trail Length	2.0 mile loop
Location	Black Canyon of the Gunnison National Monument South Rim/Montrose
Elevation	8,160 to 7,800 feet
Bloom Season	late May to July
Peak Bloom	June
Directions	Take US 50 east for approximately 8 miles from Montrose, travel north on County Road 347 to the monument visitor center for access to the trailhead. Be prepared to pay a fee.

THE UTES were able to explain Black Canyon of the Gunnison in one appropriate word—*Tomichi,* which means "land of high cliffs and plentiful water." The word "breathtaking" should precede the word "land." Magnificent, stirring, stimulating, and stunning would work, too. Geology sometimes takes on magnificent qualities. While a monumental story in stone can be gleaned from many points on the south rim drive, Black Canyon of the Gunnison National Monument offers a loop trail that takes the hiker down to a more personal encounter with the mystic gorge. The wildflowers along Oak Flat Loop add an intimate quality.

Oak Flat Trail begins on the rim top at the national monument's handsome visitor center. The loop's undaunted topography takes in two miles of woods, wildflowers, an impressive river at work, and the sheer awesomeness of the Black Canyon. Descending for most of the way, the trail reaches a great heap of gargantuan boulders which allows hikers to perch and absorb the dynamic vista—2 million years in the making. The last trail segment zigzags steeply but quickly back up to complete the loop.

Ample parking is at the visitor center. Pets are not allowed on Oak Flat Trail.

Before your hike, consider stopping at the visitor center, which is well-stocked and offers a wealth of information. From the building's long veranda, head west down the steps to encounter a sign pointing the way to Oak Flat Loop. Though "Flat" in the name is an illusion, "Oak" is accurate: Scrub or Gambels oak (named for 1840s pioneer botanist, Bill Gambel) is evident everywhere as you begin walking. The best way to hike the loop is clockwise.

In addition to grasses in the scrub oak understory, **silvery lupine** and **showy** or **aspen daisy** turn up bushlike with cool purple flowers. The oak is also favored by **white peavine**. The relaxed foliage sports winged, keeled, and bannered blossoms early in the season.

A gravel path comes in from the east, while the loop heads right. Continuing to an open spot on the left exhibits **showy daisy** at its best. **Hoary aster** is budding for its mid-summer bloom. The narrow path introduces the soft, gray-green leaves of **arrowleaf balsamroot**, whose sunflower blooms generally light up in May. In the same vicinity is **narrow-leaved paintbrush** with pop-up green "toothpick" flowers cupped by striking red bracts. Also, look for snowy **northern bedstraw**. This was a favorite find of settlers searching for mattress stuffing. A lot of **ballhead sandwort**, with its tight clusters of white stars, appears as well.

Next, the slightly declining trail offers a peek of the Black Canyon. The trail passes **serviceberry** shrubs whose fruit were sought by Native Americans and mountainmen. The berries were especially esteemed for inclusion in pemmican—a fatty, but sustaining—crude version of a granola bar.

A rocky path arrives at a junction where the river-access route goes right, but heading left is the optimum way to travel Oak Flat Loop. This direction exposes a bit of **prickly pear** cactus and, when in bloom, this well-armed cactus unveils glorious blossoms of silky, pale yellow.

ARROWLEAF BALSAMROOT
Balsamorhiza sagittata

Up to two feet tall, balsamroot's clumps of gray-green leaves produce huge 4-5 inch sunflower-like blooms. The basal leaves are covered with soft hairs, giving the aromatic foliage a felted appearance. With a lifespan of a half century, balsamroot clumps emerge from a stout taproot and don't flower until they are about five years of age. A cousin is mule's ears *Wyethia amplexicaulis.*

Native Americans discovered many uses for balsamroot: eating the young leaves and peeled stems, roasting the root and seeds, preparing a root remedy for insect bites and rheumatism, and making cough syrup from the sap. This sandy soil lover also provides forage for deer, elk, and sheep.

A few steps over some bedrock, a spiny clump of incredibly beautiful **claret cup cactus**—an endangered species—emerges. The collection of these luminescent, scarlet goblets is a sight to behold when blooming in May or perhaps early June. **Pink pussytoes** and the up-facing rosy inflorescence of **sagebrush onion** may be nearby.

Before the trail ascends a bit, look left in a vernal damp spot for an early-blooming pocket of **onions**. **Lupine** paves the way to brighter **Rocky Mountain penstemon**: the tubes are dark blue suffused with violet in each throat.

Off to the right, a yawning chasm catches the ear as well as the eye, and the deep-voiced river announces its intentions to continue its eternal vocation—canyon carving, which has taken about 2 million years of relentless work so far.

The steep north slope makes Douglas fir happy, and they in turn provide shelter for **heartleaf arnica**, **tall pussytoes**, **purple daisies**, and happy-go-lucky **American vetch**.

A bit farther along the path, a "social" spur offers a postcard-perfect

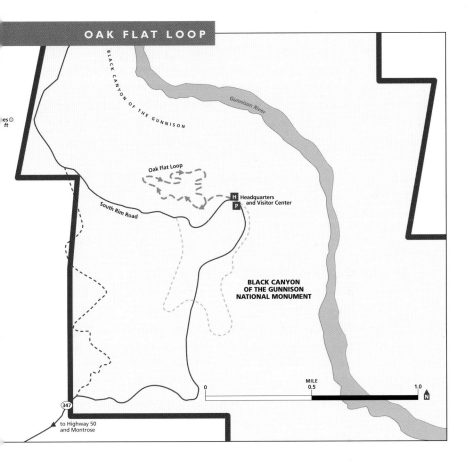

view of the gorge and the Gunnison River. Almost 2,000 vertical feet separate canyon rim from river bottom. Ranks of colossal tarnished cliffs and pinnacles reveal volcanic origins and ongoing erosion.

Cut into the steep slope, the scenic trail curves around to give hikers even more intimate views west into this geologic wonder. Fragrant **wild rose** is in the foreground. Once again the welcome shade of Douglas fir provides a fine environment for a brigade of **tall pussytoes.** Their whitish bracts are soft like a kitten's paw at first, but turn papery with age.

The trail narrows and drops with the topography, passing **heartleaf arnica**, and a few gnarly aspens. The next segment traverses scrub oak interspersed with ripening **serviceberry** bushes. East-facing **aspen sunflowers** stand tall in the oak as does white-umbelled native **Porter's lovage** or **osha,** once serving as a perennial pharmacy for Native Americans. This member of the parsley family has strong-smelling foliage—rather like pungent celery.

In fact, its leaves were used as a flavoring. Concoctions treated everything from colds and colic to headaches and snakebite.

The next segment's vegetation almost feels jungle-like. The area is entwined with magenta **American vetch**, rampant **meadow rue**, and fruiting **chokecherry**. Bridging a dry ravine, a plank calls attention to fresh pink **wild geranium** and **lupine**. Two mints may be encountered: one, seldom seen, is **false dragonhead**. It takes a hand lens to appreciate the tiny two-lipped pink corollas.

Oak Flat Trail eventually decends via switchbacks to find 30-inch-high **Rocky Mountain penstemon**, **arrowleaf balsamroot**, and faithful **lupine** loafing in an open spot.

Sounds of the river beckon as the trail travels through Douglas fir to another switchback, via steps, to reach a lichen-encrusted boulder. There, early-blooming **false Solomon's seal** bears graceful creamy racemes. A quaint bridge spans a ravine where more of this glossy-leaved plant arches its long stems.

Building a trail on an estimated 60-degree sideslope is a feat, but even more impressive is the fact that a small section is cantilevered. Beneath the canyon's rim, ever more dramatic vignettes of jagged spires and sheer walls appear.

At the base of a small wall, **alumroot**, **arnica**, and **baneberry** (with poisonous, glassy red berries) find a niche. Encroaching vegetation, dominated by **serviceberry**, hems hikers in before the trail thins to welcome more **silvery lupine**.

Any number of whisk-tailed chipmunks dart about along the gentle descent to a hundred-foot-high lichen-spattered cliff face. The towering wall, streaked with bright orange, shelters more **baneberry** and some **currants**. Early season here exhibits **violets** and **creeping grapeholly**, and in the late season, **fireweed**.

You'll see dramatic chasm views off to the east as the trail switch-backs into the ever-deepening Black Canyon and passes **ballhead sandwort** and **pussytoes** on the way to a spot where, at last, it turns right.

At this point, a wonderful opportunity calls for an inspiring rest. Off to the left is a huge pile of boulders sheltering **wax currant** and **rock spirea** bushes. Find one that suits your criteria for seating. From this lofty vantage point, relax, enjoy the view, listen to the Gunnison, and watch streamlined black and white swifts cleave the air at speeds nearing 200 miles per hour. Linger long enough to absorb some of the Black Canyon mystique before heading back. Across the way, the almost perpendicular granite walls are ribboned with a network of pale intrusions. In between are serrated and fissured ramparts guarding the rapids of the Gunnison. This is a canyon like no other.

Heading back into the scrub oak, the rule of thumb is what goes down must go back up. And so, via S-curves, switchbacks, and a right at a junction, shady Oak Flat Trail rises unbelievably quickly, bringing hikers back to the rim in short order.

It bears repeating: Black Canyon of the Gunnison is like no other. It is no wonder that it was declared a national monument in 1933. Accompanied by a sweet collection of wildflowers, the Oak Flat Loop Trail offers an intimate way to get the majestic feel of the great, almost overwhelming maw of the Canyon called Black.

Wildflower Hike 6

Spring Creek

Wildflower Alert: This trail starts right off with globes of lavender ballhead waterleaf and peppermint striped onions.

Spring Creek Trail begins along an old abandoned road with cathedral stands of aspen along the way.

Trail Rating	easy to moderate
Trail Length	4.2 miles out and back
Location	Steamboat Springs
Elevation	8,240 to 7,200 feet
Bloom Season	mid-June through August
Peak Bloom	late June through July
Directions	Take US 40 to the east end of Steamboat Springs. Turn north onto 3rd Street. Proceed for one block, and turn right at Fish Creek Falls Road. Bear right on County Road 36, and turn right onto County Road 38 (Forest Road 60) until you reach a sign for Buffalo Pass/Dry Lake. Go approximately 3.5 miles to the trailhead on the right.

IN THE LATTER HALF OF JUNE, a paradise of vibrant wildflowers—one of the best drive-by displays in Colorado—decorates the Buffalo Pass area north of Steamboat Springs. Buffalo Pass Road winds up the pass with the last few miles to the crest passing through extravagant displays of wildflowers. In a good year and at the right time (particularly the third week of June), the place is a wildflower lover's Valhalla.

The jumping-off place for Spring Creek Trail may be found on the way to Buffalo Pass at the Dry Lake trailhead. This is the north end of the trail and by far the most flowery part. In late June, about 80 different kinds of wildflowers may be experienced. Much of Spring Creek Trail passes through quaking aspen, making an autumn hike a golden journey.

From the Dry Lake trailhead (located across the road from the Dry Lake campground entrance), Spring Creek Trail begins along an abandoned road, level at first, then dropping to span the first of many stream crossings. About halfway into the hike, the gradient changes to a steeper descent before levelling out to the turnaround point. This description turns around at the tenth creek crossing, retracing the 2 miles back up to the trailhead. However, with two vehicles, a through-hike of about 4 miles can be planned.

Parking is adequate at the north trailhead.

Stately aspen start off the trail along an old abandoned road, unveiling a dozen wildflower species within the first hundred feet. Among them are **western valerian**, **ballhead waterleaf**, **blue columbine**, **wild candytuft**, and yellow **upland** or **canary violet**. Short cutbanks lead into the open where the candystriped globes of stubby **Brandegee's onion** seem to be everywhere. Sprinkled among them are the white picket-fence petals of **woodland star**.

Serviceberry bushes in bridal-white thrive on the shrubland hillside. And on the roadsides, you'll see the numerous, distinctive three-part pods of the **glacier lily**. Early season displays the yellow lilies themselves. **Mountain balm** shrubs and **mule's ears**, both with shiny leaves, signal a descending angle for Spring Creek Trail.

On view to the northeast is 10,804-foot Soda Mountain; to the southeast is Buffalo Mountain. Traverse down towards the sound of running water, and you'll pass columns of creamy-yellow beaked **bracted lousewort** and blue-spired **lupine**. Scrub oak along with **chokecherry**'s hanging racemes of white flowers make way for the perfect buds of **wild rose**, which, upon opening, offer a celestial perfume.

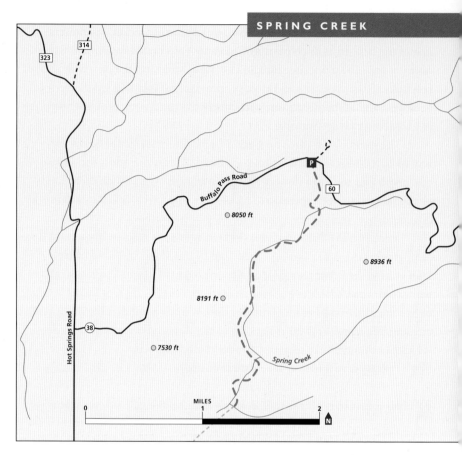

Quaking aspen hold sway once again where the trail curves into a lush environment of **cow parsnip**, **white geranium**, and **false hellebore**, lit by some **scarlet paintbrush**. At a seep, **white bog orchids** deserve a close look and a sniff to see why another common name is **scent bottle**.

At the burbling creek, the character of the vegetation takes on a jungle effect with plush clumps of **tall chiming bells**, **cow parsnip**, **monkshood**, and **twistedstalk**. Walking among smooth-barked aspen is like being in a cathedral constructed of blond wood. Sprays of **blue columbine** decorate the altar.

A granite outcrop on the right mixes aspen and evergreen trees, providing ideal habitat for **Canada violet** and **heartleaf arnica**. Cross the creek via a bridge overhung with willow trees, followed soon by another crossing with **tall larkspur**, more **monkshood**, and **white bog orchid**.

Along the winding trail, the north-facing aspect nurtures **canary violets** and **ballhead waterleaf** before you cross the creek again and the landscape switches to a more xeric environment.

The change to a warmer southern exposure uncovers an uncommon plant camouflaged in dappled aspen shade: **leopard lily**. Hung with a dozen purplish-speckled bells, this infrequently seen lily is 20 inches tall here. Also called **purple fritillary**, its odd odor attracts flies as pollinators. Abundant **blue columbine** shares the same venue, as does shrubby **red-berried elder** with its creamy racemes. Both white and pink **geranium** and attention-getting **scarlet paintbrush** brighten the aspen stand.

Span the stream to see a flurry of wildflowers plus white **bittercress**, a relative of watercress. Three colors of **violets**—yellow, blue, and white—find calm harbor among the "quakies" (an affectionate term for aspen trees), whose bark feels like soft skin, partly due to a protective "yeast" powdering the trunks.

Stepping across a diminutive sidestream bubbling over rocks puts hikers in the vicinity of **false Solomon's seal**. An outcrop of rugged gold granite precedes an S-curve where, once again, the creek is bridged. **Thimbleberry's** big leaves and few flowers appear next. They will later be accented by **fireweed**. The trail is now in Spring Creek Mountain Park.

Prepare now for a steep section where footfall

BRANDEGEE'S ONION
Allium brandegei

Like a ball of peppermint candy, the globe of Brandegee's onion's red-striped flowers catches the eye (actually, it is each flower's six tepals which bear the reddish line). And like peppermint, onions have a very distinctive odor that can be mistaken for nothing else. The spherical inflorescence nestles low in the two- to six-inch foliage (although there is also a taller form). This particular species was named for Townshend Brandegee, who was a nineteenth-century botanist with the Hayden Survey.

The *alliums* served Indian populations not only as food and flavoring but as remedies for respiratory ailments such as pneumonia. The pungent odor led to their use as an insect repellent. The bulbs were a welcome addition to the bland diet endured by the Lewis and Clark Expedition. Squirrel, deer, elk, and bear all find the onion palatable.

choices are important; keep your senses alert for descending mountain bikers as well.

Leveling out after a steep pitch, the trail advances to a bridge where the real Spring Creek comes in, quadrupling the flow of crystalline water. The next bridge over the roaring creek takes hikers into an area where everything seems oversized: the water, the trees, the flowers—even the butterflies.

Open skies greet the following crossing with the usual coterie of **monkshood**, **cow parsnip** and company, joined by yellow-petaled **bur avens**.

Rustic rails enclose the next bridge, which places hikers back into a cooler northern exposure. The shade canopy offers a tranquil opportunity for a bit of rest and relaxation before turning around to retrace your steps back to the upper trailhead.

Not far north of Steamboat Springs, Spring Creek Trail from the north end makes a worthy early summer hike. After enjoying the variety of wildflowers and picturesque stream crossings, extend the wonder by driving up to scenic Buffalo Pass with its full complement of wildflowers.

East Shore/Continental Divide Scenic Trail
(Rocky Mountain National Park)

Wildflower Alert: Pretty pocket meadows and marshes accompany this flowery jaunt along the Colorado River in Rocky Mountain National Park.

Serene water surrounded by stately pine and towering mountains is the setting for over 90 species of wildflowers on this trail.

easy	*Trail Rating*
3.0 miles out and back	*Trail Length*
Rocky Mountain National Park/Grand Lake	*Location*
8,370 to 8,480 feet	*Elevation*
June to August	*Bloom Season*
mid-June to early July	*Peak Bloom*
Take US 34 south from Grand Lake to Road 663 (Green Ridge Complex/Shadow Mountain Dam road south of milepost 12). Turn left and go 1.7 miles to the trailhead. There is parking at the west end of the dam. An alternative route is to go 11.9 miles north of Granby on US 34.	*Directions*

THE MIGHTY COLORADO RIVER begins its long journey as a brook in the northwest corner of Rocky Mountain National Park. Gathering myriad tributaries as it goes, the river meets its first man-made barrier as it flows into Shadow Mountain Lake. Between this lake and the far larger Lake Granby to the south, the Colorado River runs free for a brief time.

This wildflower hike travels along this free-running section, a segment of the Continental Divide Scenic Trail simply wonderful both in waterscapes and wildflowers. About 90 flower species may be tallied on a late June or early July hike.

Once you cross the Shadow Mountain dam top, you begin a genial walk through a number of habitats along the east bank of the Colorado River. One brief elevation gain takes the trail above Grand Bay, which is the arm of Lake Granby that meets the incoming river. Lively Columbine Creek coursing down from 12,121-foot Mount Adams is the turnaround point for the hike.

Parking is available at the west end of the dam.

The top of Shadow Mountain dam provides a wide platform for taking in a splendid panorama of peaks and water. The lake extends about 4 miles north to the town of Grand Lake, and peaks rise in every direction.

From the kiosk sign on the far end of the dam, the East Shore Trail heads right, leading down into lodgepole pines. Under these slender evergreens, splashes of starry **Rocky Mountain phlox**, along with **alpine milkvetch** and **loose-clustered milkvetch**, start off the floral parade. The decomposed granite soil supports lavender **cutleaf fleabane** and yellow **leafy cinquefoil** as the trail dips down to a meadow.

Along the meadow's edge, look for pale-yellow **western paintbrush** and **white bog orchid**. Out in the open, the sun shines on rich blue **Rydberg's penstemon** and **tall polemonium** or **Jacob's ladder** with its purple corollas exposing yellow stamens. **Littleflower penstemon**—its blue tubes rather small —grows here too. Observant hikers may spot **blue-eyed grass**, an iris relation, winking especially bright at high noon. **Burnt orange dandelion** lift their coppery heads on long stems in the same area. **Tall valerian** may hardly merit notice, but the silvery foliage and hot magenta beaks of **showy** or **woolly locoweed** do.

Cool yellow **paintbrush** pop up among gold-bloomed **shrubby cinque-foil** and willow on the way to a sign stating that no horses are allowed beyond this point. **Pink plumes** thrive by the sign. Bushy bog birch heads the trail to a built-up section, avoiding a slog through a sedge marsh.

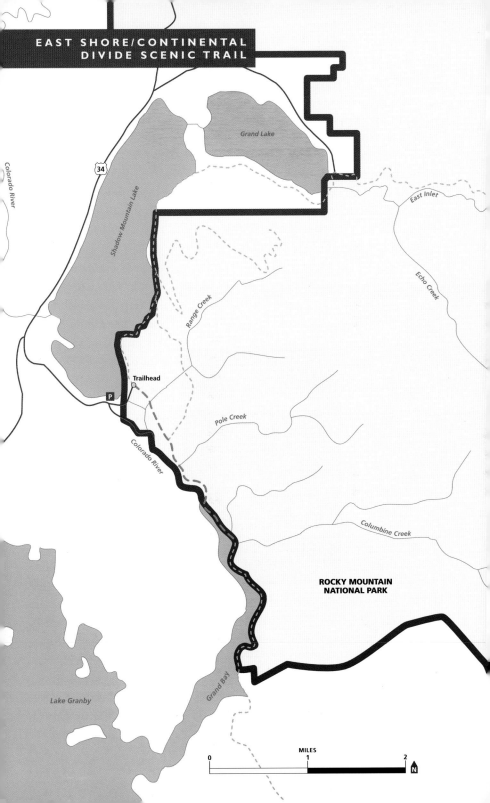

EAST SHORE/CONTINENTAL DIVIDE SCENIC TRAIL

Colorado River

34

Shadow Mountain Lake

Grand Lake

East Inlet

Echo Creek

Range Creek

Trailhead

P

Pole Creek

Colorado River

Columbine Creek

ROCKY MOUNTAIN
NATIONAL PARK

Lake Granby

Grand Bay

MILES

0   1   2

N

When you reach a junction where dark leathery leaves of **marsh marigold** bloom early, take the right path.

As the woods come into view, look for **western valerian, buttercups,** and more **pink plumes.** Another signed junction sends the East Shore Trail right again. This finger of north-facing mixed forest returns hikers to a shady habitat, just the place for **heartleaf arnica.** Keep a keen eye out for occasional pink **Calypso orchids** rooted in rich duff. **Lesser wintergreen** hangs its whitish parasols here. Creeping mats of **twinflower** lift slender stems, forking to dangle paired bells, joined by nodding lanterns of **western red columbine.** Beyond the tree shadows, the clear Colorado River flows.

Continue on to where open skies beam on a meadow filled with rangy **western valerian,** its white heads of tiny flowers spouting pincushion stamens. **Shrubby cinquefoil** lead a flowery procession. **Northern bedstraw, lupine, pink pussytoes,** and fragrant patches of **phlox** join the parade. Also marching along are **creamy buckwheat, early larkspur,** and more of the vivid nibs of **showy** or **woolly loco,** all leading into a fairyland of **phlox.** This well-drained environment encourages **wild strawberry** and Indian-named **kinnikinnick** to cover large areas of ground. **Scarlet gilia** fall into step, too.

Now wide as a road, the trail curves toward the sound of the river, and a big barn appears across the way. Back under the lodgepole pines, **heartleaf arnica** add sunny touches, and

PINK PLUMES
Erythrocoma triflora

Several other descriptive names attached to this unlikely looking member of the rose family are prairie smoke, old man's whiskers, pink avens, and fairy duster. All parts of this downy plant are a dusty rose-pink, whether in flower or seed. The inverted urn-shaped flowers turn upright upon fertilization, and these pink plumes, who like their own company, splash color from the plains to the open subalpine zones. Latin nomenclature defines *Erythrocoma* as "red mane" and *triflora* as "three-flowered." An unusual cousin is purple avens *Geum rivale.*

Native Americans found this plant useful as a beverage, an eyewash, and a component in their sweat-lodge preparations.

bright-clustered, rosy-purple **wild onion** hide in fallen timber pockets (pinch a leaf for proof).

With the river running close by, "social" trails abound. Follow the one near the water, passing an open meadow on the left. After a dab of forest, the trail opens to display **many-rayed goldenrod** before heading into willows. Where a few **littleflower penstemon** show up, cast about for **blue-eyed grass** and the hot pink arrows of **shooting stars**. **Larkspur** adds to the nectaring choices for tiger swallowtail butterflies. Thick willow clumps shelter a colorful procession of wildflowers, **pink plumes** numerous among them.

To the right, the strong flow of the Colorado River glitters in the sun. Even if it's only for a mile or so, a walk along this vital 1,450-mile-long river opens the big picture for the hiker. Don't let the encroaching willow trees and an uneven trail, perhaps even boggy footing, dissuade you from continuing—let the river sound keep you near the water. The marshy zones reveal wandering herds of **little pink elephants**, each flower mimicking the head of its namesake.

The trail becomes obvious again as it enters a stand of pines. From the left, a rivulet, on its way to join the Colorado, sports **tall chiming bells**, **bittercress**, **white geranium**, and lacy **cowbane**. Don't miss the **wild roses**, which are most fragrant when newly opened.

Winding through lodgepole and alder shade, the path comes to a creek, easily crossed on stepping stones. The route now passes more "**elephants**" and **wild onion**, both in spirited rosy-pink. Check out the short stalks of white **alpine bistort** with its tiny red bulblets—reproduction insurance—substituting for its lower flowers.

Pass angular debris from a rock outcrop on the left. Coming up is a great spot to do some river watching before the Colorado loses its river status to become an arm of Lake Granby.

Going on, the trail rises over log waterbars to where a hillside of beautiful **blue columbine** bid the river farewell. **Aspen sunflowers** cheer up the scene.

High above the water now, watch for a glimpse of a snow-capped peak, and on the steep trail bank look for **purple fringe** and **Whipple penstemon**. On a mossy northern exposure, **dainty western clematis** and **golden draba** cling to the soil, as do early-blooming **pasqueflowers**. When mature, their lilac tulips turn into wispy seed plumes.

Gold granite underfoot takes the trail down toward lake level and towering spruce, where an occasional **spotted coralroot** or last year's stalk of **pinedrops** (both saprophytic or lacking chlorophyll and therefore dependent on soil fungi) poke up under the conifers.

Sloping toward **shrubby cinquefoil** bushes decorating the water's edge, an open area boasts pastel yellow **antelope brush**, an important browse plant. Next you'll reach a lake-level meadow where **wild blue flax** greets morning hikers.

Off to the right and a bit farther on is a quiet bay. On the left, look for **creamy buckwheat, scarlet gilia, phlox,** and **larkspur**. A painted hillside of red, white, blue, purple, and yellow takes you up to golden-bedded Columbine Creek—the goal of this hike.

Before retracing your steps, take a look at the tints of the **Rocky Mountain phlox** on the hillside: lavender, pink, and white. Where the creek flows past a stand of evergreens, look for the red and yellow sconces of **western red columbine** lighting up the shade.

A wonderful experience awaits the wildflower enthusiast on the western fringe of Rocky Mountain National Park. The short section of the Continental Divide Scenic Trail that makes up this hike is loaded with blooms in early summer. And the walk along the crystalline Colorado River is memorable, putting this hike in the winner's circle.

Booth Falls
(Eagles Nest Wilderness)

Wildflower Alert: A variety of nonstop wildflowers
accompanies you from trailhead to falls.

*Just outside of
Vail, this some-
what rigorous
hike brings you
to a spectacular
waterfall.*

WHILE THE ELEVATION OF BOOTH CREEK TRAIL puts it in
the montane zone, the stream-cut valley evokes images of a trek in the Alps.
In two miles of trail, 1,100 vertical feet translates to a fair increase, but the
scenery is grand, the wildflowers abundant, and the falls a worthy finale. For
those so inclined, an additional four miles beyond Booth Falls continue up
to Booth Lake.

Booth Falls

Trail Rating	moderate to strenuous
Trail Length	4.2 miles out and back
Location	Vail
Elevation	8,500 to 9,600 feet
Bloom Season	mid-June to August
Peak Bloom	mid-July to early August
Directions	Take I-70 west to east Vail at exit 180. Turn left onto the north frontage road for 0.8 mile. Turn right onto Booth Falls Road for 0.2 mile to the trailhead. A small parking area is on the right.

The first part of the trail rises steeply before easing through flowery areas and then continues ascending, most sharply as it nears Booth Falls itself.

Located on the edge of a Vail residential area, trailhead parking fills very quickly on weekends. Be sure to arrive early.

Behind the trailhead sign, which includes a handy butterfly primer, Booth Lake Trail begins climbing immediately. Head up to find aspen trees clinging to a warm, south-facing slope where **harebells**, **fleabanes**, and **American vetch** bloom. Within the first few hundred feet, the trail gains considerable elevation as it switchbacks through ripening **serviceberry**. After reaching an open grassy space, take time to turn around to view East Vail and I-70 below.

Hemmed in by encroaching vegetation, the narrow ascending trail passes tall spires of pale lavender **horsemint** rising above deep grasses, identifiable as part of the mint family by its square stems and minty aroma. The grasses are punctuated by tall **aspen sunflower** and many-flowered **showy** or **aspen daisy**.

A rocky stretch leads up to an Eagles Nest Wilderness Area sign, followed by a cool stand of towering Colorado blue spruce. Log waterbars and foot-polished stone lead up to a somewhat more level section, where a boulder-studded hillside shows off **creamy buckwheat** and more lavender-blue **aspen daisies**. Taller aspen signal a moister habitat supporting **cow parsnip** and **wild raspberry**; less moist spots display native **orange agoseris**, sometimes called **burnt orange false dandelion**, and lavender-tinged **sego lilies**, their wide cups uniquely decorated inside.

Continuing up to reach a more genial trail segment, blue spruce and aspen trees frame a view of palisades on the left. Cool yellow **western paintbrush**, purple **monkshood**, and white-flowered **thimbleberry** thrive along the aspen-shaded trail. Occasionally, a "social" trail spur will veer off looking for Booth Creek, usually to dead end far above the water. In the lush vegetation, look for shrubs of **twinberry**. Its paired, soft gold tubes will mature into side-by-side inedible black berries, accented by red bracts. Here and there, **pink-headed daisies** bend softly wooled pink buds that open to blushed-white daisy heads.

Soon the route grows rougher and rockier as it travels into the open where Booth Creek flows in its stony bed. Spectacular scenery rises from the creek valley to introduce a whole hillside of mid-to-late summer-blooming **fireweed**, flamboyant in clear magenta, escorted by the broad white heads of **cow parsnip**. This well-endowed landscape provides a nectaring nirvana for butterflies.

The trail smooths and drops slightly to cross a small sidestream where you'll find **yellow monkeyflower**, lacy **cowbane**, and airy **brook saxifrage**. Soon the pathway wades through waist-high **thimbleberry**, shaded by quaking aspen trees, and bends toward Booth Creek, which curves around the north edge of the copse.

THIMBLEBERRY
Rubacer parviflorum

In cool, damp places, thimbleberry presents pristine white two-inch-wide, five-petaled blossoms. *Parviflorum* means "small flowered" and is misleading because the blooms, though few, are quite large. Typically growing in extensive patches in filtered shade, this member of the rose family has huge maple-like leaves attached to two- to four-foot thornless stems, forming colonies sprouting from underground roots.

While the edible but seedy and insipid fruit (called a druplet and looking like a deflated raspberry) is not especially appealing to humans, bears and birds enjoy it. Cousin wild red raspberry *Rubus idaeus* is unremarkable in the flower department, but its bright berries are a tasty find. Another cousin, boulder raspberry *Oreobatus deliciosus,* isn't much in the way of delicious, but its broad snowy blossoms are very showy.

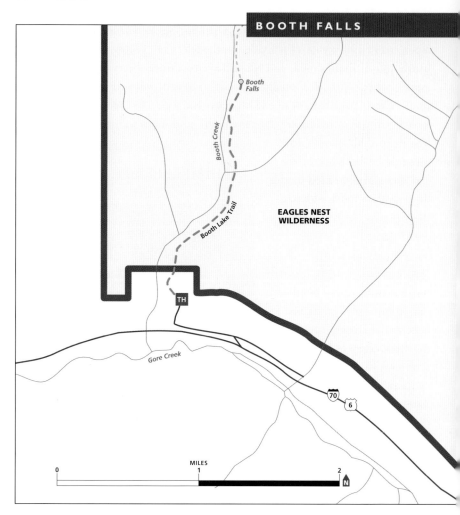

BOOTH FALLS

Booth Falls

Booth Creek

Booth Lake Trail

EAGLES NEST WILDERNESS

TH

Gore Creek

70 6

MILES

0   1   2   N

Out under open skies, the trail rises as the valley narrows. Here lavender blue **Rydberg's penstemon**, **creamy buckwheat**, and **orange agoseris** are abundant. Climbing more steeply, the trail approaches a creek and the nearby hillside boasts yellow **paintbrush**, **aspen daisy**, and a bounty of **fireweed**.

The next stand of "quakies" (a friendly term for aspen) accompanies a pleasant section of trail as **scarlet paintbrush** lights the way to raked meadows, lavish with wildflowers. Sunlight and moisture combine to provide ideal habitat for graceful **tall chiming bells**, midnight blue **subalpine larkspur**, deceptively-leafed **meadow rue** or **false columbine**, and dinnerplate-wide **cow parsnip**. Flashy **fireweed** and ranks of proud **aspen sunflower** finish the teeming meadow.

Before tackling an upcoming stiff climb, take time to enjoy the lively meadow. On the way up the incline, the trail forks. The left spur heads for an overlook. Head right, up the very steep and rocky ascent accompanied by the yellow faces of **sunflowers**.

At last the route eases as you approach a vast rockslide area. In the tumbled gray rock, clumps of lovely **blue columbine** appear unexpectedly plush. **Whipple or dusky penstemon**—both wine-colored and white—cling to exposed banks along the way, as do the moss-like mats of **dotted saxifrage**. To keep the wildflower faith, columns of **purple fringe** or **silky phacelia** with its jauntily protruding gold-tipped stamens join more **scarlet paintbrush** and **blue columbine**.

The trail continues to push up toward Booth Falls. The sound of crashing water heralds the falls, best reached from a spur trail heading left. This leads to a tilted block of ridged stone overhanging a fine view of free-falling whitewater and its dark gorge. Rugged terrain and drop-offs make it a bit precarious to find a clear view of the sixty-foot-high Booth Falls.

Booth Falls makes a fine goal, but for those who want to keep climbing, it's another four miles to reach Booth Lake, perched at 11,480 feet.

Aspen trees, sublime scenery, and vivid wildflowers make Booth Lake Trail an admirable half-day excursion to the falls from Vail Valley. Aspen are so prevalent on Booth Lake Trail that an autumn hike makes for a golden opportunity.

*Wildflower
Hike*
9

Cascade Falls
(Rocky Mountain National Park)

Wildflower Alert: This trail provides a look into Rocky Mountain National Park's backcountry and montane zone wildflowers.

Over 80 species of wildflowers dance along this trail that leads to thundering falls.

Trail Rating	easy
Trail Length	7.0 miles out and back
Location	Rocky Mountain National Park/Grand Lake
Elevation	8,540 to 8,840 feet
Bloom Season	late June to August
Peak Bloom	early to mid-July
Directions	Take US 34 to the Grand Lake turnoff. Turn right and travel for 0.3 mile, then left on West Portal Road for 0.9 mile. Go left to the trailhead.

THE WEST SIDE of magnificent Rocky Mountain National Park has some lesser-used trails that push into the park's backcountry. About 90 percent of famed "Rocky," as locals call it, is wilderness, including its expansive heart. With 265,354 acres within its boundaries, that is a lot of heart.

Though the trek to Cascade Falls covers just three and a half miles, the North Inlet Trail, which accesses the falls, continues on. Backpackers can span the park by hiking up and over the Continental Divide, eventually ending up at Glacier Gorge Junction. The description treated here doesn't accumulate much in the way of elevation gain, unlike the long haul across "Rocky." Another plus is its location in the montane zone, making for less strenuous hiking.

An early mid-July hike may turn up over 80 species of wildflowers sprinkled along the North Inlet drainage. The clear waters of the charging falls bump over huge boulders and several miles of winding waterway to pour into Grand Lake.

Parking at the trailhead is limited and fills fast on summer weekends. Additional parking may be found back along West Portal Road at the trailhead turnoff.

Even the trailhead restrooms are embellished by wildflowers, **Rocky Mountain locoweed** and **heartleaf arnica** among them.

A neighboring sign on the gated road states: Summerland Park 1.2 miles, Cascade Falls 3.5 miles. Small aspen and conifer trees lead the way down the road, passing **leafy cinquefoil** and **wild roses**. Across from a meadow featuring **bistort**, a south-facing hillside features **creamy buckwheat**, **Parry milkvetch**, and **harebells**. **Littleflower penstemon's** deep blue tubes, crowded into clusters, sag a bit. Among the rocks are

WESTERN RED COLUMBINE
Aquilegia elegantula

Like fluted lanterns, the red and yellow corollas of western red columbine most often are found lighting up spruce-fir forests, although they also grow in the open. Known in some locales as redbells, western red columbine will, on occasion, hybridize with blue columbine *A. coerulea*. The offspring take after the latter parent. The spur petals of western red columbine rise straight and almost vertically above the yellow sepals. With smaller flowers and narrowed spur tips, in addition to an earlier bloom time, this red columbine is harder to spot than its big blue cousin. Another cousin is the rare dwarf columbine *Aquilegia saximontana*.

pink pussytoes and **shrubby cinquefoil**. The gold coins of **shrubby cinque-foil** complement **wild blue flax**, whose bits-of-shattered-sky petals tremble on morning breezes.

Coming up, look to the right in the willow breaks for intense blue **Rydberg's penstemon**. Larger horizontal tubes help differentiate it from its cousin, **littleflower penstemon**. The moister habitat nurtures **monkshood**, **tall chiming bells**, and tall **Jacob's ladder**. The opposite habitat, dry and rocky, crowns an outcrop to the left with such appropriate denizens as **stonecrop**, **early blue daisy**, **bluemist penstemon**, and **bracted alumroot**. Leaving the meadow area, the flat road passes **Parry Lousewort's** creamy beaks and the nodding urns of **pink plumes**.

Entering a lodgepole stand, keep an eye out for leathery-leaved **kinnikinnick** and round-leaved **twinflower** mats draping over a suitable boulder. Where the buck-and-rail fence ends, search for a nice group of bright pink **shooting stars**.

A view opens where North Inlet, a fast-flowing, golden-bedded river, meets the trail. Cool and pale as butter, **western paintbrush** creates a pastel landscape along with **tall chiming bells** and **white geranium**. **Little pink elephants** animate the canvas with their pink ears and supple maroon trunks.

Pass more outcrops which demonstrate the contrast between the damp environment to the right of the trail and the xeric one on the left. You'll continue to hear the river long after the trail has led you away from the water.

The roadway cruises into Summerland Park. By Colorado definition, a park is a broad expanse of open land that can vary from a half-mile to forty miles in length. But it's not just a manicured area of grass. In the vicinity of the park's willows, arrows of **shooting star** aim toward earth, but upon fertilization, point heavenward. On the east end, a cabin stands. At this juncture, the trail narrows and travels into short aspen trees, and in their dappled shade grows the shapely **blue columbine**. Evergreen trees join in providing duff for **green-flowered wintergreen**, its erect reddish stems dangling pale bells.

Coming down from the north, a chatty little rill is spanned by a bridge. Quaking aspen shade is the choice of **pink pyrola**, another wintergreen family member with much the same growth habit as its green-flowered cousin. Just up the trail is a hoary, lichen-hung outcrop, its crevices crammed with clumps of **bracted alumroot** and the base perfumed by **wild rose**. A quick whiff must suffice, since the outcrop's nearest neighbor is a swamp where mosquitoes wait in ambush.

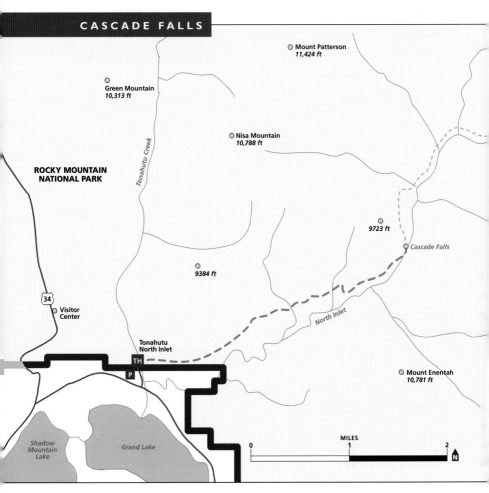

CASCADE FALLS

Mount Patterson
11,424 ft

Green Mountain
10,313 ft

Nisa Mountain
10,788 ft

Tonahutu Creek

ROCKY MOUNTAIN
NATIONAL PARK

9723 ft

Cascade Falls

9384 ft

34

Visitor
Center

North Inlet

Tonahutu
North Inlet

TH

P

Mount Enentah
10,781 ft

Shadow
Mountain
Lake

Grand Lake

MILES
0   1   2

N

The next outcrop exposes the red pigmented bracts and narrow chartreuse flowers of **narrow-leaved paintbrush** growing at the rock's base, a scene which can appear to have been brushed onto the landscape by a surrealist artist.

The trail comes upon **beauty cinquefoil**, and growing just up from here, on the right, is bright rosy **wild onion**. Cozying up to boulders on the forest floor, mats of **twinflower** display dainty pink and white bells. Offering its delicate fragrance to passing pollinators, this member of the honeysuckle clan was the favorite flower of Carolus Linnaeus, the originator of the Latin binomial system of taxonomic classification.

As the trail rises, you'll see an avalanche path exposed to the south. Crossing worn granite affords a chance to see **woolly** or **silvery cinquefoil**. The ensuing evergreen trees provide the organic duff for **spotted coralroot orchid**.

Lacking chlorophyll, the upright stalk of perfectly formed miniature orchids must tap into soil fungi for sustenance. It does so with roots branched like stubby coral.

A shoulder-brushing wall of granite is hung with **dotted** or **moss saxifrage**, where the sound of water accompanies the contouring trail. Spruce shadows guide you across a log spanning a creeklet and is the signal to keep an eye peeled for the luminous red and yellow lanterns of early-blooming **western red columbine.**

Teasingly, river sounds continue while a sign indicating Twinberry Backpack Camp is to the right. Not much farther on, North Inlet does, in fact, come rushing into view as well as a big slice of Rocky Mountain grandeur.

Rocky is also the character of the next section of trail, but the harsh footbed is softened by the alluring scent of profuse **wild rose**. As the canyon narrows, the outcrop wall rises until the confined river roars down in white fury. Also white is **sandwort**, perching its stars on wiry stems and stiff grass-like leaves.

The whitewater rears like teams of snowy horses chomping at the bit to begin a chariot race to the sea, and cantilevered dry-stack stone walls pass a sheet of granite with **stonecrop**, **leafy cinquefoil**, and **bracted alumroot** clinging to its slanted surface.

At the base of one of these walls is a sign: Cascade Falls. To view the thundering falls from the top requires ascending a rough, rocky segment. Near the goal, **Whipple penstemon** defines dusky wine with its inflated tubes. Giant boulders provide fine viewing of the metamorphosis of a topaz river into a frothing rage of whitewater.

Rocky Mountain National Park's North Inlet provides access to a bit of backcountry on an unbelievably easygoing trail. With Cascade Falls' wildly energetic whitewater as the objective, wildflower enthusiasts are treated to a variety of landscapes and wildflowers along the way as well as "Rocky's" thundering heartbeat.

Bighorn Creek
(Eagles Nest Wilderness)

Wildflower Alert: This trail features an inviting combination of aspen and wildflowers.

This trail follows the rushing waters of Bighorn Creek with an overlook of the East Vail Valley along the way.

SEVERAL CREEKS BORN OF HIGH ALPINE LAKES, each with an attendant trail, pour into Gore Creek as it winds through Vail Valley. Bighorn Creek Trail is the least taxing of them—except at the onset. Incorporating some eighty wildflower species along its first two miles, this is a good montane zone starter trail for Vail hikers.

Bighorn Creek

Trail Rating	easy to moderate
Trail Length	4.0 miles out and back
Location	Vail
Elevation	8,600 to 10,000 feet
Bloom Season	late June to August
Peak Bloom	mid-July to early August
Directions	From Denver take I-70 west to the East Vail exit 180. Turn left under the freeway and then left onto Bighorn Road. Proceed for 1 mile, and turn left onto Columbine Drive. Continue through the one-lane underpass to the trailhead parking, which is on the left near the end of Bighorn Creek bridge.

With the exception of the initial sharp half-mile ascent, the trail eases up a long scenic valley, alternating between shade and sun. Quaking aspen trees, some of great girth, dominate the route. In autumn, a hike under the aspen would be like a journey down the aisle of a natural cathedral streaming with golden, ambient light.

Parking is extremely limited at the trailhead adjacent to Bighorn Creek, so plan to arrive early. Arriving early also helps you avoid the violent afternoon thunderstorms of summer.

The hike begins near a small sign reading Bighorn Trail and passes lavender **harebells**, **creamy buckwheat**, and fruiting **serviceberry** and **chokecherry**. Rushing Bighorn Creek and the interstate compete with the warm, summer-day buzzing of cicadas in the stunted aspens. Behind you, rising to 11,000 feet, are striated sandstone cliffs decorated with aspen whose fall gold is a striking contrast with the maroon rock.

Climb farther, and you'll see a sign designating the Eagles Nest Wilderness. A soothing diversion on this steep pitch are the purple, cream, and cool whites of **asters**, **creamy buckwheat**, **sego lily**, along with the rich blue-purple of **Rydberg's penstemon**. An occasional **scarlet gilia**, sometimes called **skyrocket**, offers its bright trumpets along the warm southern exposure. Lavender-blue describes the three broad petals of the lovely **sego lily** here. Belying their dainty appearance, clumps of long-blooming **harebells** defy drought, dust, and even a touch of frost.

As you continue up the sharp gradient, you'll see the chartreuse toothpick flowers of **narrow-leaved paintbrush** poking out of scarlet bracts. The trail zigzags up to a level spot overlooking the East Vail Valley, which marks more gentle grades ahead. Douglas fir trees shade some little **green orchids** on the left before you again reach an open area. Taller **Rocky Mountain penstemon** display plush open-throated tubes near patches of shrubby, shiny-leaved **mountain balm**. Fuller clusters of smaller flowers and papery-edged sepals are diagnostic of strong-hued **Rydberg's penstemon**. The occasional **antelope brush** has duck-foot shaped leaves and teardrop seedpods that follow pale-yellow flowers.

Off to the right, an aspen glade supports **meadow rue** and **false Solomon's seal**. Highway noise is replaced by sounds of the creek and the trail cruises through white-barked quaking aspens. The varnished leaves of evergreen **mountain balm** are a good foil for the frothy, creamy white racemes of starry flowers.

Wide skies shine on **scarlet gilia** as the trail heads into lodgepole pines interspersed with aspen. The forest floor establishes a soft footbed for **heartleaf arnica** and carpets of evergreen **kinnikinnick**. **White peavine** and **American vetch** are interspersed.

Increasing in height and girth, the pale "quakies" (an affectionate term for aspen trees) are responsible for the common naming of **aspen daisies** and **aspen sunflowers** growing here. The dappled shade suits **white geranium** and cool **western paintbrush**, and where conifers join in, **spotted coralroot**. A close look at each perfectly-formed orchid reveals dark flecks on the ruffle-edged lower lip.

Ascending for a stretch, the trail passes patches of **thimbleberry**. Green-barked aspen form a line down a steep slope toward clear-running Bighorn Creek. Apparently needing less moisture than many of its kind, the little **green orchid** reappears. The aspen grow so thickly through here that you feel enclosed within a stockade. They thin out as the trail rises. The rocky trail curves up, passing both white and purple **monkshood** as well as **pearly everlasting** and **northern bedstraw**.

A little seep presents **white bog orchid**. Look for **creamy** or **sticky cinquefoil** just a bit farther. A flowery hillside responds to sunlight, lifting the trail back into **sego lily** territory and filtered shade. Also enjoying the shade are bracken fern and **red-berried elder**. The understory tightens where **baneberry's** airy, creamy racemes develop into glass-shiny fruit clusters — but remember that they're poisonous, whether they are fire-engine red or opaque white.

Cross a tiny rivulet where **white bog orchid** and **pink willowherb** decorate the upstream side, while downstream **cow parsnip** and **arrowleaf senecio** grow alongside **fireweed**.

Once again, as the aspen grow thinner the trail grows rockier and steeper. The alpine jungle is vegetated with stately **monkshood**, saucer-sized white **cow parsnip**, pleated-leaved **false hellebore,** and yellow **arrowleaf senecio**.

Close to the two-mile point, a "social" spur on the right leads to an overlook high above Bighorn Creek. The main trail circumvents the dark ooze. Look to the left and enjoy the rock outcrops and cliffs ultimately rising to 12,000 feet.

Conifers create heavier shade along a level section, pocketing a bit of sky with **tall chiming bells** in pink-budded, blue-flowered bloom. Cascading through a grove of towering spruce, clear topaz-bedded Bighorn Creek flows shallowly next to the trail. If you stop to look in the thick shade by the water, you may find **twistedstalk** and green **mitrewort**. At the northeast edge of the grove, a mossy boulder may present the wonderfully perfumed **shy wood nymph**.

A big rockfall strewn with fallen tree trunks is the locus for **fireweed** and woolly-budded **pink-headed daisy**. Alders and willows lean over the path as the noisy creek tumbles through boulders. On the shaded north bank, look for **queen's crown**, **bittercress**, and intensely pink **Parry primrose**.

You'll need to clamber over a few rocks as the canyon walls grow closer. Straight ahead, the craggy peaks of the Gore Range reach to the sky. Lavender **harebells** and **asters** enjoy the quiet company of **creamy buckwheat** and **sego lilies**. The latter sometimes sports differently designed interiors, sometimes maroon-banded, sometimes plain, but always with a ring of refined golden stamens.

Down to the right lies a still pond, its bottom emerald with trailing algae. To get there, travel through the jungle effect of **yellow monkeyflower**, **cow parsnip**, **tall chiming bells**, **monkshood**, and alders. In mid-to late summer, the scene will be ignited by huge spires of **fireweed**. Struggling aspen make their way into a pile of pink granite to show off fragrant **wild rose** and spurred **blue columbine**.

MOUNTAIN BALM
Ceanothus velutinus

Imaginative names such as snowbrush, velvety buckbrush, sticky laurel, and soapbloom are attached to this member of the buckthorn family. Creamy clouds of miniscule flowers appear above aromatic evergreen leaves in mid-summer. Often forming patches, the sprawling shrub's sticky foliage contains a volatile oil, making mountain balm a danger-ous plant in forest fire scenarios.

Found from British Columbia to Colorado, buckbrush has seeds that may remain viable for 200 or more years before — perhaps not surprising — fire germinates them. A deciduous cousin in the region is Fendler buckbrush *Ceanothus fendleri.*

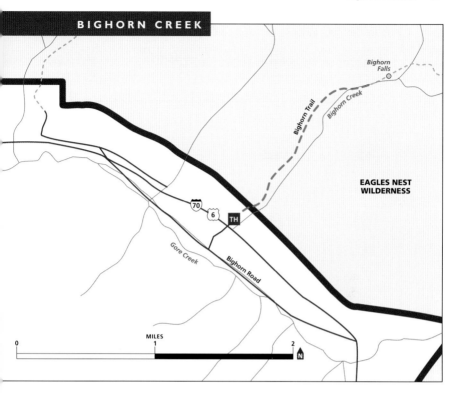

To stay on the route through the boulder field, look for well-placed cairns and be wary of unstable rock. Soon you'll see **blue columbine** in the shade of ivory-trunked aspen. Here too is **twinberry**. The rockfall reappears on the way to a view of Bighorn Creek cascading over black rock in a long fall of whitewater. You'll be captivated not only by the cascade, but by very tall, **tall chiming bells** and pink **wild geranium** and **white geranium**. If you listen carefully despite the plunging water, you might hear the thrilling trill of the broad-tailed hummingbird. As you move on, great clumps of **columbine** nestle among the tumbled stone as the trail begins to climb steeply.

For those not wishing to make the ascent—one that climbs 900 vertical feet for another mile and a half ending at an old cabin—this is a fine place to turn around. Before doing so, find a likely boulder on which to relax and contemplate water sound, skyscape, and columbine.

Bighorn Creek Trail beckons you with its diverse ecosystems and colorful montane wildflowers. The sound of rushing Bighorn Creek invites hikers to explore the lovely canyoned valley—all within a short distance of Vail.

*Wildflower
Hike*
11

Lower Cataract Lake
(Eagles Nest Wilderness)

Wildflower Alert: This trail takes you to a flowery eden featuring a glen profuse with blue columbine in early summer.

A pleasant two-mile loop around the lake showcases blue columbine, wild geraniums, and over seven dozen other wildflowers.

Trail Rating	easy
Trail Length	2.0-mile loop
Location	Silverthorne/Heney
Elevation	8,630 to 8,670 feet
Bloom Season	June through August
Peak Bloom	early to mid-July
Directions	From Denver take I-70 west to the Silverthorne/Dillon exit 205. Turn right onto US 9 and continue for 16 miles. Take a left onto Heney Road for 5.3 miles, and then take a left onto Cataract Creek Road to the trailhead. Fee required.

LOWER CATARACT LAKE is a wildflower lover's nirvana. In addition to over 80 blooming species along the two-mile trail looping the lake, an extravagant hillside of lush blue columbine highlights the gentle hike.

At the end of Cataract Creek Road, this pleasing walk is rarely out of the sight or sound of water. The cascades, which pour into the lake, may be roaring with spring runoff or burbling secretively as summer wanes.

The parking area of this popular trail fills up on summer weekends. An early arrival not only makes parking easier, but the lake waters are serene and the light best for photography.

Begin the hike by crossing log style — two steps up, two down — and then turn left along a split rail fence to pass through a pastel watercolor show of blue **penstemons** and pink **wild geraniums**. Patches of **littleflower penstemon**, richly clothed in the intense blue-violet of "nautical twilight" (that clear sky color achieved about a half-hour after sunset), grow in expanding colonies nearby. Compared to the generous tubes of most other penstemons, the dense whorls of smallish trumpet flowers bear out the name littleflower or **clustered penstemon**.

Drop down to a wide-plank bridge crossing crystalline Cataract Creek, and travel along the path entering Eagles Nest Wilderness Area. The

BLUE COLUMBINE
Aquilegia coerulea

A study in floral gracefulness, the blue columbine or Colorado blue columbine was chosen Colorado's state flower in 1899. Five lavender-blue petals sweep back to form spurs, and their tips become swollen with nectar. Designed for long-tongued humming-birds or hawkmoths, the elusive nectar repositories have driven frustrated bees to nip holes in the knobs to steal the sweet liquid. Colorado blue columbine was first discovered in southern Douglas County by physician, botanist, and aficionado-explorer Dr. Edwin James. He was an important member of Major Stephen Long's 1820 expedition.

A couple of close cousins found in the region are western red columbine *Aquilegia elegantula* and golden or yellow columbine *Aquilegia chrysantha*. The latter native, propagated in the nursery trade, is a superb garden plant with an unbelievably long season of bloom.

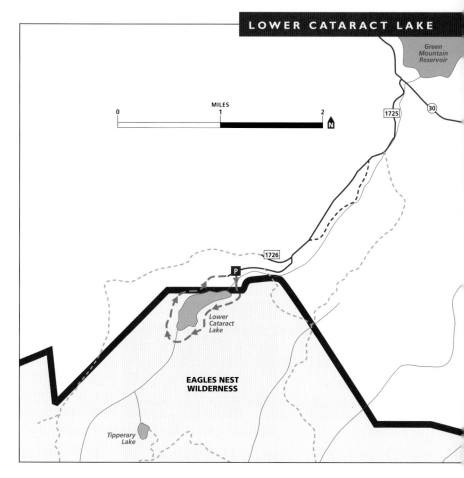

boundary is guarded by a wood post cow-excluder, barely wide enough to accommodate a backpack.

Keep straight to arrive at an aspen-topped, flower-cloaked hillock plush with **paintbrush**, **scarlet gilia**, **larkspur**, and **Rocky Mountain locoweed**, as well as a host of other wildflowers showcasing mother nature's innate gardening talent. Just down from the colorful hill is a short peninsula, which has a swampy, mosquito-guarded inlet on its southern edge. This plant-choked inlet, oddly enough, is adjacent to drought-resistant sagebrush and **creamy buckwheat**. Under overhanging willows, the inlet supports a trio of diverse swampmates. Tall **purple avens**, a mauvy member of the rose family, nods over the short, erect stalks of **pink pyrola** of the wintergreen clan. In their company, mid-sized **saffron senecio** or **groundsel** presents its scarlet-orange striped buds, opening into golden rays with orange-red reverses. A member of the extensive sunflower family, which comprises one-fifth of Rocky Mountain wildflowers, **saffron senecio** is hard to find compared to many of its more prolific brethren.

Mosquitoes move in for the kill, but being territorial, they are easy to outmarch. Continue on to encounter a plush theater of Colorado's elegant state flower, the **blue columbine**. The trail levels as it enters a curtain of aspen and evergreen trees, and the lake provides a pretty backdrop for a profusion of graceful columbines. The spurred blossoms have a gentle honeysuckle scent.

As you peruse the columbines, look for the dusty pink inverted urns of **pink plumes**. Also known as **pink avens**, among other common names, the same dusty pink shows up in the mature seed plumes, ready to take off on the wind. Downslope toward the inky depths of the lake are yet more columbines.

The trail contours around a couple of bends to cross a hillside brushed with tall **western larkspur**. The widely-spaced flowers are a muted blue. **Creamy buckwheat** and **wild blue flax** provide more pastel tints, set off by the unabashedly sun-loving faces of **sunflowers**.

The pathway descends into the cool shade of towering Colorado blue spruce to arrive in a tangle of roots and fallen trees. Take a moment to pause over the cool, cascading water on the railed, dogleg bridge.

Nearby, on the stream's banks, look for **twistedstalk** with a kinked flower stalk secreted underneath its leaves and similar appearing, but more generously belled, **wartberry fairybell**. In the deep forest duff, keep an eye peeled for bits of snowy-bracted **bunchberry**—a shorter member of the dogwood family— and **shy wood nymph** with her white head bowed to the earth. An early season visitor might even discover a pink **Calypso orchid** or two in the thick shade. In the vicinity, especially in June, stray rays of sun may light up the red and yellow hanging lanterns of **western red columbine**.

Continuing on into the open now, there is a veritable jungle of what is casually, but erroneously, called skunk cabbage. This vast meadow of head-high plants is actually populated by **false hellebore**, sometimes known as **corn lily**. Pyramidal clusters of tiny, greenish flowers top the whopping stalks with their pleated leaves—as toxic to livestock as the flowers are to insects. After negotiating the corn lily mass, the level trail passes the inflated snowflake heads of **cow parsnip**, delicate sky-blue **wild blue flax**, and perky **sunflowers**.

The trail then heads uphill a bit, passing clumps of **Rocky Mountain penstemon**, its full-blown, violet-throated tubes an impossibly hot blue. Where the trail forks and **chokecherry** and ripening **serviceberry** shrubs grow by a boulder, turn to the left. The hillside angles down to the western end of the lake, and the trail pushes on to the welcome shade of quaking aspen trees, signaling a cool saunter back to the trailhead.

The easygoing two-mile loop of Lower Cataract Lake is a winner in the world of wildflower viewing. In a good year, an astounding cast of at least seven-dozen species color the way. This congenial, child-friendly trail should rank high on any early summer wildflower hike list.

Wildflower Hike **12**

Crystal Creek Overlook
(Curecanti National Recreation Area)

Wildflower Alert: Larkspur leads this early season, off-the-beaten-path hike to a great canyon overlook.

This colorful, incredibly diverse trail leads to a breathtaking overlook.

Trail Rating	easy to moderate
Trail Length	5.0 miles out and back
Location	Curecanti NRA/Black Canyon of the Gunnison North Rim/ Montrose
Elevation	8,675 to 8,894 feet
Bloom Season	late May through July
Peak Bloom	early to mid-June
Directions	From Gunnison take US 50 west for 28 miles. Turn right onto State Route 92, proceeding for approximately 24 miles. Continue to the signed trailhead on the left.

THE NORTH RIM of Black Canyon of the Gunnison is far less visited than the south rim. Both offer astounding views into the depths of the intriguing dark chasm. Abounding in wildflowers, the genial Crystal Creek Trail winds up at an overlook high above Crystal Lake, a slender body of green reservoir water.

Despite its higher trailhead elevation, Crystal Creek Trail to the overlook begins its bloom season early in June. Actually located within the Curecanti National Recreation Area's west end, the two-and-a-half-mile hike travels through diversity, both in scenery and plant communities. The route drifts down, then works back up before a final descent to the impressive overlook. Early morning or late afternoon is a good time to hike here.

Adequate parking is adjacent to Highway 92.

The trailhead is defined by a three-rail fence overhung with **chokecherry** and **serviceberry**. Surrounding the fence are **geranium**, **chiming bells**, and **ballhead waterleaf**. Tall **western valerian**, with heads of dainty white flowers spouting impertinent stamens, poke through the wood rails.

It isn't long before a pocket garden stuffed with white-umbelled **Porter's lovage**, **chiming bells**, and **ballhead waterleaf** appear directly behind the trailhead sign. Scrub oak shields the pink stars of **spring beauties**.

Lining the path as it drifts down are more of the prolific **chiming bells**, as well as **early larkspur** and **ballhead waterleaf** with perky stamens issuing from lavender trumpets. Keen observers may pick out the minuscule white stars of **northern rock primrose** or **fairy candelabra**.

Continue along the winding trail, which is flanked by **early larkspur** in varying shades from intense purple through light lavender-blue. Sticky clumps of shiny-leaved **mule's ears** pop up ready to present their sunflower type blossoms. Now at peak bloom, **serviceberry** shrubs are covered with white, oval-petaled flowers.

Looking over the scrub oak toward the Black Canyon's Precambrian spires, the power of time and water are evident. Trailside gardens grow in lush colors. One such area, though obviously vegetated with **lupine** and **larkspur**, claims an uncommon wildflower: **purple fritillary** or **leopard lily**. The latter best describes the camouflaged nodding bells of this member of the lily family. Later in the summer, the cube-shaped seedpods of this rare "find" are easier to spot.

A concrete waterbar signals a splendid view ahead of 14,309-foot Uncompahgre Peak and the San Juan Range to the south. Near here, **scarlet gilia** adds a bright touch.

Cruising into the open, the trail passes native **false dandelion**—perky stamens pointing skyward—and pretty **longleaf phlox**. Fond of xeric places,

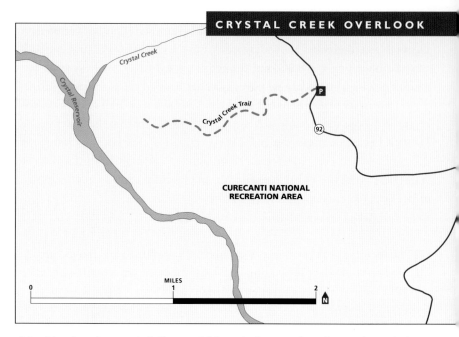

CRYSTAL CREEK OVERLOOK

Crystal Creek

Crystal Reservoir

Crystal Creek Trail

P

92

CURECANTI NATIONAL
RECREATION AREA

MILES
0   1   2
N

this phlox has showy, pink flowers (although they can be white or lavender) that require a sniff to detect their sweet fragrance.

Look to the south for a wide open view of the magnificent mountains. You'll find **arrowleaf balsamroot** at your feet. Springing from clumps of felt-like gray-green leaves, these golden flares centered by darker disk florets light the way. Crystal Creek Overlook Trail is a good place to compare mule's ears and balsamroot. Though their flowers are similar, the leaves are markedly different.

Descending through scrub oak, the trail passes fragrant **wild rose**. The trees then part at a flat area to reveal a more in-depth look at Black Canyon of the Gunnison.

This inspiring vista is followed by a change as the trail rises quickly via switchbacks. Wrapping around to a Douglas fir-shaded northern exposure with lots of white **mountain candytuft**, the trail cools briefly before pushing out into the open. On the way up to a bench overlooking moss green Crystal Reservoir and the West Elk Mountains, sunshine encourages **northern bedstraw** to bloom.

Generally level now, the trail follows the contour of the ridge just below its crest. **Fendler senecio, early white fleabane, balsamroot,** and a touch of **scarlet gilia** decorate the area. Bare spots encourage the huge, fragrant blossoms of **tufted evening primrose** to unfurl its pristine petals at the close of day. Strong-red **desert paintbrush** blooms here and there on the southeast-facing slope among scattered piñon pines. You'll also see bright **golden aster** and fading **balsamroot**.

Back into the scrub oak and serviceberry community, a side spur of Black Canyon comes into view shortly before the trail crosses a wide ridge. It then tilts up, weaving between exposures and tree types.

You'll come to a fork, where the left side climbs to a bench on an exposed hilltop. The right spur continues the Crystal Creek Overlook Trail. A stand of aspen sheltering **heartleaf arnica** precedes a 70-acre area that burned in 1974. Reclaiming the fire-affected slope are young aspens, patches of **mountain balm**, and **creeping grapeholly**.

Back into Douglas fir, the trail descends, then lifts momentarily before dropping via a switchback to reach a beautifully rustic overlook built on a prow of rugged rock. Guarded by the gnarled arms of an ancient juniper, the overlook invites you to look down to the deep curves of Crystal Reservoir's pent-up waters and the 1,500 vertical feet of great pewter spires and spears that embellish the shadowy walls of the Black Canyon of the Gunnison. It's a long way down, but white-throated swifts lance the air at speeds up to 200 miles per hour. While firmly attached to terra firma, stretch your mental wings and soar with them.

Hikable early in the season, Crystal Creek Overlook Trail is a memorable journey through time and space and offers a wealth of wildflowers, especially in spring.

BALLHEAD WATERLEAF
Hydrophyllum capitatum

This plant's common names, pussy-foot, woolen breeches, and dwarf waterleaf, are as richly descriptive as ballhead waterleaf. These names paint word pictures of a short, hairy-leaved, round-headed, soft plant. The round inflorescences explode with light purple trumpets, which in turn burst with five stamens. Broad teeth tip the softly-haired leaves, making them appear gray-green. When only a few inches high, this waterleaf blooms early, keeping its globular heads tucked near the base of the leaves.

From southwestern Canada to western Colorado, the charming ballhead waterleaf is fun to find in spring and early summer. Cousins in Colorado are Fendler waterleaf *Hydrophyllum fendleri* and purple fringe *Phacelia sericea*.

Gore Creek
(Eagles Nest Wilderness)

Wildflower Alert: Stately monkshood lead a "century" parade on this lovely trail.

This trail follows the descent and crystalline rush of Gore Creek and is a nice respite from the busy town of Vail just minutes away.

Trail Rating	moderate
Trail Length	6.0 miles out and back
Location	Vail
Elevation	8,680 to 9,840 feet
Bloom Season	late June to August
Peak Bloom	July
Directions	From Denver take I-70 west to the East Vail exit 180. Turn left under the interstate and left again onto the south-side frontage road. Continue along for approximately 2.3 miles to the trailhead, which is adjacent to the Gore Creek bridge just west of Gore Creek Campground. Find parking along the paved road if the small trailhead parking lot is full.

CRYSTALLINE GORE CREEK is full of whitewater until it reaches the
Vail Valley, where it serpentines gracefully through the length of the renowned
resort. The trail, which follows the river, offers visitors to the Vail area a chance
to taste subalpine ambience while actually hiking at montane zone elevations.

Popular Gore Creek Trail, traversing a variety of habitats, offers a
"century" wildflower viewing experience in Eagles Nest Wilderness Area. At
peak bloom—about mid-July—the hike not only offers many different flower
species, but Gore Creek is in full spate, creating a pleasing combination.

On the west side of the frontage road bridge, the trail starts climbing at
a fairly even pace on its 1,200-foot vertical gain to a lush meadow. On its way
to the meadowed slope around the three-mile turnaround point, the route
encounters a variety of terrain, including some rather rocky stretches. Gore
Lake can be reached in 6.4 miles with a 2,700-foot elevation gain from the
trailhead for those with an early start and plenty of stamina.

Parking is limited in the trailhead lot, but more spaces are available
along the shoulders of the black-topped road by Gore Creek bridge. More
information on this and other trails in the region is available at the Holy Cross
Ranger Station on Highway 24 just off I-70 in Minturn, not far west of Vail.

On the north side of the Gore Creek bridge, the trailhead sign and register
is set back in the willows. Take Gore Creek Trail, and immediately you'll
see tall **cow parsnip** with its wide white inflorescences. Climbing through sparse
aspen, the trail presents plenty of mint family member **giant hyssop.** Conical
mauve heads spout pale trumpets.

The south-facing slope wanders through **harebells** and **showy** or **aspen
daisy.** A well-watered small meadow down by the creek displays both white
and the typical deep-purple **monkshood.** A level section of trail offers a fine
opportunity to examine the interior design of the lovely **sego lily,** often a
luminous shade of lavender here.

The Eagles Nest Wilderness Area sign appears quickly. Off to the right,
the golds of **shrubby cinquefoil, aspen sunflower,** and **orange sneezeweed**
brighten the stunted aspen. Stay right on the Gore Creek Trail where a sign
points left to Deluge Lake. More shade and moisture support robust **false
hellebore** and more **monkshood.**

A rocky section sparked by **yellow stonecrop** leads into the shadows of
mixed conifers and aspen cooled by soft yellow **western paintbrush.** Back in
the open, **scarlet gilia, aspen sunflower,** and **showy daisy** combine into a nice
color medley. Early season hikers will pass **arrowleaf balsamroot's** sunny rays.

Up the way, the rustling shade of quaking aspen trees serenades **white bog orchid, monkshood,** and some of **pink pyrola's** dangling bells. More xeric conditions at the top of an outcrop are right for **creamy buckwheat** and **narrow-leaf** or **Wyoming paintbrush.** Up here, the fruit of **chokecherry** and **serviceberry** are forming.

Now rougher underfoot, the trail climbs a pitch, reaching shade where **false Solomon's seal** briefly captures your attention. Zigzag up into the open to reach a spot of pink granite, where a pause and an about-face brings East Vail into view. Shiny-leafed and evergreen, **mountain balm** or **velvety buckbrush** sport clouds of tiny-flowered racemes. More gray-green, felty-leaved **arrowleaf balsamroot** thrives on the dry slope. At the top, the Gore Creek valley stretches toward distant mountains.

On a downward trend, rocks step the trail back into aspens where a seep on the left nurses lacy **cowbane** and **white bog orchid.** On the right, **wild geranium, wild rose,** and **cow parsnip** join more **bog orchids.** Note the several tints, including lavender, that **monkshood** produces. **Tall coneflower** is appropriately named as characterized by cones of disk flowers at eye level.

Leaving shade behind, the trail passes the brilliant yellow umbels of **sulphurflower** and dark blue-purple wands of **Rydberg's penstemon.** Another moist area gathers into a creek to be crossed where **brook saxifrage, bittercress,** and **arrowleaf senecio** harmonize.

Up to the left are the gnawed stumps of an aspen copse. In the same vicinity, **fireweed, harebells, showy daisy,** and **orange agoseris** or **burnt orange dandelion** join

WHITE BOG ORCHID

Limnorchis dilatata subspecies *albiflora* (previously in *Habenaria*)

Even more alluring than the exquisite blossoms of white bog orchid is the heavenly fragrance. Some compare the perfume to gardenias; others say it is spicy sweet, hence names such as scent bottle and scent candle. Each perfectly formed waxy white orchid is attached to a spike-like raceme, typically rising one to two feet or more. Long-tongued insects, often moths, are lured onto the curving flower lip that arcs to the rear-forming nectar-filled spur. Touched on its forehead by the orchid's pollen column, the nectar-seeker becomes a pollinator. The fleshy, tuberous root was boiled by Native Americans for food.

the growing chorus. A new beaver pond down to the right explains the pointed stumps.

A knoll brings the trail to a patch of imported **oxeye daisies** and another beaver pond with Gore Creek in the background. Here, the **sego lilies** are white, the **wild rose** a deeper pink, and the rambling **American vetch** a saucy magenta. **Salsify** heads are as big as softballs.

Bigger aspen means more shade, which pleases **false Solomon's seal** and **wild geranium**. You'll reach a stream to be crossed on stones, the surrounding area replete with **tall chiming bells**. At a rockfall, a good show of clear, magenta **fireweed** leads to rocky footing right beside the white rush of Gore Creek. An upcoming outcrop is home to the bright red-bracted **narrowleaf paintbrush** and its protruding chartreuse flowers.

Narrowed by vegetation, the trail displays a full contingent of **monkshood** close-up, and on a lower level, **green bog orchid**. Boulders stud a bank edging the foaming creek, which is a nice place to view more spires of **fireweed** and other flowers appealing to local butterflies. Stay only until the biting bugs find you.

A rockfall leads to a muddy section where taller **white bog orchids** within sniffing range offer the perfect opportunity to check out the name **scent bottle**.

Leading into conifers before switchbacking, the trail widens to a barren spot where hikers can watch the force of thundering Gore Creek battering mid-stream boulders. An exposed rock garden spangled with **stonecrop**, **harebells**, **pussytoes**, and **creamy buckwheat** rises trailside.

Lodgepole pines provide shelter for cool yellow **western paintbrush**. An aspen copse leads to open skies and a pretty spot filled with lavender **showy daisies** and the yellows of **beauty cinquefoil** and **stonecrop**. Continuing up, the trail sails into conspicuous **Rydberg's penstemon** and **aspen sunflowers**. Less obvious is **woolly** or **silvery cinquefoil** at your feet.

High above Gore Creek now, the trail grows easier and you'll need to negotiate a damp area, passing the purple and white combo of **monkshood** and **parsnip**. A bit farther on, watch for **little rose gentian's** starry flowers, looking as though they were cut from Victorian satin.

With roots as natural steps, the trail opens to worn granite outcrops on the north wall of Gore Creek Canyon. It weaves into deep spruce shade where a golden-bedded brook signals a search for **shy wood nymph**. Here, in the rich forest duff, its fragrant white flowers are a find.

Climbing once again, the rocky trail approaches a serious rockfall softened by clumps of **blue columbine**. Where the little golden creek is left behind, look

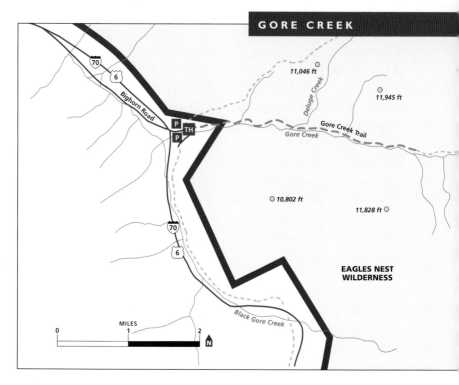

for the red and yellow sconces of **western red columbine**. Stone steps appear shortly before the path aims for head-high **cow parsnip** and waist-high **tall chiming bells**. Soon, towering spruces bring on lanky **twistedstalk** and **arrowleaf senecio**. A colony of diminutive green-flowered **mitrewort** enjoys its mossy bed. "Social" trails abound in the shadowy grove, but head to the right to cross a creek on a log bridge. Again, on the far side, look for the **shy wood nymph.**

Farther along, both **white** and pink **wild geranium** join recumbent violet-rayed **Colorado tansy aster**. Toothed leaves are a dark green. Where **fireweed** prepares to explode, check the area for **white hawkweed's** small flowers on disproportionately tall stems. **Mountain death camas'** green-based white stars grow here, too. Granite lifts the trail through conifers where the keen eye may detect the perfect miniature-orchid blooms of **spotted coralroot** on the left.

Near a pool of green water, a seep nurtures **yellow monkeyflower** and a **little pink elephant** or two. Before heading into lodgepole pines, look for **pink pyrola** and **pearly everlasting.** On the far side, the view widens to include rugged granite cliffs rising to 12,000 feet.

The trail overlooks Gore Creek below. Where newly-opened **wild rose** offers its intense perfume, expect an open hillside of willows spotlighting a burbling brook lined with **tall chiming bells, bittercress,** and **cowbane**.

An even segment through lodgepole introduces the quiet side of Gore Creek, which in turn introduces a broad vista. Both **western** and **scarlet paintbrush** point the way to a panoramic vista of what the Rocky Mountains are all about—rock. Closer at hand, the granite rock garden is highlighted by **blue columbine** and **scarlet paintbrush**.

Willows shelter a flowery haven of **bracted lousewort, bistort, little pink elephants,** and the burnt-red inflorescences of **king's crown**. This could be the **monkshood** trail for the frequent appearances of that stately—but deadly—wildflower. Accompanying it are **cow parsnip**, native white **Coulter daisy**, rich blue **subalpine larkspur**, and masses of shoulder-deep **false hellebore**.

At this point, take a moment to immerse yourself in beauty before turning to head back.

The Gore Creek Trail offers insight into a wilderness area just beyond the busy and sophisticated town of Vail. A tumbling creek entertains the wildflower aficionado, making this a wonderful "century" hike.

GREEN BOG ORCHID
Limnorchis hyperborea
(previously in *Habenaria*)

Also known as northern green rein-orchid, this moisture-loving flower is a member of the world's largest genera with some 20,000 members. Found from Alaska's Arctic Circle south to New Mexico, green bog orchid emits a musky aroma that reportedly mimics the mating scent of some insects. Its soft green, spurred flowers bloom from June through August. The species name *hyperborea* translates into "beyond the north."

Beckwith Pass

Wildflower Alert: This hike presents a myriad of wildflowers, highlighted by lush swales wallowing in giant corydalis.

One of Colorado's most abundantly bountiful wildflower displays, the Cliff Creek Trail to Beckwith Pass passes through meadows and forests with spectacular mountain views along the way.

Trail Rating	easy to moderate
Trail Length	5.0 miles out and back
Location	Crested Butte
Elevation	8,820 to 9,970 feet
Bloom Season	July through August
Peak Bloom	early to mid-July
Directions	From Crested Butte, go west on Kebler Pass (County Road 12) for approximately 12 miles. Near milepost 20, turn left by the bridge at Cliff Creek Trailhead.

KEBLER PASS, west of Crested Butte, is justifiably famous as an "autumn gold" drive. It could also qualify as a flower-filled drive. And better yet, as an access to wonderful wildflower trails, such as the Cliff Creek Trail to Beckwith Pass. "Bountiful" describes both the flowers and the landscape on the approach to the pass.

Popular with horseback riders, the trail navigates some muddy spots and alternates between open meadows and spruce-fir forested areas. Over 70 species of wildflowers and excellent scenery grace the thousand-foot vertical gain.

The aspen-girt trailhead parking area will accommodate vehicles as well as horse trailers.

From **coneflower** to **wintercress** and **waterleaf** to **cinquefoil**, over a dozen different kinds of wildflowers divert the wildflower enthusiast—and that's just between the parking area and the trailhead sign.

Shaded by old-growth aspen (which can expect about the same life-span as we humans), the moist environment produces head-high **tall larkspur**, **monkshood**, and the fascinating **Case's fitweed** or **corydalis**. Plaited perfectly like the well-fitted ends of a log cabin, the tidy racemes of white to pink flowers rise high on unbelievably lush, almost tropical foliage. Petite **American speedwell** and **longleaf chickweed** are footnotes among the willows. In the white-barked woods, check for **orange sneezeweed** and **aspen sunflower**.

As you negotiate a damp section of trail assisted by log planks, you'll pass **arrowleaf senecio** and what looks to be a crude rangy buttercup named **bur avens**, which is a lesser light in the rose family.

Rising from the verdancy, the trail approaches a spruce-fir forest where **glacier lilies** are among the first flowers to bloom. Running water greets the ear where pale, cool yellow **western paintbrush** and **heartleaf arnica** introduce their less noticeable compadres, **Canada** and **mountain blue violet**. Beyond them, the lazy suns of **orange sneezeweed** brighten the landscape. Toxic to livestock, especially sheep, this hardy plant is a bane to ranchers.

The incline increases briefly where Cliff Creek runs down to the left. Scattered about is big-leaved **thimbleberry**. Continuing the ascent, the trail passes **cow parsnip**, more **corydalis**, and lissome **wild blue flax**, backdropped by a talus-covered berm. The reward for ascending is a view of handsome East Beckwith Mountain straight ahead.

Aspen trees once again shelter legions of **tall larkspur** and **tall chiming bells**. Snowy accents are found in **white geranium**. In the vicinity, the rough, robust **western coneflower** raises its brownish-maroon conical head.

Crossing a little creek, the trail wanders up to a hillside meadow packed with **Porter's lovage** or **osha**, highlighted by **aspen sunflower** and **blue flax**, a pleasing medley. Next up, **scarlet gilia** enlivens the scene, and it won't be long before **fireweed** adds its magenta pizzazz. In the next few steps, **tall Jacob's ladder** and **lupine** bring lilac blue touches to this gay garden.

Reaching a ridge where a small stream burbles off to the left, the trail S-curves up toward **pink-headed daisy**, which displays its signature woolly pink buds, and the white-rayed **Coulter daisy**. Soon a sweet glen of **blue columbine** deserves a momentary pause. An about-face reveals the warm-tinted peaks of the Ruby Range.

More conifers precede another meadow where the trail switchbacks to another stand of lusty **Case's fitweed** or **corydalis**. Though locally abundant, this captivating wildflower is partial only to the southwest quadrant of Colorado's Rockies. The route eases with the arrival of a meadow full of **scarlet gilia, sneezeweed, lovage,** and **tall Jacob's ladder**. Both East and West Beckwith peak stand over the evergreen-studded landscape. The views turn to vistas as they sweep a full 180 degrees.

The bountiful color parade continues and a bench of mesmerizing **corydalis** strikes a strong pink tone. The bench ends at a little willow-girt pond south of the trail. Spears of evergreen trees create thick shade, allowing snowbanks to linger long enough to offer blooming **glacier lilies**, even in mid-summer.

Keep right as the trail pulls out of the forest and into a petaled sea, whose bounty creates the illusion of treading in wildflower waters. Pale **paintbrush** borders the path.

Forest dominates the next pitches, introducing an occasional **ballhead waterleaf**

CASE'S FITWEED OR CORYDALIS

Corydalis caseana

According to a Crested Butte botanist, "Lushmoe" is a colloquial moniker used by locals and it suits this plush plant perfectly. Case's fitweed is a robust member of the fumitory family, which includes the garden favorite, bleeding heart. Case's fitweed is a standout with packed racemes of white to pink spurred flowers, sometimes purple tipped, topping glaucous (bluish-green) masses of crocheted foliage. Thick hollow stems, often head high, crowd out the competition and create large patches where mature pods "shoot" their shiny black seeds, propelling them to further increase their turf.

The Latin name comes from *Corydalis,* meaning "crested lark," and *caseana,* honoring the plant's discoverer, E.L. Case. The fumitory family that also includes low growing golden smoke *Corydalis aurea* is rife with toxic members, and Case's fitweed is loaded with poisonous alkaloids. Growing in the Pacific Northwest as well as eastern Asia, corydalis is a find.

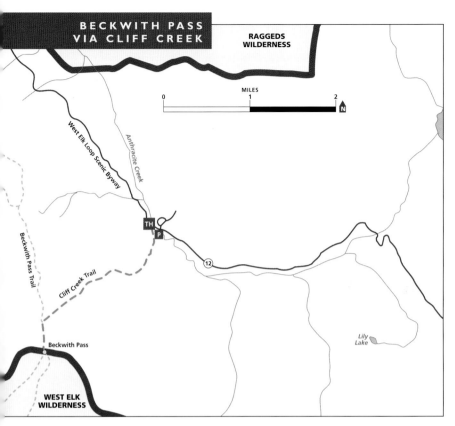

and **twistedstalk**. You'll reach a junction, at which point Beckwith Pass is only one-half mile straight ahead—and the trail rises accordingly. The cooling sound of a creeklet beckons, although crossing it is difficult due to a slippery morass that needs to be hurdled.

The messy segment is left behind with the arrival of open skies and possibly the tip of a peak in the Anthracite Range. Farther on, a **columbine**-dusted meadow waves along a gentle section of trail. Enjoy the tranquility here before tackling another arena fit for mud wrestling.

Traverse an open slope edged by a seep to gain Beckwith Pass and West Elk Wilderness Area Boundary. At nearly 10,000 feet, Beckwith Pass offers grand views, afforded by a level walk east along an old buck-and-rail fence. About 100 feet along the fence, the saw-toothed "Castles" make a jagged distant skyline, anchored by the 13,035-foot West Elk Peak.

The grand stands of wildly lush **corydalis** are reason enough to make Cliff Creek Trail to Beckwith Pass a worthy adventure, but add wildflower-filled meadows and secretive forests of petaled jewels, and it becomes a top priority. Wildflower enthusiasts should place this Crested Butte area hike high on their mid-summer lists.

Wildflower Hike

15

Brush Creek

Wildflower Alert: A bright Persian carpet cloaks the east slope of Crested Butte Mountain.

An old dirt road turns into a gentle loop trail that features over five dozen varieties of wildflowers.

Trail Rating	easy
Trail Length	3.0 mile keyhole loop
Location	Crested Butte
Elevation	8,960 to 9,300 feet
Bloom Season	June to August
Peak Bloom	early to mid-July
Directions	From Crested Butte, take Highway 135 south for 3 miles. Turn left onto East River Road (at the sign for the Crested Butte Country Club) for 2.5 miles to the trailhead, which is on the left.

CRESTED BUTTE is blessed with numerous trails that justify its promising designation as "The Wildflower Capital of Colorado." There are a number of short, easygoing hikes to introduce the wildflower enthusiast to this floristically endowed region, including the early-to-bloom Brush Creek Trail just 10 minutes southeast of town.

Stroll along an old dirt road, flanked with flowers, to enjoy sunshine and the colorful sloped meadow on the backside of 12,000-foot-plus Crested Butte Mountain. A path turns left, curving up through aspen trees and on around to rejoin the road forming a "keyhole" loop. Following this loop will allow you to view about five dozen different kinds of wildflowers.

Located up on the west side of the East River, the Gunnison National Forest signed parking area is more than adequate.

A cornucopia of color starts off the genial hike with imported **wild chamomile**, looking much like a feathery-leaved white daisy, followed by bright natives such as **silvery lupine** and **scarlet gilia**. Heading north on an old road, the aspen-crowned slopes of Crested Butte Mountain's backside rises to the left, and on the right are rolling ranchlands which frame the supple East River.

An early evening hike allows you to experience a stained glass effect, translucent with red, white, pink, blue, and yellow backlit petals and accentuated with soft gray-green sagebrush. Woven into the design are **wild blue flax**, **scarlet gilia**, and cool purple **lupine**. In unworn

MULE'S EARS (NORTHERN)
Wyethia amplexicaulis

The size and shape of the resin-varnished sticky leaves of this member of the populous sunflower family do indeed resemble the generous ears of mules. The one to two dozen rays of the four-to six-inch wide flowers are crisp gold, and the top bloom is the largest. The sizable, mostly basal-leaved clumps may set whole hillsides aglow, especially those which have warm exposures or are overgrazed. Nineteenth-century fur trader-explorer, Nathaniel Wyeth, is commemorated by the genus name. The species' *amplexicaulis* translates to "embracing the stem," in reference to the leaf base attachment.

Native Americans heated the strong-smelling roots prior to fermenting them for consumption. Black bears and deer relish the emerging foliage of spring.

spots, this wildflower carpet glows with the amethysts of **lupine** and **tall western larkspur** complemented by golden **mule's ears**.

Strolling down the road, listen for the trill of a hummingbird and note **wild roses** and clumps of blue **Rocky Mountain penstemon**. As you come to an alder-sheltered rivulet, the whites of hefty **cow parsnip** and delicate **cowbane** light up the shade. A tired old fence signals an entire slope gleaming with **mule's ears**, interspersed with more **gilia** and **flax** and woven together by sprawling **white peavine** and **American vetch**. The silvered oxbows of East River below snake through emerald pastures, a classic image of the high-country West.

INDIAN WARRIORS
Pedicularis procera

Despite its height of up to four feet and the fact that it is sometimes referred to as giant lousewort, this is a subtle plant even when viewed at close range. The spike-like racemes of red-streaked, muted-cream flowers have a pronged galea (helmet or hood) shielding a wide-lobed lower lip—an unusual characteristic—and then there is the intriguing name, Indian Warriors. Found in montane woods or spruce-fir forests from Wyoming to Arizona and Colorado, this stately member of the figwort family has fernlike leaves up to 2 feet long. Cousins include little pink elephants *Pedicularis groenlandica* and sickletop lousewort *Pedicularis racemosa*. More distant relatives are Indian paintbrushes of the *Castilleja* genus.

Looking like overlapped shingles that were applied in the wrong direction on a conical roof, the mauvy-pink spikes of **giant hyssop** exhibit pale flowers with sassy stamens. Square stems and a sniff identify this as a mint.

A gate opening in a sagging fence is decorated with pale blue-flowered **false forget-me-not**. The roadway continues into aspen, where the sound of running water attracts the ear while **white geranium, yellow monkeyflower, bittercress**, and **monkshood** attract the eye.

In the open, the grasses thicken and the trail passes the proud heads of **horned dandelion** and coiled **scorpion weed**.

Brush Creek Trail angles off to the left on a narrow path, leaving the wide road. This "keyhole" portion of the loop enters an extensive stand of quaking aspen, accompanied by pink **wild geranium** and the yellow umbels of **Rocky Mountain parsley**. As summer progresses, **fireweed** will liven up the nearby willows.

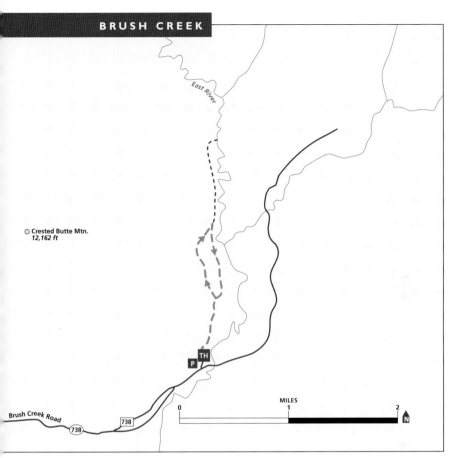

BRUSH CREEK

○ Crested Butte Mtn.
12,162 ft

East River

TH
P

Brush Creek Road

738

738

MILES
0   1   2

N

The trail reaches into the dappled shade of "quakies" (aspen) to find warm-hued **cinquefoil, pink plumes,** and sturdy **orange sneezeweed.** Cool tints hold forth in the thickening shade, represented by **lupine, false forget-me-not,** and **tall larkspur.**

The path angles up on a soft footbed to where tall but subtle battalions of **Indian warriors** stand between the pale-barked trees. Each robust spike of this penstemon relation is filled with helmeted beaks of red-streaked antique ivory.

Nearing the high point, more muted midnight **larkspur** and an occasional **wild rose** guide the leveling trail to a rolling panorama. Drifting into a broad impressionistic meadow like a Monet painting is a creeklet, which can be crossed easily on the high side. Violet **American vetch** scrambles all over its neighbors here, and early-blooming white **western valerian** stand quietly. The route curves from north to east, escorted by pale-yellow **wallflower, pink**

plumes, and **wild geranium**, to rejoin the old road. Yard-high **orange sneezeweed**, **wild blue flax**, and boldly-colored **lupine** act as foreground foils to a vista, which includes 13,209-foot Teocali Mountain in the north and 12,000-foot-plus Double Top Mountain a bit more to the east.

A second crossing of the same creek—so easily spanned before—is a little trickier here. Again, the high side works. If you linger too long, the local bug population comes calling.

An evening hike, long after the sun has dropped behind the mountain and shadows lengthen across the land might bring a coyote chorus on the return trip.

Early morning, when the sun lights the east-facing back slope of Crested Butte Mountain, or evening, when the wildflowers are backlit, are both enchanting times to walk Brush Creek Trail. Convenient to town, but far away in feeling, this short hike is a fine introduction to the wonders of Crested Butte wildflower viewing.

Old Dillon Reservoir

Wildflower Alert: A bounty of fragrant wild roses leads to pretty views of Dillon Reservoir and a serene scenic pond.

Not far from Denver, you'll enjoy pretty lake views with a backdrop of the Continental Divide on this pleasant hike.

easy	*Trail Rating*
1.5 miles out and back	*Trail Length*
Dillon/Frisco	*Location*
9,100 to 9,240 feet	*Elevation*
June through August	*Bloom Season*
late June to mid-July	*Peak Bloom*
From Denver take I-70 west to exit 205. Turn east onto State Route 6 and then right onto Dam Road for another 1.6 miles to the trailhead. Access is on the north side of the road.	*Directions*

OLD DILLON RESERVOIR

WHILE MOST VISITORS focus on prominent Dillon Reservoir, nearby is a small but charming body of water, which is the goal of this short, easy hike. Not only is the slightly elevated locale of Old Dillon Reservoir a scenic one, but the trail is lined with fragrant wild roses in late June and into July.

The gentle trail climbs only 140 feet in three quarters of a mile to offer a view of Dillon Reservoir below as well as the many mountains beyond. The goal is a tranquil pond reflecting massive Buffalo Mountain.

Tucked into lodgepole pines and willows, the signed trailhead entrance is hard to spot from a fast-moving vehicle. On the north side of the Dillon Dam Road, the parking area lies just east of the entrance to Heaton Bay campground. An early arrival on weekends makes it easier to find a parking spot.

Old Dillon Reservoir Trail begins at the northwest corner of the parking area and travels under lodgepole pines scattered with **lupine**, **senecio**, and **penstemon** to reach the foot of a hill. Angling across the hillside, the trail passes patches of evergreen **mountain balm** or **velvety buckbrush** decked out in frothy creamy white racemes in early summer. The trail rises easily through more shrubs, including **antelope brush** and **mountain lover**. When in bloom, **dogbane** presents pale pink hanging bells here.

The path carries the hiker quickly through downed lodgepole where trailing **wild strawberries** hint at yummy things to come. The careful observer may spot the pale greenish urns of **one-sided wintergreen** hidden by a sheltering stone or rotting log.

As the route evens out a bit, a wonderfully extravagant display of **wild roses** covers a logged-over slope. The lovely five-petaled pink blossoms with their plethora of golden stamens soak up the sun, only to give it back as an intoxicating perfume. All along this section, a veritable rose garden cloaks the steep slope between aging stumps.

As the trail ascends, Dillon Reservoir can be glimpsed to the south past sparsely-foliaged, tall **false forget-me-not**, which show off light blue flowers the color of a summer sky at high noon. As small aspen trees appear, views of the lake may be eclipsed by thigh-high clumps of sensational **Rocky Mountain penstemon**. Along with four or five dozen other wildflower species, Old Dillon Reservoir Trail sports several species of **penstemons**. The tall **Rocky Mountain Penstemon** is the showiest and is among at least 150 of its genus found in the Rockies. An additional 100 species are found in the rest of North America, leaving almost none for the rest of the planet.

The mineral soil and open southern exposure along the next section of trail combine to sustain

WILD ROSE
Rosa woodsii

Surrounding a center of multiple pistils and stamens, the five wide petals of the wild, Wood's, or dog rose cling to a cup whose ovary will mature into vitamin C-charged rosehips. Rose petals were sought by Native Americans and ground up to create a soothing powder for sore throats; also a tea and jelly. Some 35 species of rose are native to the U.S., including the wonderfully perfumed rose here named for British botanist Joseph Woods.

The history of the rose goes back 40 million years to a fossil found at Florissant National Monument in central Colorado. In the fifth century, the Greeks cultivated the rose, the chosen flower of the goddess Aphrodite. It could even be said that a rose was responsible for the discovery of America. Apparently Columbus' ship was becalmed in the sinister Sargasso Sea and ready to turn back home when a crew member spotted a rose branch floating in the water. The date was October 11, 1492.

all manner of wildflower, including **pink-headed daisies, narrowleaf paint-brush, creamy buckwheat, harebells,** and opulent **sego lilies.** The bulbs of this flared-petaled beauty once provided a nutritious food source for Native Americans. They shared their knowledge with newly arrived Mormon settlers long ago and thus saved the newcomers from starvation that first winter in Utah.

The open trail levels to present an outstanding panorama of Dillon Reservoir below and peaks forming the Continental Divide beyond. Most weekends, this wide view becomes animated as fleets of sailboats skim the blue waters. A memorable photographic shot is achieved from a low angle, catching a foreground of wildflowers as rainbow spinnakers billow from racing boats.

A slight rise brings the trail up to even ground while retaining the stunning view to the south. Looking north, Old Dillon Reservoir, built in the 1930s, glistens through the trees.

The flat trail eases through short aspen, some of which ended their growing career as stumps chiseled by beavers. Among the quaking-leafed trees are **lupine, red globe anemone,** and **cinquefoil.**

The west end of Old Dillon Reservoir is anchored with a large stick and mud beaver lodge. Beyond the lodge rises Buffalo Mountain to the west. Often its warm-tinted reflection gleams in the reservoir during the early morning hours when alpenglow strikes the mountain's 12,777-foot bulk.

A pleasant stroll counterclockwise around the reservoir's grassy marshes may turn up **littleflower penstemon, buttercups, rosy pussytoes,** and **shrubby cinquefoil.** Growing directly in the path are minute pink stars sprinkled on thready-leafed mats: **Nuttall's sandwort.** Leading you around to the east side of the little lake are **silvery cinquefoil** and aptly named **pearly everlasting.** Here, once again, over legions of spired evergreens, Buffalo Mountain looms on the far horizon.

The wide, gravelly trail comes around to drop down into the canal-like depression where **wild roses** and **fireweed** cloak the inlet's bank. Also perking up the vicinity are magenta **American vetch** and **white peavine,** both rambling members of the legume or pea family.

As you finish the circuit, take a look at what appear to be indented inlets, but are actually slipways down which the nocturnal beaver slides. If you arrive early, when the morning mist still rises in ghostly wisps from the still waters, you may find the beaver just finishing his nightshift.

Take time to memorize the enticing fragrance of the exuberant wild roses while heading back down to the car park. The memory may be as absorbing as those views of Buffalo Mountain reflected in Old Dillon Reservoir. This short summer hike, just an hour and a half from the bustling Denver Metro area, is a great starter trail with many things to interest children and adults alike.

Lily Pad Lakes
(Eagles Nest Wilderness)

Wildflower Alert: This trail offers lovely sego lilies and yellow pond lilies in mid-July.

Floating on the water, the heart-shaped leaves of yellow pond lilies can grow to be 18 inches across.

moderate	*Trail Rating*
3.2 miles out and back	*Trail Length*
Frisco	*Location*
9,090 to 9,900 feet	*Elevation*
June to August	*Bloom Season*
mid-July	*Peak Bloom*
From I-70 go west to Frisco exit 203. Turn right and then immediately left onto a dirt frontage road, which ends at the trailhead.	*Directions*

LESS THAN AN HOUR AND A HALF from the Denver Metro area is a short hike that reaches into the Eagles Nest Wilderness Area. Along the way, over 50 species of wildflowers line the trail, ending at a pair of evergreen-surrounded lakes, one of which has many of the yellow pond lilies blooming in July.

The Meadow Creek Trail access to Lily Pad Lake and its adjacent, but much smaller sibling, gains about 800-vertical feet in just over a mile.

The parking area, just off the Interstate, is accommodating.

The rocky, rising Meadow Creek Trail begins in the filtered shade of aspen and conifer trees and is full of birdsong and **white geranium, yarrow, mouse-ear chickweed, cow parsnip,** and **northern bedstraw.** The pinks are represented by **wild rose** and **wild geranium,** the blues by **tall chiming bells, harebell,** and **wild blue flax.**

A signed junction soon appears where Meadow Creek Trail turns left, while the path to Lily Pad Lakes heads right toward the sound of rushing water.

As you reach a bench, the trail overlooks rangy plants with droopy, orange-gold ray flowers: **orange sneezeweed.** Ranchers detest this member of the sunflower family because of its toxicity to livestock. Except for isolated areas in the Pike's Peak region, **orange sneezeweed** is mostly found west of the Continental Divide. Growing near the sturdy sneezeweed, refined **wild blue flax** titillates the morning hours with its silky sky-blue petals.

The trail continues to rise confidently, flanked by stately quaking aspens with enticingly fragrant **wild roses** and sprawling **white peavine** in the understory.

Gaining in girth, aspen shade the way to a level terrace where the trail pushes into a solid stand of lodgepole pine. Little grows in this type of forest, but **heartleaf arnica's** occasional sunny flare glows in the cool shade. Most of the eight or so arnica species in the Rockies prefer sunshine. The yellow flowers of heartleaf arnica were steeped for healing chapped lips and wounds.

Just before crossing lively Meadow Creek on a well-built bridge, scan the undergrowth on the right for the dangling scarlet and yellow lanterns of **western red columbine.** This Western Slope beauty has five red petals which elongate into straight, nectar-bearing spurs. The yellow sepals cup a bundle of extended stamens.

Where the ascending trail opens to a grassy hillside, be on the lookout for a variety of butterflies sipping from wildflowers scattered around gray sage-brush. Among the aromatic sage are the wide chalices of lovely **sego lily,** often

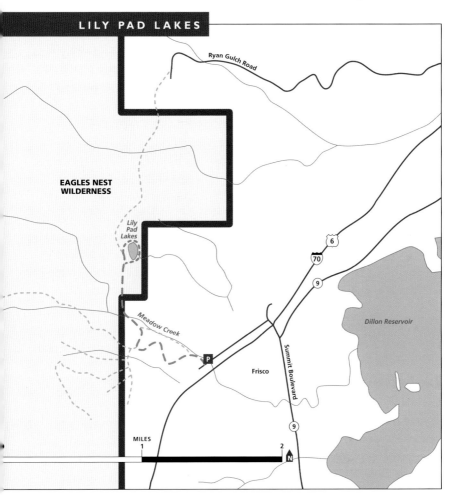

tinted lavender-blue here. A neighboring plant is the **creamy** or **subalpine buckwheat**, which changes its youthful ivory to warm rose as it ages. Most of the fifty buckwheat species in the Rocky Mountains tend to be yellow—all are a fine honey source.

Still pulling up, the trail passes an old beaver dam whose pond has evolved into a lushly grassed pocket meadow. A pause here cues in Dillon Reservoir and the mountains beyond.

Be on the watch for an open hillside rife with the delicate bi-colored heads of **western red columbine**. Observant hikers will spot one, then two, then many of this pretty wildflower during its typical mid-July bloom. The more moisture in the ground, the better the display.

Don't dally, however—standing too long to admire the flowers brings out the mosquitoes from nearby wet areas. This is ideal habitat for two tall, slim members of the hellebore family: **monkshood** and **tall western larkspur**, both richly-hued and toxic—the monkshood being deadly in all parts.

The trail advances toward thick evergreens that cloak the slope leading up to the larger lake. Before beavers moved in and raised the water level by damming the outlet, Lily Pad Lake had extensive patches of pond lilies floating on its surface. When the beavers claimed the lake and built a substantial lodge, the lilies disappeared. To see these floating flowers, however, continue around the southeast shore of the lake and climb the berm dividing the upper and lower lakes.

The upper lake is more of a pond, but in July its dark surface is a mass of **yellow pond lilies**. Rising from the platter-sized leaves, big globes of gold sepals cup toadstool-shaped pistils and scads of stamens. A pair of binoculars are helpful for examining flower structure if the lilies are far from the shore. Pond lily stems may be six feet long from their sinuous rhizomes, anchored in bottom muck, to their floating leaves. Fishermen know that pond lilies mean the water will be over their waders. Indian peoples found the lilies a nutritious food source—from the thick submerged rootstocks harvested by bare toes to the ripe seeds roasted like popcorn.

YELLOW POND LILY
Nuphar lutea subspecies polysepala

Spatterdock, Wokas, and Rocky Mountain cow lily also describe widespread yellow pond lily, a member of the waterlily family. Blooming in mid-summer, big globes of golden yellow sepals cup a bevy of maroon-ish stamens and a prominent disc-shaped stigma. The leathery leaves grow in size up to 18 inches and are shaped like rounded hearts. They lie floating on the surface or submerged beneath the water.

Though harvesting the plants was not easy, Native Americans found yellow pond lilies a nutritious food source. Prying the king-sized, sinuous rhizomes from the thick muck with their toes, Indian women boiled snaky roots for stews or porridge. The seeds—called "wokas"—were roasted and said to taste like popcorn, although most were made into flour.

Return to the lower lake and find a boulder upon which to perch. Perhaps the nocturnal beaver will make an appearance and slap his flat, fleshy tail on the water to warn intruders.

As you continue on, gingerly circling around the lake, look along the marshy edges for **shooting stars, white bog orchids,** and **little pink elephants.** As the water level rises, many of these bog areas will disappear and with them the flowers.

After heading back down the trail to the parking area, watch the sides of the road for **Rocky Mountain locoweed** as you drive off. Flourishing in tints from pale-lavender through violet, the erect racemes are a showy diversion along the road. A member of the pea family, this locoweed is also called **silverleaf loco** due to myriad silky hairs lining the ladder-like leaves.

The fast-growing Frisco-Dillon area still has a number of close-in getaways for hikers. Lily Pad Lakes, from the Meadow Creek Trailhead, has a convenient access and, in well-watered years, is a nice trek through a colorful wildflower garden to a pair of scenic forest lakes.

Gold Hill

Wildflower Alert: Flurries of starry phlox are nature's snow-in-summer on this short, early season trail between Frisco and Breckenridge.

Lush meadows, tall lodgepole pine, and views of the Tenmile Range mark this easy-going hike.

Trail Rating	easy
Trail Length	1.4 miles out and back
Location	Frisco/Breckenridge
Elevation	9,200 to 9,400 feet
Bloom Season	June to August
Peak Bloom	early to mid-July
Directions	From I-70 go west to the Frisco exit 203. Turn onto Highway 9 and proceed south for approximately 5 miles. Park on the right at corner of County Road 950 (Gateway Drive), and the trailhead is across from Gateway Drive.

FOR THOSE WHO DESIRE A SHORT EASY JAUNT to preview a nice collection of about 50 different kinds of wildflowers, Gold Hill Trail is just right. In early summer this montane-zone hike produces an especially fine phlox display—an illusion of heat-proof snow. Glimpses of the Blue River valley surrounded by mountains are an added attraction.

Shaded for the most part, Gold Hill Trail rises gently to a level meadow area. In the first half of June, calypso orchids hide here and there in forest duff, followed by flurries of phlox in July. The trail description here covers only the flowery portion of Gold Hill Trail, which is a small segment of the ambitious Colorado Trail. A longer hike can be achieved by ascending through "doghair" lodgepole pines to a clear-cut area and connecting with Miners Creek Trail.

There is plenty of parking at the trailhead sign on the corner of State Route 9 and Gateway Drive. The trail itself is accessed by crossing Gateway Drive.

The Gold Hill Trail displays about 20 different wildflowers in the first few yards of the sagebrush-flanked trailhead, including gold-flowered **shrubby cinquefoil**, supple **wild blue flax**, full-headed **creamy buckwheat**, rambling **American vetch**, long-blooming **scarlet gilia**, and sleek **tall larkspur** as well as spatters of **Rocky Mountain phlox** which lie on the ground like crocheted doilies.

The trail angles up into lodgepole pines where **lupine** exhibits its choice blue, pea-type flowers. This widespread plant is an important nitrogen-fixer in the nutrient-needy mineral soil often associated with these spare pines.

Come to a meadow full of pastel **Rocky Mountain locoweed**, brilliant **scarlet gilia**, and the wide cups of **sego lily**. Also called **mariposa lilies** (Spanish for butterfly), the three showy petals range from white to lavender-blue and even a soft wine.

Spring bloomers, such as **golden banner** of the prolific pea family, **mountain blue violet** in its edible clan, and **bluemist penstemon** (related to paintbrush) are scattered here and there. Joining them are **harebells**, **red globe anemone**, and **wild rose**.

Level now, the trail travels through an exquisite snowfall of pristine **Rocky Mountain phlox**, each pale star secreting a delightful fragrance. A more open path heads into a moist environment perfect for **pink plumes**, that unlikely-looking member of the rose family. Whether in the inverted urn, tri-flowered stage, or a mass of feathery seed plumes, the color is a distinctive dusty rose-pink. Growing from the foothills to subalpine, it is sometimes called **pink avens**. Look in the same vicinity for the brighter pink of up-facing **Geyer onion**. Nearby, in early July, stately **wild iris** sends up its signature lavender-purple blossoms. Easy to identify because of its similarity to the garden variety, this wildling is the only iris native to the Rockies. Here and there, **bistort's** white bottlebrush heads wave on long stems. Lighting up the landscape is a smattering of **blue columbine**.

Skirting private property, the trail comes into cool yellow **western paintbrush**, more **pink plumes**, and **littleflower penstemon** with its rich blue-purple whorls of tubular flowers. The ray and disk flowers of proud **aspen sunflower** add petaled sunshine to the scene.

The trail roams through evergreens including Colorado blue spruce. Summits of the lovely Tenmile Range are visible through the trees; these shapely crests vary from Peak One's 12,805 feet on the north to Peak Ten's 13,633 feet on the south.

ROCKY MOUNTAIN PHLOX
Phlox multiflora

The needlelike foliage of the widespread Rocky Mountain phlox forms spreading mats that frame five-petaled pastel stars. Sweet scented, the salver-shaped flowers may be white or blushed, even pale blue or lavender. Armed with tiny stiff bristles, the leaves feel rough, and this plant likes dry habitats. Another moniker is many-flowered phlox. *Phlox*, meaning "flame" in Greek, is the genus moniker; *multiflora*, "many flowered," is the easily translated species name. Colorado cousins include longleaf phlox *Phlox longifolia* and alpine phlox *Phlox condensata*.

As you walk toward a large lodgepole pine on the left, the trail may expose some basal-leaved clumps of **mountain death camas**. The whitish tepals form broad stars. This attractive plant is toxic in its entirety. An opening finds soothing **western paintbrush** and serene white and lavender **sego lilies**.

An open area brings the beautiful Tenmile Range back into view. To the southwest, in the shadow of Peaks 7 through 10, are the runs of Breckenridge Ski Area.

You'll come upon a field of upright **aspen sunflowers** interspersed with **golden banner** and **creamy buckwheat**. **Wild blue flax**, the color of the sky on a clear day, is best observed in the cool hours. Though the fibers of this plant were once

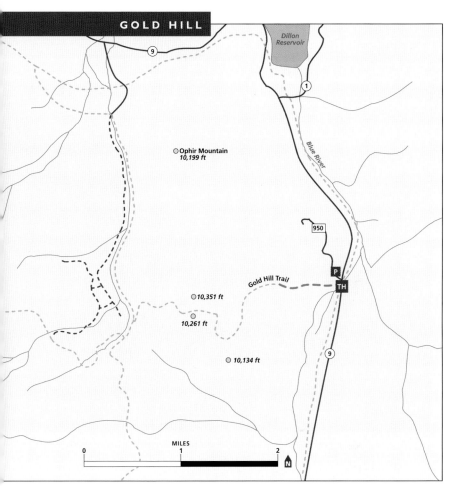

used by Native Americans for fishing nets and cordage, the fragile petals last but a day, often dropping by afternoon.

The next gap reveals a sight for which the Blue River valley is famous—huge piles of tailings, evidence of humanity's quest for precious metal. Underfoot, roots take the trail back into evergreen shade, which means fewer wildflowers, although **mountain death camas** continue to thrive even here among the lodgepole pine. Fallen trees increase, as does the gradient, until they mass into a chaotic deadfall. This is a good turnaround point.

Short, but sweet with flurries of **phlox** and pools of **iris**, Gold Hill Trail is a good choice for a wide range of hiking abilities. Views of the Tenmile Range add interest to this pretty little foray of convenient summer wildflower viewing.

Wildflower Hike

19

Tenderfoot Mountain

Wildflower Alert: This south-facing lakeview trail brings on wildflowers early in the season.

Cool aspen stands, open hillsides, and sweeping views characterize this trail, with a bench at trail's end for time to reflect.

Trail Rating	easy
Trail Length	2.5 miles out and back
Location	Dillon
Elevation	9,280 to 9,800 feet
Bloom Season	June to late July
Peak Bloom	late June to mid-July
Directions	From Denver take I-70 west to the Dillon exit 205. Take a left onto US 6 to the stoplight. Turn left and then immediately right onto County Road 51 for approximately 0.5 mile to the signed parking just below Dillon's water tank facilities.

TENDERFOOT MOUNTAIN TRAIL offers wonderful views of Dillon Reservoir and the peaks of Tenmile Range beyond a flowery hillside. Thanks to a south-facing slope, this easygoing hike is especially fine on early season mornings and evenings.

Traversing cool aspen copses, sagebrush-studded open hillsides, and lodgepole pine stands, this one-and-a-quarter-mile trail heads up at a fairly steady pace. Wildflower menus change with alternating habitats throughout the trail. A bench is located at the end of the hike for enjoying marvelous views of the water, flowers, and peaks.

Parking is usually adequate at the designated trailhead.

Timber steps find plush swabs of **Rocky Mountain locoweed** leading into a lodgepole forest on the high side of the roadway. Also in the pea family, **standing milkvetch's** tidy racemes bloom a bit later along the way.

As the trail passes through a quaking aspen grove, rambling magenta **American vetch** and **white peavine** prime the canvas for stately **tall larkspur** and comely **blue columbine**. Perfumed **wild rose** adds a tantalizing pink touch. Roses have been enticing pollinators for 40 million years with their inviting scent.

Out in the open, **creamy buckwheat** and **sego lilies** decorate the sagebrush on this south-facing slope. A sign sends Tenderfoot Trail up to the left. Take a moment for a sweeping view of Dillon Reservoir and its foreground marina to the sawtoothed Tenmile Range beyond.

CREAMY OR SUBALPINE BUCKWHEAT
Eriogonum subalpinium

This wild buckwheat is found at higher elevations, while species of cousin sulphurflower run the gamut from plains to tundra. Creamy or subalpine buckwheat's packed ivory age gently into salmon and finally a rich rusty red. Fond of mineral soil, buckwheats attract bees, making them fine honey plants. Cousins include sulphurflower *Eriogonum umbellatum* and cushion buckwheat *Eriogonum ovalifolium*.

Considered a valuable medicinal source by Native Americans, creamy and yellow buckwheats also provide food for wildlife.

Purple **showy** or **aspen daisy** and **scarlet gilia** embellish the sage- and **antelope brush**-dotted hillside. Creamy buckwheat's cousin **sulphurflower** lifts hot yellow umbels on bare stems to perk up the steadily rising trail. Watch for the washed-out blue stars of spindly **sticky gilia**. This undistinguished member of the phlox family is closely related to the showy **scarlet gilia** or **skyrocket**.

Contouring around the hill, the trail heads past **goldenrod** and a splash of **Rocky Mountain phlox** into the domain of grasses and an aspen copse. Lodgepole pines zig the trail by **mountain lover** shrubs and creeping **kinnikinnick** and into straggling aspen and prickly common juniper.

Sagebrush accompanies a view of Buffalo Mountain on the right. On the left, numbered one through ten, peaks of the Tenmile Range crest over Dillon's wide lake waters. Sages are often the host plant of choice for **naked broomrape**. Early season hikers might spot this fleshy (both in color and texture) parasite poking up its oddly attractive tubular flowers. Tolerating xeric conditions, **showy daisy**, **scarlet gilia**, **creamy buckwheat**, **lupine** and the ragged bracts of **sulphur paintbrush** sweep the open slopes around you with a color-charged brush.

Beneath spacious skies, a bench beckons. Take a moment and experience the expansive mountainscape. The ragged pinnacles of the Gore Range are visible along the northwest and west. Next is 13,189-foot Red Peak and in front of the Gore Range is the worn summit of 12,777-foot Buffalo Mountain. Also included in this majestic melody is the Tenmile Range with 12,805-foot Peak 1 to the southwest and 13,633-foot Peak 10 to the south.

Continuing up the trail, **aspen sunflowers** with white daubs of **Rocky Mountain locoweed** and **phlox** appear—both often display pastel tints. A level section travels into an aspen-shaded ravine with cool **western paintbrush** on its banks. A dab of a **wild rose** or two along the steadily rising trail are intertwined with close-growing lodgepoles, referred to as "doghair." Sagebrush and **snowberry**, with its delicately-blushed white bells, stabilize the granular soil and are aided intermittently by ultramarine-pigmented **Rocky Mountain** and **bluemist penstemons.** As the pathway pushes into the shimmering shade of "quakies" (aspen), artistic **harebells** dangle lilac thimbles.

Pine trees guide you to a sturdy split-log bench. Curve up just a tad to find low clumps of **early blue daisy**, **bluemist penstemon**, **silvery lupine**, **yellow stonecrop**, and **standing milkvetch** adorning the dry slope overlooking Dillon Reservoir. Far below, watch for the graceful glide of white-winged sailboats. The bench makes a good turnaround point. Along the southern horizon, the Continental Divide adds a finishing touch to this satisfying scene.

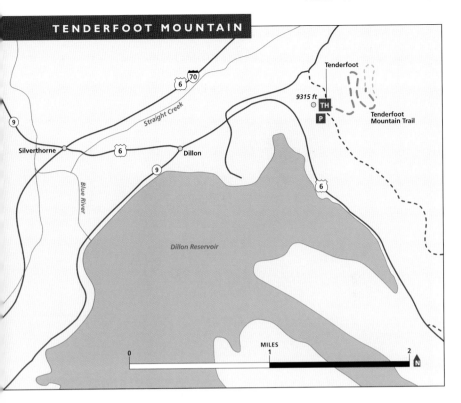

This short, easy hike is as much about water and mountain vistas as it is wildflowers. Perfect to begin or end a day in the Dillon-Frisco-Keystone area, Tenderfoot Mountain Trail is like your first paint-by-number kit: quick, simple, colorful, and gratifying.

Wildflower Hike

20

Blue Lake
(Rawah Wilderness)

Wildflower Alert: A vale of golden-bedded brooks harbor perfect capes of Oriental gardens.

This spectacular trail stretches for nearly five miles and encompasses great diversity.

Trail Rating	moderate to strenuous (for length)
Trail Length	9.8 miles out and back
Location	Rawah Wilderness Area/Colorado State Forest/Fort Collins
Elevation	9,520 to 10,840 feet
Bloom Season	late June to August
Peak Bloom	mid- to late July
Directions	From Ted's Place, which is approximately 10 miles west of Fort Collins, go west on State Route 14 for 55 miles. The trailhead is located on the right, which is the opposite side of Long Draw Reservoir Road.

THERE ARE A NUMBER OF BLUE LAKES in Colorado. This one sits in a golden bowl in the lovely Rawah Wilderness Area west of Fort Collins. While the handsome lake itself is in the subalpine zone, surrounding areas soar into the alpine zones. Nearly 90 wildflower species may be encountered on the 4.9-mile trek, which may slow down the ambitious wildflower aficionado. It also happens to be the most easily accessed lake in the Rawah Wilderness.

The trail begins along a forested rushing river, then curves up, via an old road, through evergreens. Climbing through a rocky area, it reaches small springs and creeks of great charm before ascending to a level segment above Blue Lake.

Parking is generous in the paved area adjacent to the highway. Restrooms are across the way at the Long Draw Winter trailhead.

Wide enough for two people, the trail to Blue Lake begins on a slant through lodgepole pine down to the north fork of Joe Wright Creek, which is more of a river by high country standards. The surging whitewater is crossed on a sturdy bridge.

The path ambles along the north side of the river in the shade of mixed conifers, where the royal purples of **monkshood** and **subalpine larkspur** put in an appearance. Openings allow the sun to nourish **arrowleaf senecio** and **cow parsnip**.

Where a little seep crosses the trail, alders shelter **white geranium** and **white bog orchid**. The trail winds up and widens. On its edges, look for slender **white hawkweed** and later-blooming **fireweed** and **goldenrod**.

Far above the river now, left with only its rushing-wind sound, the trail turns onto a northern exposure. Here **one-sided wintergreen, lesser wintergreen**, and a patch of **prince's pine** or **pipssisewa** enjoy the cooler aspect. Another seep area is home to colonies of papery-bracted **pearly everlasting**.

On parallel logs, cross a small creek which chimes in from the left, and proceed to another seep. This one is populated by both **green** and **white bog orchids**. In addition, **pink pyrola** with its pendant corollas and **lesser wintergreen** with whitish ones flourish in the mossy environment. On the bank above, the keen eye might find **twinflower**'s dainty pink and white bells.

Along this partial road, peek through the close trees for a glimpse of mile-long Chambers Lake below and a snow-patched peak ahead.

Bits of **scarlet paintbrush** lead to the place where Blue Lake Trail takes off to the right. Heading up the single trail, white **sickletop lousewort** calls for scouting a nearby mossy bank to find **twayblade**, a little fork-lipped green orchid that is easiest to spot by locating its single pair of opposing leaves.

Approach another well-built bridge to span Fall Creek's whitewater cascade. **Tall chiming bells**, twistedstalk, tall **arrowleaf senecio**, **bittercress**, and

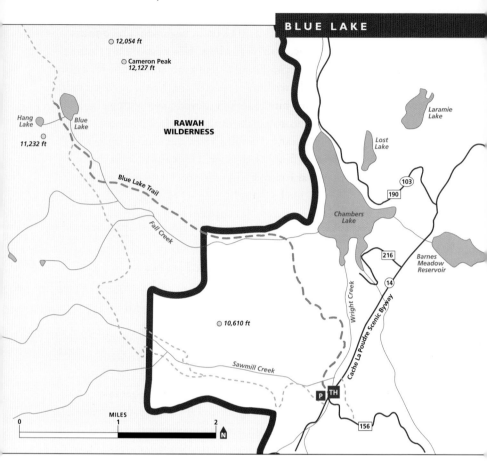

cowbane flank the leaping creek. Just uphill from this show, about two miles from the trailhead, a sign welcomes the hiker to the Rawah Wilderness Area.

No longer easygoing, the trail grows rocky as it rises, and like many high country trails, this one climbs and levels many times. The next segment is a level one.

Unlike the sparse understory of lodgepole pine, spruce-fir understory is full of verdant pockets of meadows. In this meadow is **mitrewort** (a hand lens brings out the maroon tracery in the green snowflake flowers) and more **twayblade**.

Underfoot, a bit farther on, is an old road that takes the hiker through a pocket meadow featuring **monkshood**, **cowbane**, **white geranium** and **arrowleaf senecio**. Continuing on, lovely **blue columbine** and **pink-headed daisies** pop up in spots of shifting sunlight. In damp places along the roughening trail, **foamflower**, a delicately-flowered member of the saxifrage family, thrives in moist habitats.

Sometimes shallow water runs onto the trail, but it's nothing a pair of sturdy hiking boots can't handle. Patches of **alpine milkvetch**, with white pea-type flowers tipped in blue, occur trailside. Leveling out somewhat, the trail passes three-paneled pods of **glacier lilies**, which bloom soon after snowmelt.

Racemes of green-tinged white **mountain death camas** line the way to forested vignettes of a peak-surrounded bowl. Climbing to a creeklet that mumbles through rocks, look near the trail for the hanging parasols of **pink pyrola**. The pathway begins drifting down to a mossy tangle of old wood and rock where a display of **fringed Parnassia** is a treat to the eye. Its pearly buds develop into five waxy petals, finely fringed on the inner edges with each rising high on straight stems.

Downhill a bit, a grass-choked meadow spouts **little pink elephants** on the left, and, on the right, a seep featuring **yellow monkeyflower** and more **Parnassia**. Named after Greece's Mount Parnassus, this attractive mid-summer bloomer favors subalpine wet places.

As you come into an area rife with creeklets, pause to enjoy the serenity. Early season hikers will find **Parry primrose**, **marsh marigold**, and **globeflower**, whose long stalks terminate in a multi-podded seedhead that resembles a tiny overblown artichoke.

The Blue Lake Trail pulls up a moderate pitch and fluctuates with the lay of the land. **Sickletop lousewort** or **parrot's beak** insert racemes of white coils in the shady forest.

You'll recognize the rocky character of the trail in glimpses of a cornice-ringed bowl of raw-sloped peaks. Numerous sandy-bottomed brooks appear, and the verdant banks of some are overhung with **queen's crown**. Among the stones look for swatches of early-blooming **pink bog laurel**. The meadowy spaces between the sparkling creeklets support **blueleaf cinquefoil**, **bog orchids**, **alpine speedwell**, **Parry clover**, and **subalpine daisy**. The latter with its wider petals looks more like a cool pink aster than the fleabane daisy it is.

Forest again holds sway, allowing some **broad-leafed arnica** the role of little suns. Running water courts the distinctive brick-red heads of noble **king's crown**. Look for **little pink elephants**, **subalpine daisy**, **white bog orchids**, yellow **subalpine** or **woolly arnica**, and tall **arrowleaf senecio**.

These sky-blessed areas hold great charm. One crystal-clear brook is home to **Parnassia**, **moss** or **compass gentian**, dusky-purple **star gentian**, and tight overlays of sub-shrub **pink bog laurel**.

Roots and rocks clutter the trail as it climbs higher and then eases, passing sloped meadows of **tall chiming bells**, **king's crown**, **bistort**, **homely buttercup**, and **Gray's angelica**. The drier uphill side supports **Parry clover** and lots of **black-headed daisies**.

Where snow lingers, look for both **marsh marigold**—its white tepals tinged steel blue underneath—and showy **Parry primrose** before the shimmering green waters of Blue Lake below divert your attention.

Rising above the lake to the northeast is smooth-looking 12,127-foot Mount Cameron, and to the southwest is 12,951-foot Clark Peak. Directly west are rugged outcrops jutting into the sky, and due north is 11,000-foot Blue Lake Pass.

A subalpine crazy quilt of cool yellow **western paintbrush, scarlet paintbrush, subalpine arnica, subalpine larkspur**, and **bistort** drapes color on a bit of hillside stretching down to the lake.

The trail is flat along the terrace high above Blue Lake. Snowbanks linger here and the evidence is a prime swatch of yellow **glacier lilies** with its signature curved tepals. Perhaps a **snow buttercup** will give away the location of the last snow to go.

To catch more of the floral offerings of this lovely place, continue on the trail to mossy seeps nurturing **pink willowherb** and **rosy paintbrush**. A burbling creek flows across the trail. After an appreciative sweep of dainty **brook saxifrage**, hot pink **Parry primrose,** and cold water-loving **marsh marigold**, retrace your steps to complete the trek to Blue Lake.

While rather long, especially for day hikers who happen to be wildflower aficionados, Blue Lake Trail offers a fine hike with access to the Rawah Wilderness Area. With about 90 different flower species to view, you will enjoy both the scenic variety and the petaled variety of this hike. Set your sights on this grand subalpine trail west of Fort Collins.

GLACIER LILY

Erythronium grandiflorum

Appearing as the snowbanks melt, the six golden-yellow tepals of glacier lily arc back from six pendant stamens. This showy wildflower, sometimes congregating in the hundreds or even thousands, is also called the avalanche or snow lily. A pair of smooth, elliptical leaves emanate from the base, and below is a bulb-like corm. These bulbs when boiled or dried were relished by Native Americans. Rodents dig them up for winter food. The 3-paneled green pods are foraged by deer, elk, bear, and bighorn sheep. A spectacular but seldom-seen cousin is the wood lily *Lillium philadelphicum.*

Crater Lake *via West Portal*
(Maroon Bells-Snowmass Wilderness)

Wildflower Alert: Over 100 species make this "century" trail a floristic fantasy.

Just outside of Aspen, this trail shimmers with color and features stunning views of the famous Maroon Bells.

moderate	*Trail Rating*
4.5 miles out and back	*Trail Length*
Aspen	*Location*
9,540 to 10,076 feet	*Elevation*
late June through August	*Bloom Season*
early to mid-July	*Peak Bloom*
	Directions

From Aspen take State Route 82 west. Turn left onto Meadow Creek Road, which ends at Maroon Lake. Watch for the West Portal trailhead on the right just before the road's end. Note that travel by shuttle is required from 8:30 a.m. to 5:30 p.m. —cars are not allowed. Check locally for details. A fee may be charged for entry to the Maroon Lake area.

COLORADO IS RENOWNED for stunning landscapes, and awe-inspiring Maroon Bells reflected in Maroon Lake is one of the top contenders. Great layered heaps of deep red sandstone, including 14,165-foot Maroon Peak, make up the intriguing formations known as the Maroon Bells.

Hikers going beyond Maroon Lake to Crater Lake get to see the "Bells" much more intimately. The hike to Crater Lake is a "century" trail, meaning at least 100 species of wildflowers appear along the trail at peak bloom. This description begins at West Portal Trailhead, which rises and then drops to a view of Maroon Lake. The Maroon-Snowmass Trail takes the hiker up to Crater Lake. The one-way distance is two and one quarter miles from the West Portal to Crater Lake. Be alert for adverse weather, especially in the afternoon— clouds build quickly into thunderheads.

Considering the extraordinary beauty of the Maroon Bells area, it's not surprising that the limited parking lot could not accommodate all visitor vehicles. A shuttle bus originating in Aspen solves the problem. At the time this book was written, private vehicles could drive in before the entrance station opens at 8:30 a.m. They are also allowed after 5:30 p.m. To update this information, check locally before making plans.

There are restrooms and ample parking at the West Portal trailhead where this description originates.

The trail starts off on a rustic slope of quaking aspen trees. The verdant understory brushes on daubs of white **cow parsnip**, **northern bedstraw**, and lavender **aspen** or **showy daisy**. All are tied together with **white peavine** and magenta **American vetch**.

Hikers weave up on a trail flanked by vegetation so thick that a sense of adventure is essential. In damp areas, **tall chiming bells**, **Canada violet**, and **tall larkspur** flourish. Drier zones are just right for **Rocky Mountain penstemon**, **narrowleaf paintbrush**, and **few-flowered false Solomon's seal** or more simply **star Solomon's seal**.

The trail thins out from the right where **yellow monkeyflower** delight in wet feet as does snowy **bittercress**. Both plants served as salad greens for Native Americans. Modern campers find the vitamin C and A-charged leaves a nice addition to lettuce, especially the peppery taste of bittercress. Once the bittercress blooms, it gets a serious "bite" to it, explaining its common name.

More xeric-type wildflowers, such as **Rocky Mountain locoweed** and **Whipple penstemon**, grace a hump at an easily crossed creek. To the north are the ragged citadels of Sievers Mountain, topping out at 12,773 feet.

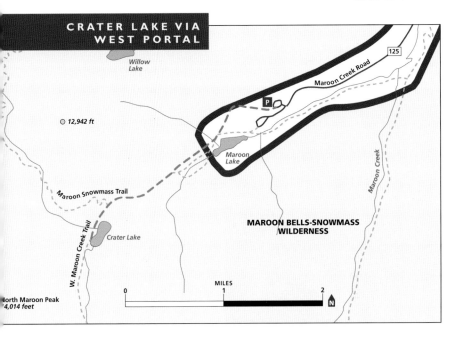

The trail crests and wades through a sea of wildflowers on the way down toward Maroon Lake. **Orange sneezeweed** in hot gold complements **monkshood** in regal purple. Though all parts of monkshood are deadly, it has fascinating flowers. Head-high specimens here invite the hiker to peer under the curved "cowl" (the top sepal) of a blossom to inspect a whiskery "face" (petals and stamens) hidden by the rim of the "hood" (other sepals). **Pink-headed daisy** and **cow parsnip** soften the effect.

The trail continues, passing through heavenly swaths of deep blue **tall larkspur** and white **cow parsnip**. A graceful slope sweeps up to the north, centered by a bright rill. Just down on the right, a good-sized patch of **giant hyssop** materializes. With warm-mauve, shingled "cones" ready to pop out tiny white trumpets, this fragrant mint is beloved by bees.

The trail narrows and drifts into soggy ground, no problem if you've worn your sturdy boots. The soil grows quite wet, and it becomes difficult to believe that there is, in fact, a trail. While debating, look up for inspiration to the rugged spires of bright rock or down at the wetfoot **yellow monkeyflower** and **pink willowherb**. Beware of clumped stinging nettles (this sector is filled with adventure). Pick your way through the "secret water garden," and reach the main Maroon Lake Trail.

Soon, a right turn onto the wide Maroon Lake Trail brings you past thriving **scarlet paintbrush** before you reach a creek crossing. The great

Maroon Bells tower over the jade lake. Shortly thereafter, a sign that posts camping regulations prepares hikers for entering the Maroon Bells-Snowmass Wilderness. Cross another creek, and the trail comes up to the Wilderness boundary and a junction. From here you'll head straight to Crater Lake.

SPOTTED OR DOTTED SAXIFRAGE

Ciliaria austromontana (Saxifraga bronchialis subspecies austromontana)

This plant is also commonly known as prickly saxifrage, a name that alludes to its spine-tipped compact leaves. Jammed into moss-looking mats of mini rosettes, the leaves are awl-shaped and the airy, five-petaled white stars are suspended on wiry stems. The petals are spotted with tiny dots, and a hand lens will reveal colors ranging from orange and purple to crimson and yellow. Growing from Alaska to New Mexico at lower elevations, spotted saxifrage appears on dry forest floors. In the subalpine and alpine zones, it tends to be compatible with rock.

The genus name *Ciliaria* derives from the Latin word for eyelash, and the species' *austromontana* translates as "of southern mountains." A cousin is the true or nodding saxifrage *Saxifraga cernua*.

As you hike, you'll see the beacon "Bells" ahead, and it's not long before the open skies of a southern exposure encourage **narrow-leaved paintbrush** and **fireweed**. **Showy** or **aspen daisy** like this warm slope, too.

Rocky underfoot now, the trail ascends above the white cascades of Maroon Creek and passes quaking aspen. Thickets of white, large-flowered **thimbleberry** and tiny-flowered **red osier dogwood** shrubs find aspen shade perfect. Pink **wild rose** adds a touch of enticing fragrance.

A Crater Lake signboard opens the trail to a rockfall graced with healthy clumps of **blue columbine**. Just up the way, blue-green pools reflect the rugged ramparts of the "Bells." Blue and suffused with violet is **Rocky Mountain penstemon**. **Cutleaf fleabane** is found here as well.

A rock slide brings out the intensity of pink **wild rose** and its matching perfume. **Spotted saxifrage**, with needle-like mats clinging to the ravaged slope, tempers the raw rock, as does poised **blue columbine**. Quarter-sized rosettes of **golden draba** and the blushing bells of droopy-leafed **dogbane** do their part, too.

The trail takes you beneath aspen trees and leads to **heartleaf arnica** and a sign warning of sudden weather changes. Crater Lake/Maroon-Snowmass Trail heads up to the right at this point, accompanied by **scarlet paintbrush** and **golden senecio**. The steep ascent is hampered by sharp-edged rocks underfoot.

The next incline leads up to aspen where **white peavine**, decidedly pink, grows. The trail is now on a north-facing slope where conifer shadows optimize the occurrence of **mountain blue violets** and the red and yellow lanterns of **western red columbine**.

Open skies reveal the splendid glory of the Maroon Bells. The trail crawls through gigantic piles of tumbled stone with patches of flowery rock gardens scattered among them. **Blue columbine** adds a touch of elegance to these rocky retreats.

The sound of falling water comes from the west where later-blooming **black-tipped senecio** displays its big gray-green leaves and flat golden heads.

The trail is brightened by yellow **alpine wallflower** and **shrubby cinque-foil**. The ventriloquist pika, about the size of a hamster, sounds off in his rock-bound home. He may be mowing down wildflowers for his winter "haystacks."

Straight ahead is the highest "Bell," but watch your footing through the rocky garden. Through this delightful passage you'll find **red globe anemone's** cerise cups, **greenleaf chiming bells'** dangling cobalt tubes, and **scarlet paintbrush** lifting flaming bracts. Plush heads of lilac-trumpeted **sky pilot** nestling in the lee of boulders is worth looking for. A rocky rise and decline, followed by an aspen copse, take the trail to its objective—Crater Lake.

West Maroon Trail guides the hiker down through a flowery meadow and spruce trees toward the lakeshore. A little trailside exploring, under the expressive brows of the Maroon Bells, turns up **wild blue flax**, **orange sneeze-weed**, **white geranium**, and **many-rayed goldenrod**. Typically a late summer bloomer, the royal blue **Parry** or **Rocky Mountain gentian** may have opened its shapely goblets among the spruces.

Crater Lake is masterfully cradled by two "fourteeners": Pyramid Peak rising to 14,018 feet on the south and 14,156-foot Maroon Peak to the west. The water-side trail wanders to a flower-filled peninsula of mostly white, with noble touches of purple-blue **subalpine larkspur** and yellow **aspen sunflower** growing along the north shore.

The majesty of the magnificent Maroon Bells reflected in Crater Lake paints the perfect finale. The trek to Crater Lake, while not long, is filled with incredible diversity, not to mention stunning beauty. Wildflowers abound, and the Maroon Bells astound.

Wildflower Hike

22

Judd Falls

via Copper Lake Trail

Wildflower Alert: A lush flowery beginning leads to rock gardens and a refreshing waterfall.

This short, two-mile hike features over 80 species of wildflowers and a dramatic view of Gothic Mountain.

Trail Rating	easy
Trail Length	2.0 miles out and back
Location	Crested Butte
Elevation	9,560 to 9,860 feet
Bloom Season	June to August
Peak Bloom	July
Directions	From Crested Butte go north past Mount Crested Butte and onto Gothic Road. Continue past the town of Gothic for approximately 0.3 mile until you reach a dirt road on the right. Park here at the junction.

A PLEASANT TRAVEL through wildflowers, this short hike ends up at an overlook of free-falling whitewater. About 80 species appear on the mile-long trail. Marvelous views of massive Gothic Mountain and a seasonal waterfall flowing down its rugged cliff face add to the enjoyment.

The trail heads east up a dirt road flanked by a flower-filled meadow, passing a seep to arrive at another parking area. It then undulates south to reach the gorge where you'll find Judd Falls.

While there is a second parking area 0.4 mile up the spur road, some of the loveliest wildflowers and the essence of the place would be missed by not walking from the bottom parking area.

With the commanding presence of Gothic Mountain over this lush valley and the high crystalline air, the scenery at the beginning of the spur road is breathtaking. The wildflower count begins when you get out of the car. Floristics start with **beauty cinquefoil**, **tall chiming bells**, and **tall valerian** that are partnered by **pink-headed daisies** and bright-pink **sticky geranium**. Look near the forest service sign for **tall larkspur** with its dark dolphin-shaped buds, white-umbelled **Porter's lovage**, and spurred **blue columbine**.

The road pulls up through **aspen sunflowers** and **wild blue flax**, piqued by **scarlet gilia** and reams of fuzzy-budded **pink-headed daisies**. **Showy** or **aspen daisy's** purple buds join the promenade.

Continuing the ascent, a little seep near stunted aspen supports **yellow monkeyflower** and lacy **cowbane** while another features **pink willowherb** and **green bog orchid**. An uprooted giant conifer makes way for **monkshood**, **arrowleaf senecio** or **groundsel**, and more **monkeyflower**. Across the way, search for **western red columbine**. Back on the right, moisture nurtures rare **purple avens**, along with **tall chiming bells**, **monkshood**, **bittercress**, and other flowers that like wet feet. Later in the season, **fireweed** will inflame the landscape.

Soon the wide road enters into an area populated by aspen and spruce and passes scattered **blue columbine** as well as yellow-snowflaked **mountain parsley**. The observant hiker may scope out an **Indian warrior** or two and a smattering of **orange sneezeweed** before the trail opens to a view of 12,625-foot Gothic Mountain.

Scarlet paintbrush enlivens the scene just before the route reaches a little creek where the high side reveals more **western red columbine**, shining like miniature lanterns in the dark ravine. Mats of **dotted saxifrage** cling to the tumbled talus.

Enjoying the disturbed soil along the roadway, a **milkvetch** displays rosy-red, pea-type flowers sitting atop fuzzy, gray, ladder-like leaves. Nearby, a different species of **milkvetch**, sporting pinkish-purple flowers, demonstrates colonizing tendencies. Both are in the prolific *Astragalus* genus.

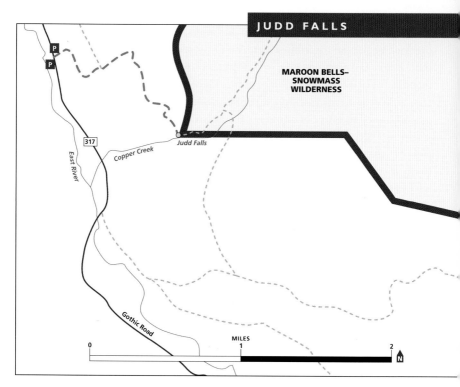

Another view of Gothic Mountain's considerable bulk brings **ballhead sandwort** to the fore, which is counterpointed by **scarlet paintbrush** along a dry slope. Aspen cools hikers in an understory of pink-budded, blue-tubed **tall chiming bells**, **blue columbine**, and some stately **Indian warriors** among a myriad of other wildflowers. A rivulet tinkling down from the left adds to the cooler environment.

The upper parking area's trailhead sign states 0.5 mile to Judd Falls along the Copper Lake Trail. Passing a vehicle barrier, the broad trail grows stony in the dancing shade of "quakies" (aspen). On the left, watch for the arched racemes of **mountain death camas**; the stems straighten as toxic death camas come into full bloom, each pointed bud opening to greenish-tinged white stars.

The route, level now, aims south with Mount Crested Butte and its ski runs ahead. The aspen-filled habitat here nourishes huge specimens of **wild blue flax** and Colorado's state flower, the elegant **blue columbine**.

Back in wide-skied ambience, the trail to Judd Falls exposes a dry, stony slope of **ballhead sandwort** and **yellow stonecrop**, brightened with **scarlet gilia**. **False forget-me-not's** light blue flowers point to **wild rose** shrubs—perfumed pink blossoms alight—next to the trail. Here too, **showy** or **aspen daisies** bask in the warmth of a southern exposure.

A sign indicates the Rocky Mountain Biological Laboratory is located to the west and below. Then the narrowing trail drifts into more aspen or "quakies" where **cow parsnip**, **monkshood**, and **tall larkspur**, all head high, dominate. A touch of **yellow monkeyflower** lights up a seep before the trail heads back into the open, finding **shrubby cinquefoil** decorated with five-petaled golden doubloons.

Rocks and roots combine to lead the hike into a damp spot where blue **American speedwell** keeps a low profile while **false hellebore** towers over it. The seep gathers itself into running water where **mountain death camas** and vivid pink **shooting stars** emerge downstream. A pocket-sized pond on the left harbors bugs eager to meet you on the trail.

Contouring the hillside on a stony footbed, the path opens to a rock garden area featuring **yellow stonecrop**, **dwarf sulphurflower**, **whiplash fleabane**, and copious **ballhead sandwort**. Red and white perks up the rocky earth thanks to **scarlet gilia**, **scarlet paintbrush**, and **northern bedstraw**.

The last pitch is rocky and unpredictable as it drops to a sign that aims the trail toward the right and to the Judd Falls Overlook. And an overlook is exactly what it does —straight down. A stout bench, shaded by a mature Douglas fir, is dedicated " . . . to the man who stayed—Garwood Hall Judd 1852-1930." Pause here for the sight and sound of Copper Creek, which sends a torrent of whitewater off a sheer precipice far below.

Even the popular road to Gothic and beyond revels in astonishing wildflower displays. The vintage town of Gothic itself, centered around the 1880 town hall built during the silver-mining era, is now the flowery home of the Rocky Mountain Biological Laboratory, a field research station. The trail to Judd Falls presents a quick opportunity to see falling water, savor grand mountain scenery, and see many different kinds of wildflowers along the way.

BALLHEAD SANDWORT
Eremogene congesta (Arenaria congesta)

"Snow ball sandwort" also describes the cluster-flowering heads of this member of the the chickweed clan, sometimes included in the same family as carnations (depending on which authority you follow). The dense inflorescences of white, starry flowers top wiry stems and are typically less than a foot high. The sharp-tipped, grass-like leaves gather into clumps in xeric habitats, hence *Eremogene* meaning "desert flower" or *Arenaria* meaning "of sand." When ripe, the minuscule, chalice-shaped seed receptacles fling their contents to the fates, hoping to beget the next generation. Cousins include the alpine sandwort *Lidia obtusiloba* and Fendler's sandwort, which is mostly referred to as sandwort *Eremogene fendleri*.

Wildflower Hike

23

Rabbit Ears Peak

Wildflower Alert: This trail showcases endless Colorado color, ranging from primary to pastel in July. You'll discover a glory of glacier lilies in early summer.

A moderate hike that begins along an old jeep road, this trail eventually leads to crumbling orange "ears"— deeply eroded volcanic plugs.

Trail Rating	easy to moderate
Trail Length	5.0 miles out and back
Location	Rabbit Ears Pass/Steamboat Springs
Elevation	9,600 to 10,600 feet
Bloom Season	late June through August
Peak Bloom	late July
Directions	Take US 40 east from Steamboat Springs. Proceed north on Dumont Lake Road 315 for 1.6 miles. Turn left at Monument Park or continue for 0.3 mile and park, or turn right onto primitive road 291 and go 0.3 mile and park under the trees.

FROM A DISTANCE, the twin prongs of Rabbit Ears Peak are aptly named. Up close, the "ears" betray their violent origins: volcanic plugs now deeply eroded. But it is the jeep-road trail up to them that causes wildflower enthusiasts to catch their breath. From start to finish, a never-ending exhibition of crazy quilt colors sweep along this hike. Early season hikers enjoy a plethora of glacier lilies. It's an "ooh and ahh" kind of place.

The old road undulates through flowery meadows before ascending at a faster pace. Weaving in and out of evergreen stands and across meadows, Rabbit Ears Peak Trail then climbs steeply to reach the base of the "ears" themselves.

Parking is up on the old highway that runs parallel to the new one, and the most spacious parking area is by the old highway monument. Just east of Steamboat Springs, this is a justifiably popular hike.

S tarting at the last parking area, look across the way for both white and pink **Rabbit Ears gilia**, interspersed with rangy clumps of slightly haphazard **Engelmann aster**. Though the buds are quite pink, fully open rays are barely blushed or even white. **Beauty cinquefoil, lupine, yarrow,** and white-umbelled **Porter's lovage** fill the flat space across from tall conifers.

An old level jeep road proceeds into the open where a drier habitat supports **golden aster, creamy buckwheat,** and **many-rayed goldenrod**. Smatterings of **scarlet paintbrush, Whipple penstemon, pearly everlasting,** and **showy daisy** add to the floral display. This rocky roadway passes meadows that exhibit cacophonies of color.

It isn't long before the road dips toward a small waterway anchored by a burned stump and backed by a hillock crowned with aspen. Around the picturesque stub, very appropriately, grows **fireweed** and yardstick-straight **aspen sunflower**. Closer to the water source, **arrowleaf senecio** and **white bog orchid** bloom where **bittercress** bloomed earlier. Another wetfoot, **little pink elephants,** stands about two feet tall, and much taller **false hellebore** claims the background.

Though the rising roadbed is cobbled now, the fullness of mother nature's gardens predominate. White **Coulter daisy** and **pink-headed daisies** prepare the way for clumps of **blue columbine**—Colorado's state flower since 1899.

The **Engelmann aster** clumps get bigger as the road continues straight for Rabbit Ears Peak. **Cow parsnip** bob above pleated-leaved **false hellebore** and early-blooming **tall larkspur**. Scrambling amongst the taller wildflowers is bi-colored **wild sweetpea** flowering in dark pink and white over narrow leaves.

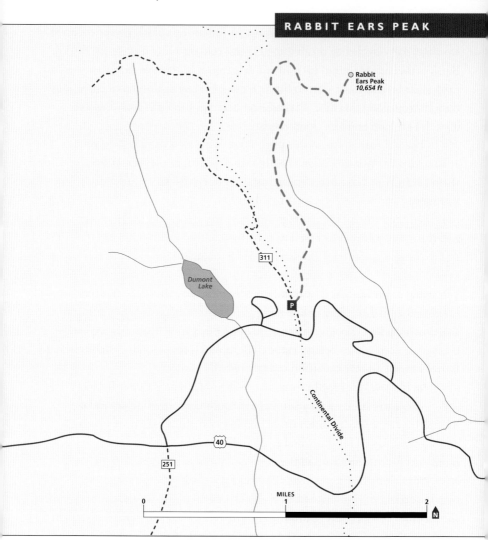

Columbine, set off by magenta **fireweed** and **creamy buckwheat**, increases in quantity.

The yellows of **cinquefoil**, **senecio**, and **sunflower** complement the purples of **asters** and **larkspur** along the next portion of the hike. The road is deeply rutted as it draws near spruces, and the landmark "ears" vanish from sight.

Where the terrain evens out on a curve through evergreens, the tips of the "ears" pop up again and merge into a single block as the trail emerges from the trees. More elevation is gained before a **fireweed** field promises to set the landscape aflame. Big, coarse **dock** turns up its dangling crowds of red seedpods. Red, purple, and gold colors dominate, tempered by pinky **Rabbit Ears gilia**.

The sweeping valley, with an occasional conical spruce, cups an almost invisible seep area off to the left. Lichen-coated boulders poke up through the thick grasses where early **marsh marigolds** start off the flowering sequence, followed in turn by **white bog orchids** and **little pink elephants**. As high summer greets August, look for the lovely purple **fringed gentian** hiding in the grass.

The roadway turns toward pocked volcanic rock as it dips to a stream crossing. Here, those first blooming buddies, **marsh marigold** and **globeflower**, greet high country spring (which may be summer by the calendar). White **bittercress** and dainty **brook saxifrage** emerge, too. Later, gilt **arrowleaf senecio** grow tall alongside deep purple-blue **subalpine larkspur** and bold **cow parsnip**.

Ascending more, the trail encounters a stony section with muted **tall valerian** off to the side, while creeping patches of **Nuttall's sandwort** sprinkle minuscule pink stars in the roadbed itself. Under open skies, radiant purple **lupine** almost overshadows white and pink **Rabbit Ears gilia**, blushing **Engelmann aster**, **Whipple** or **dusky penstemon**, and winking **golden-eyes**.

In the midst of conifers, a small open area surrounding a double-trunked spruce is home to **linanthastrum** or, easier to say, **Nuttall's gilia**. Loose bunches of sweet-smelling white flowers cap the spiky-leaved, almost bushy, little plants.

The gradient increases before leveling and passes flanking stands of spruce. Resembling a piece of enameled cloisonné jewelry, another flowery meadow full of red, purple, white, and gold emerges. A muted mix of **Porter's lovage** and **blue columbine** adds a variety to the dominant primary color scheme.

Soon another meadow-wide display of bright colors appears. **Scarlet paintbrush** is off to the left. More tranquil color and aspect emerge along the road with **subalpine larkspur**, **white geranium**, and more **lovage** growing on an even segment.

The rising and falling road to Rabbit Ears passes more subtle wildflowers, including **wild** or **mountain candytuft**, **sickletop lousewort**, and two members of the parsley family, whitish **turkeypeas** and yellow **mountain parsley**. A cupped swale features ground-hugging **sibbaldia**, a member of the rose family that turns salmon-red in the fall. Where snowbanks linger late, look for a **glacier lily** or two hanging on. Their distinctive, erect, three-paneled pods are easy to spot, and just after snowmelt, the Dumont Lake area of Rabbit Ears Pass is famous for its glacier lily show.

It's not far to the goal now. A pair of cousins, **white peavine** and **American vetch**, grow over, around, and through their more staid neighbors.

A bench along the trail allows for a closer look. **Wild rose**, a few belated **yellow violets**, and more **Nuttall's gilia** gather just as the road takes a steep pitch that goes straight up to the base of Rabbit Ears Peak. Though this pitch feels almost perpendicular, it is thankfully brief.

The reward at the top is a close-up of the crumbling orange "ears," once a solid core of red magma. Lichen-encrusted now, the plug remnants protrude another 60 feet or so above your head. The description ends here at the eroded base where **cutleaf fleabane** and **whiproot clover** cling to the jagged brick-red rock—Rabbit Ears Peak is not safe to climb. Footing is tricky in the unstable rubble, and children need to be supervised when heading around the north side of the formation—there is an abrupt drop off. Long vistas of meadows and far mountains, evergreens and still waters are a peacefully composed bonus.

The trek to Rabbit Ears Peak is a florescent one. Convenient to Steamboat Springs, this is an enchanting hike with an abundance of wildflowers representing more than 80 species.

NUTTALL'S GILIA OR LINANTHASTRUM
Linanthastrum nuttallii

Growing up to a foot high, this light-hearted member of the phlox family has fragrant flowers. Each narrow tube flares like a white trumpet and contains five yellow stamens. These delicate flowers gather on stem ends over pairs of finely-divided opposite leaves, giving the illusion of whorls of needly-looking foliage. The Latin name honors Thomas Nuttall, a versatile British botanist born in 1786 who explored the West.

Maroon Lake Scenic Loop
(Maroon Bells-Snowmass Wilderness)

Wildflower Alert: You'll find yourself wandering in a sea
of wildflowers serenaded by water on this scenic trail.

*With splashy floral colors and lofty mountain
views, this trail is truly magical.*

easy	***Trail Rating***
1.25 miles in a figure-eight loop	***Trail Length***
Aspen	***Location***
9,580 to 9,780 feet	***Elevation***
late June through August	***Bloom Season***
early to mid-July	***Peak Bloom***
Take State Route 82 west from Aspen. Turn left onto Meadow Creek Road, which will end at Maroon Lake. Note that travel by shuttle is required from 8:30 a.m. to 5:30 p.m. Check locally for details. A fee may be charged for entry into the Maroon Lake area.	***Directions***

THERE IS SOMETHING MAGICAL about the Maroon Bells. Perhaps it is their saturated pigmentation, or their lofty summits, or it could be the multifold layers of eroded sandstone. Most likely it is their magnificent setting, which is mirrored in jeweled Maroon Lake. The Maroon Lake Scenic Loop is actually two loops formed into a figure eight. The bounty of wildflowers make this a wonderful experience for lovers of natural beauty.

As beautiful as the Maroon Lake area is, it is not surprising that the limited parking lot will not accommodate all visitor vehicles. The solution is a shuttle bus that originates in Aspen. At this writing, private vehicles may drive in before the entrance station opens at 8:30 a.m. They are also allowed after 5:30 p.m. To update this information, check locally before making plans.

During the summer, nature's plans often include intense afternoon thunderstorms. So go early and be prepared.

The broad trail begins on the left side of the restrooms and drifts into the open. Immediately visitors are struck by the awesome panorama of Maroon Lake embraced by great mountains of deep red sandstone, some over 14,000 feet. As you begin your stroll into the landscape, look for wildflowers along the pathway. Prominent because of its white, dinner plate-sized heads and huge leaves, **cow parsnip** thrives in the damp ground along the outlet stream. **Orange sneezeweed** adds a sunny touch.

Although the wildflowers tend toward subalpine, the Maroon Lake Scenic Loop is in the montane zone. Under wide open skies, dashes of paint-box colors enchant the eye, including the intense cadmium red of **scarlet paintbrush**.

After crossing a creek, you'll see a sign with information about camping regulations. Another creek tumbles over big rocks and the trail continues up to the wilderness boundary and a junction where the scenic loop goes left.

Traveling under the dappled shade of quaking aspen, the hiker reaches a point where the trail S-curves down to a bridge. Along the way, **false forget-me-not**, **Coulter daisy**, **Rocky Mountain penstemon**, and **senecio** provide pleasing company. To take in the most exciting part of the figure-eight loop, do not cross the inlet bridge, but continue along the north side of Maroon Creek. Wending through thick vegetation, the trail soon passes the steep short-cut that comes down from Crater Lake. The loop path continues to wander through aspen, yielding **tall chiming bells**, **white geranium**, **Canada violet**, and **paintbrush**. As summer wears on, **fireweed** brightens up the landscape.

An inlet creek travels under the trail, ushering in delicately scented **blue columbine** and mats of dainty, pair-belled **twinflower**. Though not

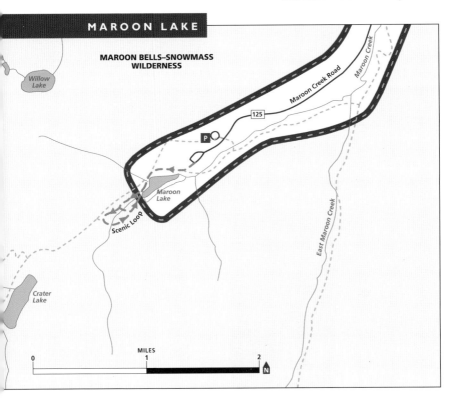

MAROON LAKE

MAROON BELLS–SNOWMASS
WILDERNESS

Willow
Lake

Maroon Creek Road

Maroon Creek

125

P

Maroon
Lake

Scenic Loop

East Maroon Creek

Crater
Lake

MILES
0   1   2
N

pleasant-smelling—and toxic to boot—**mountain death camas** is still attractive with its wide, whitish stars. Each one of its six tepals is based in a green kidney-shaped gland. Look in this moist area, particularly by a streamside boulder, for **nodding** or **true saxifrage**. An appealing innocence marks these less-commonly found wildflowers. Not only is the spindly reddish stem topped with a single white flower, but tiny red bulblets cluster in its leaf axils. **Pink pyrola**, with its pendant parasols, may also be found in the vicinity. Pink may also be spotted in **hybrid columbine** hiding in the bushes on the right. This is the offspring of the genetically dominant blue columbine and western red columbine.

   With **fireweed** and **tall chiming bells** leading the way, wide skies shine down on a province of stone adorned with bouquets of **blue columbine** and gold-coined **shrubby cinquefoil**. Vivid wands of **scarlet paintbrush** inflame the rockscape while shapely mats of **spotted saxifrage** cool the effect. Ensconced in the massive shadow of 14,018-foot Pyramid Peak, this captivating rock garden is a work of natural art. Hummingbirds frequent the area, enjoying the advantage of flight over the earthbound hiker who must negotiate jagged red rock in the trail.

In a copse of aspen is the sound of falling water. The trail becomes thick with vegetation, and as it winds up through the trees, becomes rocky as well. A field of **fireweed**—bright in bloom and brilliant in fall—flanks the loop where singing water cascades. **Pink-headed daisies** with their signature woolly buds and **giant lousewort**, named more intriguingly as **Indian warriors**, add pastel accents.

Fronting the whitewater cascade, a "social" trail leads left to an eddy. At water's edge, the palette of yellow, blue, purple, and abundant white is lushly represented by **cinquefoil**, **tall chiming bells**, **monkshood**, **bittercress**, **cow parsnip**, and **white geranium**. With the majestic Maroon Bells pushing into the sky to the west, the scene is just waiting for paint or film.

The main trail travels through aspen-sheltered **twinberry**—its flower, fruits, and bracts paired—and **thimbleberry**. Footing can be tricky during a brief pitch in the path.

Spray from the frothy creek makes for rather precarious footing on a short drop studded with worn rock. Stepping down through luxuriant wildflowers, some head high, you come toe to tempest with the edge of wild whitewater. Straight from the horseshoe cirque high on Pyramid Peak, Maroon Creek carries the cold of its snowbank origins. Two cascades join in a race around flower-crammed islands to create a scene that is nothing short of sensational.

A bridge spans the rushing creek on your left; this is the access for the eastern half of the figure-eight loop, but you should continue straight ahead. The word floriferous, meaning "bearing flowers in abundance" or "flowery," barely suffices to describe the density of pastel

NODDING OR TRUE SAXIFRAGE

Saxifraga cernua

The moniker "nodding saxifrage" stems from the Latin *cernua* which means "nodding." The genus portion *Saxifraga* translates as "rock-breaker." True, this family is often found in deteriorating rock formations, but another explanation is its reported ancient use as a treatment for breaking up kidney stones.

Fond of weeping water and rocky places in subalpine and alpine life zones, true or nodding saxifrage sports a white flower atop a sticky, erratic stem. In the leaf axils minuscule red bulblets, which look like beginning buds, are sources of new plants. Cousins include dotted or spotted saxifrage *Ciliaria austromontana* and brook saxifrage *Micranthes odontoloma*.

wildflowers in this well-watered oasis. Even the trail takes on dampness where a little seep harbors **pink willowherb** and **yellow monkeyflower.**

So overwhelming is the floral opulence just left behind, that the openness of the meadow ahead is almost a relief. **Scarlet paintbrush, fireweed,** and the warm-gold droopy-rayed suns of **orange sneezeweed** catch the pastel-sated eye. A bit farther on, satiny purple **monkshood** stands tall over softly budded **pink-headed daisy.**

Waiting just ahead to tame the racing river is lovely Maroon Lake. Rambling **American vetch** refuses to be mellowed, either in its magenta flowers or its happy-go-lucky growth habit. Look for it, along with both **scarlet** and cool yellow **western paintbrush.**

Near the bridge at the west end of Maroon Lake, big pale green leaves of **green gentian** or **monument plant** form rosettes. It takes a number of years for the rubbery-looking leaves to build up enough energy to shoot up an impressive stalk of mint-green flowers.

The crystalline waters flowing under the bridge are mellow now. Just ahead on the right, **green bog orchid** looks up to tall creamy-beaked **lousewort.** Level and smooth now, the trail passes the plump heads of **Bigelow** or **ray-less senecio.** Color in capitals spells more **sneezeweed, parsnip, wild blue flax,** and a mass of **monkshood.**

Traveling on the north shore of Maroon Lake, the pathway heads back to the parking lot.

Nothing short of fabulous can begin to describe the florescent amplitude of the Maroon Lake Scenic Loop. A special slice of high country glory, the figure-eight trail is a fabulous array of mountain, water, and floral beauty.

Wildflower Hike

25

CENTURY HIKE

Rustler Gulch
(Maroon Bells-Snowmass Wilderness)

Wildflower Alert: It's no exaggeration to say that Rustler Gulch is the premier place to wade through endless wildflowers.

Enchanting Rustler Gulch boasts gentle valleys, sweeping meadows, and a reputation for some of Colorado's most vibrant color displays.

Trail Rating	easy to moderate due to length
Trail Length	6.2 miles out and back from yellow gate 8.0 miles out and back from creek crossing
Location	Crested Butte
Elevation	10,100 to 11,400 feet (yellow gate) 9,700 to 11,400 feet (at creek crossing)
Bloom Season	late June through August
Peak Bloom	mid-July to early August
Directions	Go north from Crested Butte through Mount Crested Butte on Gothic Road. Travel 6.8 miles from where the pavement ends. Turn right at the spur marked Rustler Gulch. Park before the creek or a bit further on (high clearance advised).

PREPARE TO BE DAZZLED. Filled with floods of wildflowers from start to finish, Rustler Gulch at peak bloom is a prize winner. At least 114 different kinds of flowers may be seen during prime-time bloom, making this an extraordinary floral trek. Maroon rock formations, talus-sloped peaks, pretty creeks, inspiring views, and mining relics add to the hike's allure.

If you choose not to drive up the steep and sometimes-slippery access road, the first mile utilizing the road itself is the toughest part of the hike, but even this segment is awash in waist-high flowers. When you reach a locked, yellow metal gate, the trail inclines steadily but gently. One, perhaps two, challenging creek crossings must be negotiated to reach the high country's floral glories of Rustler Gulch.

Note that parking your vehicle is slightly problematic—the road is a challenge.

Beginning about a half mile before the gate, the road wades between banks of meadow-loving flowers such as rich, purple-blue **subalpine larkspur** and **monkshood**, white **cow parsnip**, pastel **tall chiming bells**, and both **sawtooth** and **arrowleaf senecio** or **groundsel**. A white, rock-crested ridge makes a pretty backdrop.

The trail heads into a mixed conifer and aspen forest. Floral offerings continue with umbel-headed white **Porter's lovage** or **osha**, a valuable plant to American Indians, cheerful lavender **showy** or **aspen daisy**, fuzzy-budded **pink-headed daisy**, and **aspen sunflower** standing at attention. Later in summer, **golden-eyes** or **sunspots** toss their yellow disks about like drops of shattered sunbeams. **Fireweed** and **Engelmann aster**, with its tousled rays, bloom about the same time.

LITTLE BEEBALM
Monardella odoratissima

Also called cloverhead mint, this sensory-stimulating plant pops out in bursts of lavender pink, narrow-tubed flowers, beneath which you'll find papery purple bracts. The interesting fragrance of a rubbed leaf calls for a second sniff. With a fondness for rocks and gravelly soil, clumping little beebalm's Latin genus name commemorates a botanist-writer of sixteenth-century Spain, Nicolas Monardes. Relatives such as beebalm *Monarda fistulosa var. menthifolia* and giant hyssop *Agastache urticifolia* are part of Colorado's mint family.

Also called coyote mint, Native Americans made extensive pharmaceutical use of this plant, using the leaves as an insect repellent as well as for flavoring tea.

Mount Bellview's twin summits of 12,473 and 12,519 feet probe the sky to the north, while 13,000-foot gray stone molars bite out a chunk of the eastern skyline. By turning south, you can see the broad bulk of Gothic Mountain, and further off is the apex of Mount Crested Butte. The western view introduces the deep red sandstone of the Maroon Bells formation.

Soon the road forks, and a left turn heads up the Bellview spur toward the Silver Spruce Mine. Continue to head up the right path, passing richly-hued **harebells, scarlet paintbrush**, and **beauty cinquefoil**, to a slanted parking area and just beyond it, the yellow gate. Ensconced in a damp forest, a weeping bank sports **bittercress** and **foamflower**, which is a saxifrage family member. Both **broadleaf** and **heartleaf arnica** thrive in the shade here.

The trail begins its passage through the Maroon Bells-Snowmass Wilderness Area, passing dark conifers and amethyst **lupine, larkspur**, and **monkshood**. Around a bend, **cow parsnip** and **white geranium** counterpoint the purples, which meet their complementary color in **orange sneezeweed.**

WESTERN SWEETVETCH
Hedysarum occidentale

Chainpod, the second common name for this plant, is unmistakably descriptive of the linked sequin-sized pod sections, each containing a single seed. Each round "link" displays a network of veins framing the dark seed, like the shed skin of a snake. Full racemes of relaxed pea-type flowers stand above sturdy three-foot clumps. The cousin northern sweetvetch *Hedysarum boreale* is found at lower elevations. Preferring higher mountain meadows, western sweetvetch roots are favored by grizzlies.

Emerging into sunlight, the trail exhibits thicker vegetation near a seep that features **yellow monkey-flower, pink willowherb**, and open-faced lavender **seep speedwell**. It isn't long before a wide stream challenges your resourcefulness. You can take off your boots or build a makeshift bridge with rocks. Another alternative is to bushwhack a hundred yards upstream and hopefully find a convenient downed tree to bridge the waterway.

The trail passes through big evergreen trees where a keen eye may pick out **western red columbine** before the valley opens up to an endless brigade of wildflowers. Marching alongside the majestic gulch are the rocky flanks of 12,653-foot Mount Avery on the right and the eroding strata of the Maroon Bells sandstone on the left.

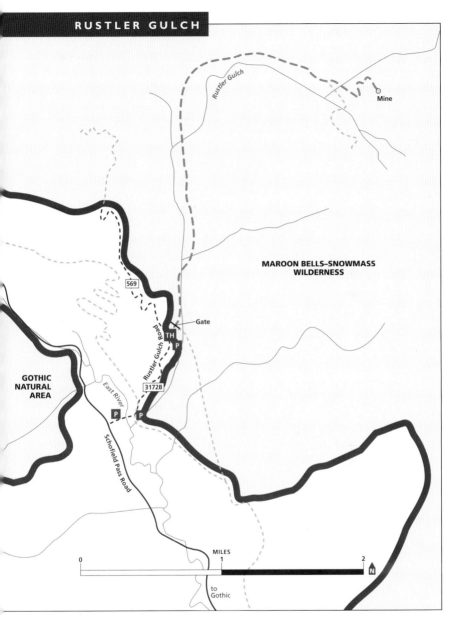

A momentary change of pace comes as the trail approaches an interesting stream—this one sheeting smoothly over broad-stepped layers of water-worn sandstone. While coming to terms with this creek crossing, let your thoughts be diverted to the vivid pink plant clinging to the south cut bank, **alpine** or **broadleaf fireweed**—quite different from the spires of its common cousin. Balance yourself on the rocks and a tree trunk to reach the far side, and the reward is a mossy bog next to the trail displaying **star gentian**, **fringed gentian**, and **fringed Parnassia**.

Curving steadily to the right on the sweeping valley's south flank, the lush trail proves that Rustler Gulch is as good as its gets. The raging abundance of lush **lupine**, one of about 50 species in the Rockies, and **orange sneezeweed** testify to the valley's bounty. **Western sweetvetch** or **chainpod** (examine a pod and the name becomes perfectly clear) show off splendid racemes of fresh pink flowers. To top off the kaleidoscope growing at your feet, look up to a crescent of colorful summits, which are all over 13,000 feet and include 13,360-foot Precarious Peak. Towering over the head of Rustler Gulch, these bright mountains were prospected for precious metals. A far-off fall of whitewater once provided the steam power for the boilers that ran the mining enterprises.

In exposed, sun-facing areas, look for **ballhead sandwort** and **sulphur-flower**. Near willow-girt seeps look for **little rose gentian** and more **fringed gentian**. In groups of redstone or other rocks, watch for low clumps and plump kettle-shaped buds of aromatic **little beebalm**. A leaf rolled in the fingers leaves an intriguing scent. A spherical starburst of warm lavender flower heads is like finding a minty fourth-of-July sparkler. At the right time (typically July), the trail wades through a sea of **blue columbine**.

In cool spots with lingering snowbanks, floral spring can be revisited. One stretch may boast **ballhead waterleaf**, **yellow violets**, and nosegays of **lavender violets**—all violets are edible and a good source of Vitamin C. Where the snow has recently retreated, **snow buttercup** and **glacier lilies** may be in evidence.

The trail travels up to the left toward old mine ruins, an incredible valley vista, and more and different wildflowers. It then pokes through an old rock-fall where bright blue clumps of **dwarf chiming bells** flourish along with an occasional **purple fringe**.

The trail ascends through an alien rockscape and arrives at a little creek where **Parry primrose** and **marsh marigolds**—usually among the earliest of bloomers—thrive. **Rosy paintbrush** and sweet-smelling **Parry clover** are sheltered in the willows on this last pitch.

The end is close. Just up ahead hidden in willows are the walls of an old stone structure and a huge rusting boiler, evidence of man's quest for gold. A big flat outcrop just off to the right marked with an iron pipe makes a fine place to pause and absorb the views in every direction.

Rustler Gulch is an awe-inspiring place, not only with its wildly boun-teous masses of wildflowers but scenery that can't fail to lift your spirits. A trek through its ever-changing landscape is just the thing for wildflower enthusiasts as well as for those who are seeking a perfect hike.

Wheeler Lakes
(Eagles Nest Wilderness)

Wildflower Alert: A great diversity of flora and scenery give this convenient trail an edge.

A blanket of wildflowers leads to Wheeler Lakes, with views of the Tenmile Range rising in the distance.

moderate	*Trail Rating*
5.6 miles out and back	*Trail Length*
Copper Mountain/Frisco	*Location*
9,760 to 11,050 feet	*Elevation*
early July to August	*Bloom Season*
mid- to late July	*Peak Bloom*
Take I-70 to exit 195 at Copper Mountain. Park on the right near side of the freeway overpass in the pullout.	*Directions*

AT THE SOUTH END OF THE GORE RANGE are Wheeler Lakes, which lie inside the Eagles Nest Wilderness. Named for Judge John Wheeler who established an 1880s town that was destroyed by fire and avalanche, Wheeler Lakes offer a great day-hike convenient to Interstate 70. The judge's ill-fated town rests under Copper Mountain Ski Resort.

Well over 80 species of wildflowers populate the trail, which journeys through varied habitats and landscape and ends with lakeside bloomers. The beginning of the trail travels adjacent to the freeway, and then the Gore Range Trail heads up a south-facing slope, alternating between dry and moist habitats. Wheeler Lakes are reached via extensive meadows preceding a gentler final ascent.

Arrive early to secure a parking spot in the limited space at the overpass. More parking exists a half mile north, back up the trail near a fishing pond next to I-70. You can also park at Wheeler Flats trailhead across the freeway in a frontage area east of the Highway 91 and Copper Mountain Road junction.

MOUNTAIN DEATH CAMAS

Anticlea elegans

Each of the six white tepals forming the broad stars of mountain death camas has a green heart-shaped gland at its base. The bracts are nearly the length of the pedicels. The name "poison onion" was assigned by Native Americans who knew of the plant's deadly properties. Alkaloids are so concentrated in the black-sheathed bulbs that just a couple may be fatal.

Found from Alaska to northern Mexico, death camas has been tagged alkali grass, lonely lily, and wand lily. The genus name *Anticlea* was Ulysses' mother's name. *Elegans* means "elegant." A cousin, inhabiting lower elevations, may be even more toxic: death camas *Toxicoscordian venenosum*.

Find the trail behind a berm next to the overpass parking area. On the right, in earliest spring, lilac **pasqueflowers** bloom among lichened stones. Here, late summer is charged with electric-blue **Rocky Mountain** or **Parry gentian** with contrasting **creamy buckwheat** and yellow-gold **shrubby cinquefoil**.

At a fork, head right, up under open skies into silvery sagebrush. Early hikers find clumps of **wild iris** lifting purple blossoms above tough, strappy leaves. **Pink plumes**, like **pasqueflowers**, are easy to detect as long as their feathery seed plumes remain. A bit of **orange sneezeweed**, with its lax ray petals, rides above the sage.

After meeting a few lodgepole pines, the trail heads into a ravine buffered by a hillock. **Silvery lupine's** blue pinnacles lead up to a trail register. Traversing a south-facing slope—the ski runs of 12,441-foot Copper Mountain are across the valley—the azures of **bluemist penstemon** and **wild blue flax** emerge. **Yellow owl's clover**, which are actually related to penstemons, shares the scene.

Damp soil encourages bog birch as a neighbor to **fringed gentians** and **cowbane** as well as **shooting stars** and **bog orchids**. Native **false dandelions**, **mountain death camas**, and **twinberry** shrubs accompany the ascending trail. Under the aspen trees are **heartleaf arnica** and **monkshood**.

Following the sound of water leads to a creek crossing and a sign welcoming you to Eagles Nest Wilderness. Open areas bright with wildflowers include the yellows of **aspen sunflower** and **mountain parsley**, complemented with purple tints of **showy** or **aspen daisy**, **harebells**, **sego lilies**, and **lupine**. The gradient begins to ease next to **scarlet paintbrush**, and tattered log water-bars aid hikers up through flowery slopes that grow more stony. In the shade, **western paintbrush** presents its cool yellow bracts.

Mucky footing is just right for **tall chiming bells**, **arrowleaf senecio**, **cowbane**, and **white geranium**, but requires hikers to execute some fancy footwork. Where a confusion of unsightly and erosion-prone shortcuts appear, stick to the ascending main trail passing **sickletop lousewort** and **delicate Jacob's ladder** sheltered under conifers. Midway, in rich forest duff, keep an eye out for **shy wood nymph** bowing her demure white head.

The grade increases where **lupine** and **bracted lousewort** share ground. In a riparian zone, **woolly** or **subalpine arnica's** sunny heads follow the flowering season of **marsh marigold** and **globeflower**. Easing somewhat, the trail comes upon sturdy **false hellebore** overlooking both **fringed** and **Parry gentian**. **Rosy paintbrush** live above a stand of willows. Offering a distant glimpse of Shrine Ridge, a flat, colorful meadow produces **alpine speedwell**, **horned dandelion**, **blueleaf cinquefoil**, and both **alpine** and **American bistort**. As summer wanes, annual **fringed gentian** casts its purple spell among the grasses.

Standing out in the soft soil are bright rosy-lavender **subalpine daisy**, purple-suffused blue **lupine**, luminous bracts of **rosy paintbrush**, and **little pink elephants**.

Patriarch conifers guard a dazzling display of **bistort**, **Coulter daisy**, **asters**, **fleabanes**, **arnica**, and **monkshood**. Almost bashful with its dainty pea flowers, **alpine milkvetch** shares the trail sides with **lupine**.

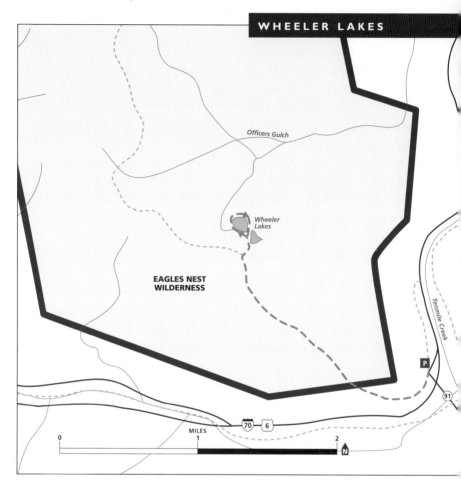

Far to the right, the Tenmile Range rises in the distance. The gradient lessens before heading into a grove of spruce. At a fork, stay right to continue on toward Wheeler Lakes; the left leg is the Gore Range Trail. Seen at several points along the way is locally prolific **fern-leaved lovage**. This member of the parsley family is topped with white-umbels of tiny flowers. Then the first meadow-girt Wheeler Lake comes into view.

Off to the side, picturesque outcrops create a rock garden consisting of **buckwheat, asters,** and **paintbrush**. On the lake's far side, re-enter woods to find **daffodil** or **nodding senecio**. Heading for the second Wheeler Lake, the pathway drifts down among **little pink elephants, rosy paintbrush, arrowleaf senecio,** and **bracted lousewort**. To avoid a bog, head left, using the forest edge as a guide, before coming to water's edge. As you near the sparkling lake, light and airy **brook saxifrage** and stodgy **bog saxifrage** grow close enough for comparison.

Along the lush west shore, watch close and low for **mitrewort**— its fascinating green snowflake flowers are touched with a trace of maroon. It takes scrutiny with a hand lens to do it justice. Easy-to-spot **narcissus-flowered anemone** leads the eye to **marsh marigold** and the pearl-like buds of **fringed Parnassia**. When the clear white flowers open, the hand lens reveals Parnassia's interesting blossom.

A peaty spot, willow-challenged, is populated with dozens of petaled rainbow shards. It is also populated by starving mosquitoes who form an instant greeting committee. Drier footing leads to the north end of the lake where the sight of **subalpine larkspur** and a grand view of Dillon Reservoir finish the hike.

Wheeler Lakes provides a fun dayhike offering a wide array of flowers, peak views, lakes, and exercise. Convenient to I-70, the Gore Range Trail, which accesses the twin lakes, provides entry into a lovely landscape, colored bright with high-country wildflowers.

Missouri Lakes
(Holy Cross Wilderness)

Wildflower Alert: This hike features wildflower, lake, and mountain landscapes worthy of calendar covers.

Set in a postcard-perfect Colorado landscape, this trail follows Missouri Creek and leads to a series of lakes surrounded by high peaks.

Trail Rating	moderate
Trail Length	6.4 miles out and back
Location	Minturn/Vail
Elevation	10,000 to 11,500 feet
Bloom Season	July through August
Peak Bloom	mid-July to mid-August
Directions	Go west on I-70 past Vail, and then south on Highway 24 to Minturn (exit 171). Proceed for 14 miles to Homestake Road (Forest Road 703) right for approximately 7.5 miles, and then travel on Forest Road 704 for another 1.5 miles. Turn sharply to the right and proceed to the trailhead, which is next to Missouri Creek.

CRADLED AT THE FOOT OF TOWERING PEAKS, Missouri Lakes attracts the expectant eye of wildflower lovers. Among some 87 other alpine lakes within the roughly 126,000-acre Holy Cross Wilderness Area, the collection of Missouri Lakes rewards hikers with majestic mountains, jeweled waters, and abundant wildflowers.

The trail begins flat through damp forest and then rises, quite strenuously in a few places, and levels periodically to reach the lake basin. Along the way are intriguing spots with a mysterious air. About 90 species of wildflowers line the three-mile hike, which leads to the first of several lakes. This description includes the largest lake situated at 11,502 feet.

Like all high-country hikes, go prepared for inclement weather that often manifests itself in lightning activity. Sturdy boots help negotiate the trail which can be muddy, rooty, rocky, and steep in segments.

Parking is adequate around the restroom area at the trailhead where a huge intake pipe moves captive water east to the Front Range metro areas.

L ively Missouri Creek sounds off by the trailhead sign where **fireweed** and **pearly everlasting** grow. August brings on the gentian clan. It takes a keen eye to pick out rare and endangered **twisted** or **fragrant gentian** along the level road-wide trail. This is the perennial dark purple gentian in the region and much less common than annual fringed gentian. In the vicinity, the family is also represented by the showy chalices of bright blue **Rocky Mountain** or **Parry gentian**.

Trail edges makes it easy for **many-rayed goldenrod** to gain a root-hold. In moist spots, **little rose gentian** may be in the company of the profuse annual, **fringed gentian**. Willows mark a mossy area, home to **little pink elephants** and the late-blooming **hooded ladies' tresses**, an orchid whose white blossoms spiral neatly up its sturdy stalk.

A vest pocket meadow in the spruce-fir forest exhibits two fleabanes: **subalpine daisy** with rosy lavender petals wide enough to mistake it for an aster and **Coulter daisy** with narrow white rays. Conifer shade nurtures four members of the wintergreen family including **one-sided**, **lesser**, **green-flowered**, and **pink pyrola**. Following a summer rain, the fascinating, but deadly, amanita mushroom with its scarlet cap—often white scabbed— emerges rather rapidly. In fact, under those conditions, the whole trail is a mushroom marvel.

The last vestiges of a log cabin on the left signals **monkshood**, **tall chiming bells**, and **arrowleaf senecio**. The saunter continues where evergreen trees

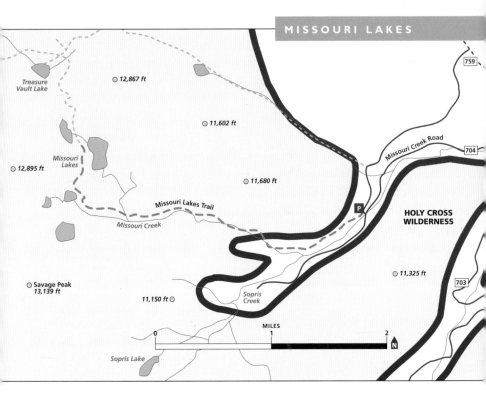

MISSOURI LAKES

Treasure Vault Lake

○ *12,867 ft*

○ *11,602 ft*

Missouri Lakes

○ *12,895 ft*

○ *11,680 ft*

Missouri Creek Road

704

Missouri Lakes Trail

Missouri Creek

P

759

HOLY CROSS
WILDERNESS

○ Savage Peak
13,139 ft

11,150 ft ○

Sopris Creek

○ *11,325 ft*

703

MILES
0   1   2

N

Sopris Lake

lean over a rotting log lined with **shy wood nymph** and **mitrewort**. In another wet spot nearby, the whites of **cowbane**, **brook saxifrage**, and **bittercress** appear.

Strolling ends where Missouri Creek glides by a sparsely-vegetated slope. Before the trail climbs, the very hairy **orange hawkweed** forms a patch on the right. Perhaps due to its burnt orange-scarlet rays, this interesting alien is also called **devil's paintbrush**. **Wild strawberries** and **wild raspberries** follow the trail up into lodgepole pines. While **bog orchids** and "elephants" are fairly early bloomers, it is later in the season when **fringed Parnassia** decorates the next bog. Leveling again, Missouri Lakes Trail parallels its heavily vegetated namesake creek. The trail rises and becomes rocky as it wanders into the open and into view of twin cascades. Fond of disturbed soil, **blacktipped senecio** grows near a diversion pipe. A peaceful pond on the left marks a trail mileage sign which disagrees with the distances given on the trailhead sign.

Upon entering the forest, **twistedstalk** dangles above a corduroy bridge. Undulating now, the trail heads to an uprooted tree sheltering **foamflower**, **shy wood nymph**, **pink pyrola**, and **mitrewort**. The creek rushes from a mysteriously primal forest and is spanned by a pair of flat-topped logs.

The trail curls up over bedrock to pause before a majestic view of rugged mountains. **Broadleaf arnica's** sunny heads poke above the trail, which heads into a tight, rugged little gorge rushing with crystalline water. The next pitch is assisted by more native stone until it comes to another corduroy bridge and levels. Left of the trail, in deep moss, is the place to search for **twayblade**, which is a descriptively named tiny green orchid.

Draped with copious moss, giant boulders display **Parry primrose** at their bases early in the season. **Daffodil senecio's** lemony rays follow that showing. **Star gentian** blooms where the trail has convenient stones for crossing a waterway. Wide planks span the next thundering creek crossing.

More elevation is gained over a rumpled footbed to reach tranquil waters and vertical rock walls. The creek serpentines through an exquisite meadow among **white bog orchids**, **queen's crown**, **rosy paintbrush**, and those wonderful **gentians**: hot blue **Rocky Mountain**, purple velvet **fringed**, and silky **star**. To the south, observe 13,139-foot Savage Peak.

A rockfall on the right escorts the level trail, passing clumps of **blue columbine**, **scarlet**, and pale-yellow **western paintbrush** before reentering the woods. Once again, the creek carves a picturesque little gorge. Sprayed with whitewater, the ragged ledges support **Parry Primrose**, **tall chiming bells**, and **arrowleaf senecio**. **Queen's crown** and **fringed Parnassia** adore this kind of water works.

Quiet water follows, and the trail S-curves up through a notch and opens

HOODED LADIES' TRESSES
Spiranthes romanzoffiana

Not only does the common name sound romantic, the Latin scientific title evokes an exotic image. Both suit the "French-braid" of white orchids languorously coiling up a proud spike. These orchids, each emerging from the axil of a leaf-like bract, are lipped and hooded, but not spurred. Blooming a little later than other native orchids, hooded ladies' tresses are sweetly perfumed. The genus part of the Latin name *Spiranthes* is derived from the Greek *spira* meaning "a coil" and *anthos,* "flower." The species portion commemorates a Russian patron of botany, Count Romanzoff who lived from 1754 to 1826. Spurred relatives in the region, sometimes found growing together, include green bog orchid *Limnorchis hyperborea* and white bog orchid *Limnorchis dilatata subspecies albiflora.*

into a meadow wallowing in wildflowers. Gentle trickles, reminiscent of tiny Oriental gardens, regale **fringed Parnassia, rosy paintbrush, bog orchid**, and an occasional **hooded ladies' tresses**.

Meadows slowly widen the landscape. Outcrops sport **yellow stonecrop, Whipple** or **dusky penstemon, harebells**, and even a **horned dandelion** or two. A sweet rill curves off amid wildflower-draped banks as the trail approaches a chaos of fallen, silvered-tree trunks. Driven by avalanche forces from the north, jumbled old trunks shelter **stitchwort** and **delicate Jacob's ladder**.

Another unrelenting ascent arrives at a stillwater meadow of purple and gold **subalpine aster** and **subalpine arnica**. Broken rock ledges, often softened by moss, house **king's crown** and **fireweed**.

Again the undulating wildflower-lined trail travels through rock-studded terrain to reach puzzle-piece tarns. Interpreting this surreal beauty would challenge any artist.

A last ridge enters into a memorable scene of a serene alpine lake held like a precious gem in rugged pewter prongs. Surrounded by sweeping slopes of bountiful wildflowers, the setting is perfect. No more could be asked of a trail than to deliver you into this place of astounding beauty.

For those who wish to experience more of this loveliness, Upper Missouri Lake lies just up the trail a quarter mile or so. Much larger and set quite differently, it is worth the extra distance.

Missouri Lakes are the epitome of Colorado's serene high-country majesty. Wildflowers are profuse and varied along the diverse trek. Water of every description and manner increases its appeal. Add this world-class trophy trail to your wild-flowering spectrum.

St. Louis Lake

Wildflower Alert: This trail showcases crazy-quilt
meadows on the way to a lovely flower-girt lake.

*This trail begins at the rushing waters of St. Louis Creek
and is filled with a dazzling variety of wildflower color
during the month of July.*

moderate	*Trail Rating*
7.0 miles out and back	*Trail Length*
Fraser	*Location*
10,000 to 11,531 feet	*Elevation*
July through August	*Bloom Season*
mid-to late July	*Peak Bloom*
Take US 40 north to Fraser. Take a left turn at the stoplight next to the Safeway on County Road 72. Turn right immediately after the railroad underpass and then left on County Road 73 (Forest Road 160). Continue for approximately 13 miles to the trailhead located at the end of the road.	*Directions*

BEGUILING ST. LOUIS LAKE straddles the subalpine and alpine zones. Not only is the lake and its flower-bedecked inlet right up the wildflower lover's alley, but the string of meadows leading to them are calico quilts of color in full bloom. Add the tranquility of deep forests, and you have a terrific high country hike.

The trail begins at the end of a long dirt road. Lively St. Louis Creek provides part-time company as the route climbs 1,500 vertical feet through conifers, then eases through flowery meadows. The trail rises and falls until the final ascent that reaches St. Louis Lake three and a half miles and seven dozen flower species from the trailhead.

Because this is a popular destination, parking can be a challenge on summer weekends. Cars line both sides of the road's end, making it difficult for large vehicles to turn around at the trailhead. Also be alert for thunderstorms that can build with amazing speed.

As you prepare to cross rushing St. Louis Creek, the wildflower parade begins at a sloped seep on the left with **rosy paintbrush**, **American speedwell**, **pink willowherb**, and **bog saxifrage**, among others. On the far side of the bridge, look for the lemon yellow rays of **daffodil senecio** under big conifers.

The trail begins pulling up over rocks, passing moist spots berthing white **brook saxifrage** and **bittercress**. Spidery green flowers touched with a trace of maroon (a hand lens bears this out) describes **mitrewort**, which has found footing in one of these choice spots. Another nurtures **yellow monkeyflower**.

A more level trail presents **tall chiming bells**, **subalpine larkspur**, and long-blooming **arrowleaf senecio** in a pleasant combination. **Scarlet paintbrush** and **bracted lousewort** come into play as the creek and trail travel side by side. Willows introduce rosy-lavender **subalpine daisy**, which superficially resembles an aster. **Colorado tansy aster** spreads wide its warm-violet blooms in mid-summer.

Leaving St. Louis Creek behind, the trail climbs through the depths of a spruce-fir forest. In the accumulated duff, look for the wonderfully scented **shy wood nymph** with her bowed white head. In the same habitat, June hikers may discover the secretive **Calypso orchid** in its cotton-candy pink perfection.

Where there are trees, there are roots underfoot. **Daffodil senecio** and **heartleaf arnica** add to the scenery. Passing pocket meadows of **scarlet paintbrush**, **subalpine daisy**, and **woolly** or **subalpine arnica**, the trail becomes rocky and uneven. Eventually joined again by the creek, this segment reveals **monkshood**.

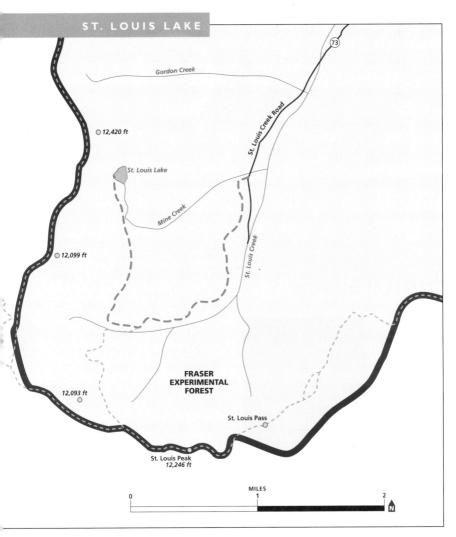

A hefty log crosses the noisy creek. On the far side, look for **little rose gentian** with tiny feathers tickling its satiny throat. Close by, low-growing **black-headed daisies** don woolly ruffs to warm their white heads.

A sloping meadow, where the trail drops to a stream, is home to **little pink elephants** and **queen's crown**. Early season openers here, **marsh marigold** and **globeflower** are a common spring combination. Before stepping onto the log bridge, look left to find dusky purple **star gentian** in the company of **rosy paintbrush**, **queen's crown**, **cowbane**, and **brook saxifrage**. Ascending from the bridge, watch for white **Coulter daisy** and, by August, the great blue chalices of **Rocky Mountain** or **Parry gentian**. The pink, white, yellow, and purple of **paintbrush, daisies, senecio,** and **monkshood** are on the left.

The golden creek courses openly, and the trail heads up and back into big conifers. The next meadow is filled with nonstop color across a broad slope. Here, at peak July bloom, every hue imaginable covers several acres. **Horned dandelions** lift their shaggy heads along the trail. A junction of the St. Louis Lake Trail is to the right. Passage through the next flowerscape, stitched together by tall purple **monkshood**, reveals the treeless summit of 12,246-foot St. Louis Peak to the south.

Round, rosy, and fragrant, **Parry clover** initiates a steepening passage through evergreens where the coiled beaks of **sickletop lousewort** or **parrot's beak** bloom. Switchbacking makes the incline a little easier as it leads to

DAFFODIL SENECIO

Ligularia amplectens

A summer bloomer, daffodil or nodding senecio is one of the most attractive in its clan. Strappy (*ligula* means "strap" in Latin), clear, light yellow rays taper to a point along with darker disk-shaped flowers to make the showy heads of this unmistakable endemic. Found in subalpine forests and meadows, the two-foot-high stems curve at the top, bowing the three-inch blossoms that emerge from dark bracts. Of the 3,000 "senecio" species around the globe, 100 can be found in North America from Alaska to New Mexico. A profuse cousin that is fond of wet places is arrowleaf senecio *Senecio triangularis*.

another patchwork quilt of **scarlet paintbrush, Coulter daisy, arnica,** and **horned dandelions**. At meadow's end, look for the low-growing vivid violet **Colorado tansy aster**.

Threading a meandering meadow, a creeklet gathers **star gentians, little pink elephants,** and fairy-influenced **brook saxifrage** at a log bridge crossing. Craggy outcrops rear into view, where evergreen shade suits **daffodil senecio** and palest blue delicate **Jacob's ladder**. Descending, hikers pass colorfully-clothed swales and eventually come upon a bright slope plaited with rivulets, which are accented with vibrant pink **Parry primrose,** white **bistort,** and **yellow monkeyflower**.

Convenient stones help with crossing a brook as you enter into a lush plot populated by midnight-blue **subalpine larkspur** and the high-noon-sky color of **blue columbine**. These trickling rills nurture **fringed Parnassia** whose white petals deserve a close look. Nearby willows court burnt red **king's crown**. Drier ground ahead takes the trail up a steep, brief pitch to more even terrain.

Western paintbrushes' cool yellow swabs, which are often suffused with red in this area, suggest probable interbreeding. Rugged mountains and a myriad of wildflowers make diverting company during the last pitch to reach St. Louis Lake. The creamy beaks of **Parry lousewort** point the way to a shallow pond rife with **little pink elephants** and brilliant **rosy paintbrush**.

Without a break in the flowery display, a ridge topped with "flagged" spruce trees opens to accommodate entry to St. Louis Lake. Backed by sky-sweeping crests, which are well over 12,000 feet, the jeweled waters dance in the summer sun.

As you head left to circle the flower-lined lake, enchanting floral interludes call for a pause. One unique spot is in the middle of a stone-studded mossy flow, accommodating wildflowers such as **Parry primrose** and **yellow monkeyflower**. Everywhere, **paintbrushes** embroider the background. Completing a circuit of 12,531-foot-high St. Louis Lake even allows you to view some tundra wildflowers.

The lakeshore is itself in bright bloom and includes **king's crown**, **columbine**, and the trumpets of **purple fringe**.

A wonderful trek for anyone seeking a good hike, St. Louis Lake Trail is special for wildflower lovers. Mark this trail as one of the best.

Wildflower Hike
29

Columbine Lake
(Indian Peaks Wilderness)

Wildflower alert: Luminescent meadows hued like sunstruck prisms lead to a lovely lake.

Plenty of moisture ensures a lush wildflower display along this colorful path.

Trail Rating	easy to moderate
Trail Length	5.6 miles out and back
Location	Fraser/Tabernash
Elevation	10,080 to 11,060 feet
Bloom Season	late June through August
Peak Bloom	mid-July to mid-August
Directions	Take US 40 through Fraser, and turn right onto County Road 83. Cross the Fraser River and turn left onto County Road 84 (Forest Road 129 or Meadow Creek Road). Proceed for 11.3 miles, and pass Meadow Creek Reservoir. Turn left to Junco Lake trailhead to access the Columbine Lake/Caribou Pass Trail.

CRADLED BY THE CONTINENTAL DIVIDE, lovely Columbine Lake is the perfect finale to a flower-filled hike in Colorado's high country. Blooming meadows, curling creeks, and tarns make outdoor enthusiasts happy and wild-flower lovers ecstatic.

Sturdy foot gear is required for hiking this well-watered trail, which begins on a rocky old road and then travels through colorful—albeit wet— meadows at a leisurely pace. It then climbs sharply along a tumbling creek to reach mountain-girt Columbine Lake just west of the Divide, all within spectacular Indian Peaks Wilderness.

After the long drive in from the main highway, it's a relief to find ample parking at Junco Lake trailhead, which is where the trail to Columbine Lake begins. Like all high-country hikes, start out early to avoid the afternoon thunderstorms. They can arrive with amazing speed.

A sizable buck-and-rail fence leads to the trailhead, and a pair of signs directs hikers to Columbine Lake and Caribou Pass Trail.

A level start sets the trail off through lodgepole pine, where **many-rayed goldenrod** and lavender violet **subalpine daisy** introduce the first of a colorful cast of petaled characters. In many parts of the high country, including here, a tiny taste treat ripens about the end of July: **wild strawberries.**

It isn't long before a bridged creek announces **queen's crown**, **arrowleaf senecio**, **white geranium**, and delicate white **cowbane**. Showing up frequently along the trail is showy **subalpine daisy**.

An old abandoned road makes walking easier. Soon a larger-bridged creek emerges, and to the left, a vest-pocket meadow which features **rosy paintbrush, cowbane, subalpine** or **woolly arnica,** and bit of brilliant **Parry primrose**. Look for the pearl-perfect buds of **fringed Parnassia**. Watch for troupes of **little pink elephants** before you cross a bog-spanning log.

The trail becomes a steady ascent along a rocky-bedded road, and this is a good section to concentrate on footing. Farther along the trail becomes muddy, and logs placed side by side allow hikers a way to avoid the mud. Then it becomes as rocky as a riverbed. A log cabin ruin appears on the right.

Inaugurated by several kinds of **cinquefoil**, a wide meadow appears where the path smooths out. Along here, about halfway into the hike to Columbine Lake, a welcoming sign to the Indian Peaks Wilderness Area materializes along with the craggy summits of Indian Peaks.

Another meadow quickly follows, costumed in pastel yellow **western paintbrush, white bog orchid,** and **little pink elephants**. Trail sides are rife with unobtrusive **rayless arnica.**

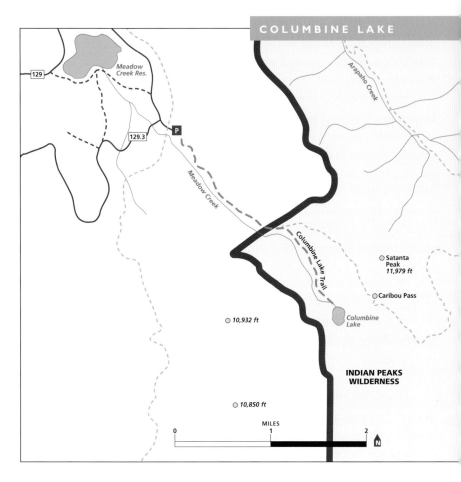

COLUMBINE LAKE

129

Meadow Creek Res.

129.3

P

Meadow Creek

Arapaho Creek

Columbine Lake Trail

○ Satanta Peak 11,979 ft

○ Caribou Pass

Columbine Lake

○ 10,932 ft

INDIAN PEAKS WILDERNESS

○ 10,850 ft

MILES

0   1   2

N

The trail narrows through a stand of conifers, reaching another flowery meadow. In addition to present bloomers, August will present **Rocky Mountain** or **Parry gentian**, its deep chalices a rich royal blue.

Circumvent a boggy spot by using the drier forest floor. Those mesmerizing peaks dominating the skyline upstage a field of complementary purple and gold.

At the right time—typically following rain—fire-engine-red mushrooms, often sporting white scabs, pop up. This deadly amanita is as poisonous as it is beautiful.

Coming up is a junction that sends Caribou Pass trail left, while the right spur continues to Columbine Lake. The next meadow fills itself with a kaleidoscope of blooming things including the proud native **horned dandelion**. A hidden creek talks to itself within thick willows before going public at an oxbow to exhibit tall purple **monkshood**. Footing is challenging through this rather sloppy area.

Not only is the meadow awash in water, but in flowers. Choose your route carefully, wending through the adjacent conifers. Then begin climbing through boulders and gnarly roots. The spruce-accompanied ascent leads past **Parry Primrose** and thick stands of earlier-blooming **globeflowers**.

The trail travels in an area of downed trees—probably a freak blow down. Up on the right, a cascade sings and a mini-meadow previews **tall chiming bells, arrowleaf senecio**, and **cowbane**. A rooty stairway pulls the hiker through dense evergreen shadows into a primeval scene of hushed expectancy.

Coming into sunshine again, the trail edges another verdant basin filled with rainbow pastels, particularly the pinks of **rosy paintbrush** and friendly looking **little pink elephants**. White **bistort** waves above it all.

You'll reach a bog where single logs assist your crossing. White **bittercress** blooms where **marsh marigold** was an early season star. At the log's end you'll find an unusual treat; an underground channel, interwoven with a ceiling of dark earth, wends below your feet. Peek inside, then catch a glimpse of reigning **queen's crown**. The main creek curves in tight oxbows as it leads to a log that ends too soon. More of these log situations are ahead.

Fronting a ridge of raw rock that tops out at 11,831 feet, a bald-faced outcrop beams down on a sweet garden. Next

SUBALPINE DAISY
Erigeron peregrinus subspecies callianthemus

One of the most commonly encountered "daisies" in the subalpine zone, especially in July or early August, is the subalpine daisy. The bright rosy-lavender rays (ray flowers) are quite wide for a fleabane, and it is often mistaken for an aster. A close-packed center consists of orange-yellow disk flowers. Typically the wide showy heads of subalpine daisy are borne one to a stem. The Latinate name may be broken down into the genus *Erigeron,* meaning "early" and *geri,* meaning "old man." The species name *peregrinus* means "wanderer," and the subspecies, *callianthemus* means "beautiful-flowered." Cousins include Coulter daisy *Erigeron coulteri* and pink-headed daisy *Erigeron elatior.*

a lively cascade appears on the right. On the left, as the trail prepares to ascend, is a nice grouping of **scarlet paintbrush, bracted lousewort,** and **bistort.** Low-growing **black-headed daisy** is soon on stage.

The next bit of trail is challenging, not only because it steepens, but route-finding is sometimes confused by "social" trails. Staying fairly close to the tumbling cascade is **Parry primrose** practically wading in the water. A little whitewater-surrounded island is picture perfect in pink, blue, and white: **Parry primrose, tall chiming bells, cowbane,** and **bittercress.**

Additional climbing offers more of the usual wet habitat wildflowers, plus regal purple **subalpine larkspur.** Each sharp pitch along the path is balanced by a shelf where you can catch your breath.

Find comely **blue columbine** in the shadow of skyscraping granite. Domes of worn outcrops take hikers over raw rock to reach a creeklet burbling down over stair-step ledges. Cross it near a big spruce on convenient logs. The trail traverses up a short granite face which houses **little pink elephants.**

The bench, marked with chocolate-swirled granite, holds several dark tarns. Lingering is not advised since bogs and bugs often go together.

Pushing on suddenly reveals the celadon-green depths of Columbine Lake. Find a flat outcrop overlooking the sparkling waters and bask in the beauty around you. Both cool yellow **western** and showy **scarlet paintbrushes** decorate the far side of the lake. Satanta Peak rises to 11,979 feet to the northeast and Mount Neva rises to the southeast at 12,814 feet.

Late July and early August are postcard-perfect times to enjoy abundant wildflowers on a warm summer day. A beautifully set lake, dancing waters, and Rocky Mountain majesty help to rank this trail close to the top of a mid-summer hike agenda.

Crag Crest

Wildflower alert: This trail leads you through head-high corydalis to a stupendous panorama.

Eggleston Lake is the starting point for this trail steeped in hip-deep wildflowers.

easy to moderate	*Trail Rating*
4.0 miles out and back	*Trail Length*
Grand Junction/Grand Mesa National Forest	*Location*
10,150 to 11,128 feet	*Elevation*
July through August	*Bloom Season*
late July to early August	*Peak Bloom*
Take I-70 to Highway 65 east of Grand Junction for 17 miles. Go south for 34.5 miles, and then left onto Forest Road 12 for another 12.5 miles. Go left at a fork in the road for 0.9 mile. Park right adjacent to Eggleston Lake. The trailhead is across the road.	*Directions*

THE RAZOR-EDGED RIDGE OF CRAG CREST rises abruptly from Grand Mesa, which is one of the largest flat-topped mountains in the world. The Crag Crest hike from the east trailhead to the ragged ridge back offers an intriguing variety of unique terrain as well as wildflowers. Nine-hundred vertical feet of elevation gain is achieved in two miles of trail. Once on top, far-sweeping vistas are in every direction.

This part of the Crag Crest National Recreation Trail is available to foot traffic only. Hikers saunter through Engelmann spruce-subalpine fir forest, pocket meadows, and flowery slopes before tackling lava-rockfalls, inclines, and switchbacks to reach the top.

On the way to the trailhead, stop by the attractive visitor center staffed by helpful personnel. Parking is generous across from the trailhead, right by Eggleston Lake.

Look for the sign leading to the Crag Crest trailhead across the road on the east edge of Crag Crest campground. A stream flows nearby, and at least three dozen kinds of wildflowers start off within a few feet of the sign, including **Case's fitweed**. This plush plant can't be missed during its typical mid-July to mid-August bloom season as it often stretches head high and is chockfull of racemes packed with plaited white or blush-pink flowers, often purple tipped.

The trail is filled with hip-deep wildflowers: **tall Jacob's ladder, Porter's lovage, white geranium, subalpine larkspur,** and later-blooming **fireweed**. As the trail pulls up from this lush beginning, look for lesser lights of **many-rayed goldenrod, western paintbrush, Coulter daisy,** and both an **arnica** and a **senecio** displaying their ray-less heads.

After this head-spinning array, the trail soon arrives at a junction. Head right, and you'll enter a spruce-fir forest. Easygoing in its ascent, the trail finds **heartleaf arnica** and **mountain parsley** with **sickletop** and **bracted louseworts** among the trees—perhaps even an occasional **blue columbine**. In damp places, **bittercress** and **homely buttercup** appear. Along the way, a pond opens the tree-shrouded sky, and the path wanders through a patch of subalpine "jungle" where wildly plush **Case's fitweed** may reach up to eight feet tall in a good year.

Leaving the evergreens for sunshine, the scenery takes in the sparkling waters of Upper Eggleston Lake, which is a destination for enthusiastic fishermen. Traveling across a slope above the lake, the trail becomes waist-deep in **orange sneezeweed, subalpine larkspur, tall valerian,** and **pink-headed daisies**.

Pocket meadows of **little pink elephants, subalpine daisy,** and a particularly vibrant shade of **rosy paintbrush** emerges during the next half mile along the flat terrain. Tucked into mossy spots may be the minuscule in-line snowflakes of green **mitrewort**.

A junction appears, and a left here heads to Butts Lake. A right takes Crag Crest Trail hikers up to overlook Bullfinch Reservoir and up further toward the hike's goal. A great fall of chunked lava rock edges the trail where **sibbaldia** carpets flat spots and **rock brakenfern**—its upper parts like green antennas— are tucked in among rough boulders. Here and there, clumps of **columbine** soften the imposing rockscape, as do divots of **early blue daisy** and **pussytoes**.

The angle increases past Bullfinch Reservoir and begins switchbacking to ease the ascent. On a west-heading switchback, watch the steep cutbanks for elongated specimens of **purple fringe** or **silky phacelia** in soft lavender. The view along here exposes mile-long Butts Lake, its south shore thickly treed, the north side a slide of raw rock. The higher the trail goes, the more expansive the views.

In places, the increasingly rock-girt trail is cut into very steep slopes with stunted aspen maintaining an astonishing root-hold. Stands of quaking aspen, whether in a flat meadow or clinging on a precarious slope, "clone" themselves— meaning that roots travel and produce suckers that form one widespread organism.

A glance up to determine where you're headed may reveal a rugged escarpment almost hanging over your head. Keep an eye on the path, however, as the encroaching vegetation might be **stinging nettles**.

ORANGE SNEEZEWEED
Dugaldia hoopesii

Also known as owl-claws and swamp sunflower, orange sneezeweed was actually named because the dried leaves, up to ten inches long, served as snuff—hence the sneeze connection.

Its tri-toothed drooping rays emanate from a convex disk flower center. Except for the Pike's Peak region, orange sneezeweed is a Western Slope species. It's somewhat ironic that this big (up to four feet) plant increases where grazing is heavy because it is toxic to livestock, causing spewing sickness in sheep. Cousins in the sunflower family include one-fifth of all Rocky Mountain wildflowers.

Native Americans ground the root for chest poultices when dealing with pneumonia and other respiratory ailments. They also garnered a soft yellow dye from the flowers. Dugald Stewart was a late sixteenth-century Scots philosopher and Josiah Hoopes was a nine-teenth-century botanist from Pennsylvania. They share the honors of the Latin name.

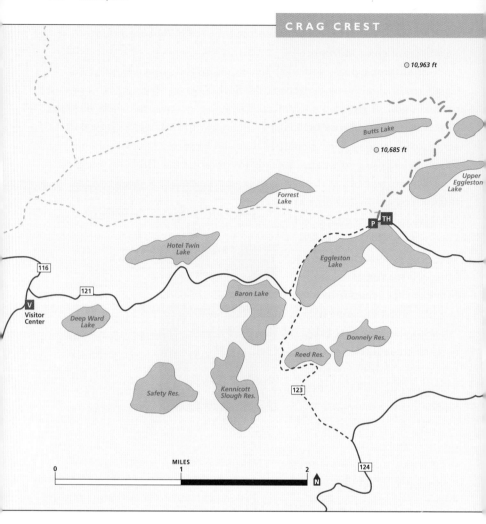

It is surprising how well-clothed Mother Nature keeps these incredibly steep slopes where rock doesn't render them barren. Pockets of collected soil support many plants including **columbine** and **senecio** or **groundsel**.

Nearing the top, the trail S-curves up a segment flanked by great heaves of porous lava jumbles. A sweet meadow retains enough moisture to nurture plants as tall as **false hellebore** or **corn lily** or as short as **little rose gentian**. The views are now vistas, and the pathway steps through more rock to reach a saddle.

Trees grow shorter, and the trail pushes up to climax at a heart-stopping 360-degree panorama. The narrow crest of craggy basalt has been broached. Take a deep breath where the trail, suddenly and narrowly, shifts from the north side of the ridge to the south. Take a moment to find a slightly uncomfortable seat on a pockmarked boulder at this precipitous and jagged juncture of primeval outcrop. Look down a double-black-diamond slope of ragged broken lava before letting your eyes lift northwest to the bare Book and Roan Cliffs in the distance. Battlement Mesa's lava-capped palisade is north. Grand Mesa's highest point, 11,234-foot Leon Peak, along with the Elk Mountains and impressive ranges in the Crested Butte region, is east. To the south are the West Elk Mountains, 14,309-foot Uncompahgre Peak, and the San Juan Range. Utah's La Sal Mountains are on the hazy horizon to the west.

When saturated with the panoramic view, look in the eroded outcrop at your elbow for swatches of moss-like **spotted saxifrage** cleaving to its rocky home. Just a tad up the trail where it widens is **dwarf goldenrod**, and maybe even a **Rocky Mountain gentian** about to burst into royal blue goblets.

Crag Crest Trail from the east trailhead is a hummer, so full of diversity that the trek up is worth bragging about. This is an easy getaway. Over 80 species of wildflowers, and a good workout add to the pleasure of this hike.

Fourth of July Mine
(Indian Peaks Wilderness)

Wildflower Hike
31

Wildflower Alert: This trail provides maximum high-country color in late July.

Not far from Boulder, this trail was originally established by early Native Americans and later utilized by prospectors and miners.

Trail Rating	moderate
Trail Length	4.6 miles out and back
Location	Nederland
Elevation	10,160 to 11,250 feet
Bloom Season	July through August
Peak Bloom	mid- to late July
Directions	Take Highway 119 west from Boulder to Nederland. Go south onto County Road 130 for approximately nine miles to the trailhead, which is located at the road's end.

LOCATED IN THE SOUTHERN PART of the popular Indian Peaks Wilderness Area, this trail is a gorgeous high-country flower hike. Early Colorado miners used this trail that was originally established by early Native Americans as a route to cross the imposing Continental Divide. Fourth of July Mine never amounted to much, but its existence is still marked by a huge rusting boiler.

Generally the well-trodden trail rises at a steady incline. It begins through spruce-fir forest, then shifts into a more open mode, exposing steep flowery slopes and finally flattening out at treeline. Along the way, stirred by a number of waterways, approximately 90 wildflower species color the magnificent mountainscape. Wildflowers at this elevation are almost exclusively perennial, which means bloom times vary. To catch spring and summer bloomers overlapping, visit in the third week of July, which typically is prime time.

If this sounds like a great hike, plan on arriving at the trailhead early. On summer weekends, parking gets competitive. Summer is also the time for afternoon thunderstorm activity—another reason for an early start.

Head up over log steps to reach the trail-sign kiosk above the upper parking area. In late summer, the sign's posts are surrounded by **white checkermallow**, a relative of cotton and okra. Follow more peeled logs to discover a meadow of **scarlet paintbrush**, **bracted lousewort**, and **pink-headed daisy**. Engelmann spruce and subalpine fir create a setting for moisture-loving **monkshood**, **white geranium**, **subalpine daisy**, and **cow parsnip**. The high-country spring duo of **marsh marigold** and **globeflower** set the pace for early season hikers.

ARCTIC GENTIAN

Gentianodes algida

The last gentian to bloom, 4 to 6-inch-high arctic gentian reportedly signals the coming of snow to the tundra in six weeks time. On the outside, each green-tinged white flower sports purple streaks made up of closely set speckles; on the inside is a green pistil surrounded by five salmon-colored stamens. Closing at night and during cloudy weather, the petals draw tight, making the shut corolla appear dark purple. Of the 300 gentians species worldwide, about 14 grow in the Rocky Mountains. Arctic gentian's Latin specific name *algida,* "frigid," refers to its chosen alpine habitat. Cousins include the rare fragrant or twisted fringed gentian *Gentianopsis barbellata* and star gentian *Swertia perennis.*

A boardwalk introduces the first creeklet, with **twistedstalk** above and **subalpine larkspur** and **arrowleaf senecio** below. The second waterway offers **white bog orchid**. Pocket meadows featuring **mountain death camas** string along the trail.

Gaining elevation, the narrowing trail opens up to include views of the Continental Divide peaks to the west. **Fireweed** ignites hillsides and **yellow stonecrop** colors the cutbanks. The trail becomes rockier, grows steep, and then eases again as the path is accented by east-facing **aspen sunflowers** and pert **harebells**. Long-blooming **sandwort** and **golden aster** adhere to the lithic soil where bristlecone pines illustrate their identity with resin-flecked needles.

SUBALPINE LARKSPUR

Delphinium barbeyi

Subalpine Larkspur are anywhere from two to five feet tall. With intense purple-blue racemes, this flower is a member of the often toxic hellebore family. The flowers of the subalpine larkspur consist of five flared sepals; the uppermost is the spur. The four petals are scrunched up under the spurred sepal. It is especially fond of spruce-fir forests and moist subalpine slopes. A cousin is Geyer larkspur *delphinium geyeri*. Another cousin, monkshood *Aconitum columbianum*, is even more toxic. Early Californios referred to larkspur as "*esuela del caballero,*" "cavalier's spur." The species name commemorates William Barbey, born in 1842 in Switzerland.

Sounding like a high wind, a waterfall sends white streamers off a cliff far to the left. An aspen copse prefaces an Indian Peaks/Roosevelt National Forest sign. Switchbacks wind past a rivulet of **tall chiming bells, subalpine larkspur, monkshood, broadleaf arnica, Porter's lovage,** and **little rose gentian**.

A charming trio of elfin falls—one delighting in whimsical **yellow monkeyflower**—are channeled, and boots stay dry. As you approach a conifer-shaded rill that can be crossed on stones, take in white **bittercress** and lacy **cowbane**.

Vistas of the peaks of the Continental Divide punctuate the western skyline. **Queen's crown** and pearly **fringed Parnassia** grow luxuriously, and shady places reveal the zigzag stems of **twistedstalk**, its orange-scarlet berries once hanging white bells. Also shade-loving but barely noticed, **mitrewort**'s tiny snowflake-like flowers deserve a hand lens for enjoying their delicate maroon and green traceries.

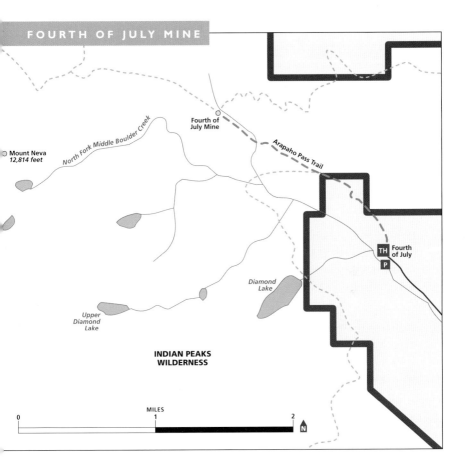

On the near side of an impressive cascade, **purple fringe**, **whiproot clover**, **spotted saxifrage**, and **alpine sorrel** enhance crumbling outcrops. Choose your crossing carefully to avoid wet feet and a precarious drop off on the left side. Not only does the water cascade, but the wildflowers follow suit. Farther on, after a bit of woods, a stony-bedded waterway sports **bistort**, **little pink elephants**, **white bog orchids**, and **queen's crown**.

At the 1.3 mile point, the lush seeps at the Diamond Lake junction send Arapaho Pass/Fourth of July Trail up a switchback. Another mile takes you to the mine site. With flowers illuminating every square foot of open terrain, the landscape looks like the pages of a Colorado high country coffeetable book.

Ascending more strongly now, **aspen sunflowers**, **cinquefoil**, and **pink-headed daisy** listen to Middle Boulder Creek roaring below. In xeric places, the intertwined roots of bi-colored **whiproot** or **alpine clover** knit the gravelly soil.

Trough-like now for a stretch, the trail shares a narrow creekbed with a small golden-granite stream. Flanking this section are **monkeyflower**, **arrowleaf senecio**, and **monkshood** in complementary yellow and purple.

Panoramas review winsome **blue columbine** on the right. Drier habitats fill in with pastels of **creamy buckwheat, harebells, pink-headed daisy**, and **yarrow**.

A long traverse across a swooping slope reaches an outcrop overlook. Along the way, swales that held lingering snowdrifts reveal **glacier lilies'** curved yellow tepals to early-season hikers. Later, erect three-paneled pods of glacier lily make choice tidbits for wildlife. Pink **pygmy bitterroot**, yellow **blueleaf cinquefoil**, and **alpine avens** bloom among the stunted spruce near the outcrop.

As you approach treeline, the gradient and rocky footing increases. Ease your mind with a glance at the cross-trail flow of handsome **marsh marigolds, Parry primrose, little pink elephants**, and **white bog orchids**. Pink **willowherb** and **yellow monkeyflower** act as foils for somber-umbelled **Gray's angelica**. Where late-melting snow delayed bloom, white **bittercress, bistort**, and **brook saxifrage** appear. On the right are **tall chiming bells**. Farther along the trail, **star gentian** and **mountain death camas** arrive with low willows.

South Arapaho Peak prods the north skyline as the the trail levels across a broad bench cloaked in spruce *krummholz*. This is a good place to watch for yellow-bellied marmots and listen for high-pitched pika voices. **Shrubby cinquefoil** and the wiry-stemmed stars of **sandwort** flank the wide pathway. **Arctic gentian** is nature's autumn countdown—six weeks until snowfall. Tucked among the tussocks of tundra grass here, the almost-translucent white goblets with their purple speckled exteriors define this last-to-bloom gentian.

Odd-shaped pools of iron-oxide-stained water, accented by rosy lavender **subalpine daisies** and both **alpine** and **American bistort**, require creative crossing. Drier areas run to early blooming tundra-dwellers such as **moss campion** and **mountain dryad**. Tight-matted **alpine sandwort's** white flowers manage to keep on going all season.

A signed junction for Arapaho Pass and Arapaho Glacier marks the site of the Fourth of July Mine. The rusting hulk of a boiler and tailing piles are all that remain. **Woolly** or **frosty ball thistle** and **purple fringe** cling to the compacted scree of the tidy piles. Nearby boulders make fine resting places to view 12,814-foot Mount Neva to the west and 13,397-foot South Arapaho Peak, north.

"Grandeur and wildflowers" could be the title of the Fourth of July Mine trek. Blooming rainbows, sweetened by moving water of all shapes and speeds, color the mountainscape pages. Convenient to the Front Range, this choice trail belongs at the top of wildflower hike destinations.

Second Creek

Wildflower Alert: This trail takes you along a flower-lined cascade as pretty as a picture postcard.

Although occasionally steep, this hike follows a tumbling creek and showcases over six-dozen species of wildflowers.

moderate	**Trail Rating**
3.0 miles out and back	**Trail Length**
Berthoud Pass/Winter Park	**Location**
10,560 to 11,400 feet	**Elevation**
mid-July through August	**Bloom Season**
late July to early August	**Peak Bloom**
Take I-70 west to US 40, and then go north to Berthoud Pass and continue 2.9 miles to a wide turnout on the left.	**Directions**

BERTHOUD PASS crosses the Continental Divide at 11,315 feet, and several scenic cirques, often white-rimmed by remnant cornices, highlight the west side of the road. One of these curved bowls is accessed by the Second Creek Trail.

The trail begins on the right side of Second Creek and penetrates heavy conifer shade before edging out to the north and ascending, generally in the open, some 800 vertical feet. The steepish hike is accompanied by over six dozen wildflower species of many colors. But the crowning glory of Second Creek Trail is found just beyond a closed Forest Service cabin: the flower-lined cascades of First Creek.

A wide turnout on the left provides ample parking for this hike. Located 2.9 miles down from Berthoud Pass, it is marked by an avalanche warning sign for cross-country skiers.

Near the beginning of Second Creek Trail, in the deep shade of towering evergreen trees and along the braided path, keep a keen eye out for **mitrewort** and **twayblade orchid**. Search in the damp forest duff for these bantam-sized plants. Both feature tiny, green flowers that under magnification are a delight. Then head streamside and look for mossy seeps, where **yellow monkeyflower** with its red-speckled throat flourishes. Historically, the oval leaves have been used as salad greens or mashed to sooth rope burns and wounds.

Head right and toward more open skies. The single trail winds up through early-blooming **louseworts** such as **sickletop**, with its coiled white blossoms, and **bracted**, with beaked cream-colored flowers. **Fleabane daisies**, some of which resemble later-blooming **asters**, dot the slopes. Next to the trail, look for **dwarf goldenrod**, whose leaves, boiled or ground into powder, have been used to heal wounds. Widespread **yarrow** lifts whitish composite heads here and there. Its pungent leaves served many medicinal purposes and are especially effective in stopping bleeding wounds—hence another common name: **woundwort**. The suffix "wort," or "wyrt" in Old English, simply means "plant."

Rising, the trail travels past several intimate bogs featuring **white bog orchid**, **little pink elephants**, and golden **subalpine arnica**—each a study in color harmony. **Little rose gentian** grows from the edges of the trail. To appreciate the feathered throats and fine petal lines of this small Victorian rose-tinted gentian, a hand lens is necessary.

A couple more short rocky pitches, and the trail evens out by a flowery pocket meadow on the left and then goes up through an old burn. Great trees

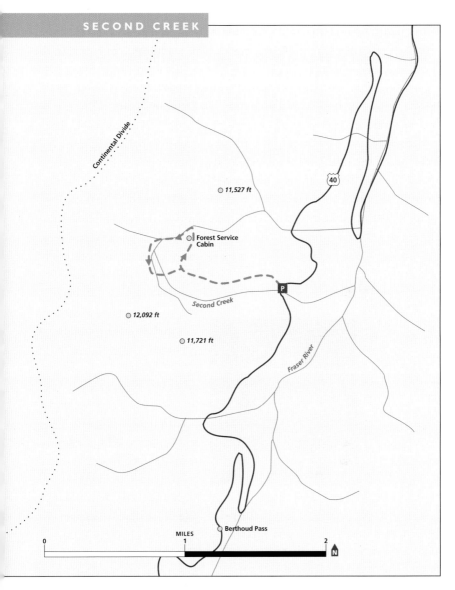

11,527 ft

Forest Service
Cabin

Continental Divide

40

Second Creek

12,092 ft

11,721 ft

Fraser River

P

MILES

Berthoud Pass

0   1   2

N

stood here before a forest fire reduced them to a few standing sentinels amid
an army of fallen trunks.

At the base of a big outcrop, sometimes topped with sunning marmots,
vibrant **scarlet paintbrush** and **fireweed** light up the pale rock. Up to the
southwest, the contours of the Berthoud Pass Ditch may be seen as the trail
curves around a pair of weather-bleached snags. Along an easy-going section
where the path is less defined, watch for a distinctive plant not commonly

encountered: **moonwort**, or more descriptively, **grapefern**, which looks like a cross between a fern and tiny green grapes. This plant begins to appear in the latter part of July here.

Moving on, hikers soon reach the closed Forest Service A-frame where a handy outhouse is just downhill to the east. **Delicate Jacob's ladder** and late-blooming **fireweed** decorate the cabin's front "garden." Now comes the best part. Ease around the front of the cabin and follow a narrow path through the trees toward the sound of rushing water. First Creek summons you to take in one of the loveliest flower-lined cascades in Colorado.

Flanked by a veritable eden of pink **Parry primrose**, soft blue **tall chiming bells**, and the brisk whites of **brook saxifrage**, **bistort**, and **brookcress**, the purling staircase commands attention. **Brookcress'** dark peppery leaves give away its watercress cousinship. The Latin name, *Cardamine cordifolia,* describes its heart-shaped leaves but also discloses its historical use for cardiac problems.

TWAYBLADE

Listera cordata

With notable exceptions, such as the Calypso and ladies' slipper orchids, most orchids in the region are small with tiny flowers.

Though twayblade orchid fits in the last category, it is fun to inspect the interesting green flowers with a hand lens and discover the apt naming of this deep shade denizen. Touching the pollen bead with a pointed object may trigger the fertilization mechanism. The sticky pollinium shoots out for attachment on what is assumed to be an inquiring insect. The genus portion of the Latin scientific name *Listera*, commemorates Dr. Martin Lister. He was a British naturalist who lived from 1638 to 1711. The specific portion *cordata*, refers to the pair of heart-shaped leaves emerging at the mid-point on the stem.

Although the footing gets a bit tricky on a side hill, persevere and you'll see **black-headed daisies** and both wine and off-white **Whipple penstemon.** Tending more toward copper and a lower growth habit at this elevation, **burnt orange false dandelion** or **orange agoseris** cling to the left bank. The adjacent creek displays fine stands of **arrowleaf senecio, marsh marigold** and **queen's crown,** all fond of wet places. **Queen's crown,** sometimes called **roseroot** due to its reportedly rose-scented root, sports rounded terminal heads of pointy warm-pink blossoms. Its light green, succulent leaves are said to be edible either raw or cooked. These will turn a luminescent red in the fall. More white-petaled **brook saxifrage** with its dark red flower parts—and later, conspicuous seedpods—accent the scene. This airy species is one of about twenty members of the saxifrage family in the Rocky Mountains.

Climb up to the lip of a derelict aqueduct ditch, and begin searching for ground-hugging **pygmy bitterroot**, with its narrow succulent leaves cradling bright satin stars of rosy pink (sometimes white or pale pink). This member of the purslane family was once considered a food source. Also edible, and growing in the same gravelly soil, is **alpine blue violet**.

Turn to the left along this old ditch and follow it either along the rim or down inside to enter an area where rocks take over. A flowery rill, mostly hidden, beckons you to drop down by a stream which flows into a smaller ditch. While descending, note the lush clumps of **rock senecio** nestled next to (what else?)—rocks. There are at least forty "senecio-related" species in the Rockies, part of about a thousand around the world. Nearby, in mid to late August, the royal blue chalices of **Rocky Mountain** or **Parry gentian** start their end-of-summer display—a memorable performance.

Follow the little creeklet through a flowery meadow with islands of willow full of midnight blue **subalpine larkspur** and **arrowleaf senecio**, in complementary purple and gold. Herds of **little pink elephants** graze in the meadow below.

While descending the slope, stay high and to the left to keep your feet dry. Walk in a southeasterly direction through grasses fresh with lavender **daisies** and **paintbrush** in order to retrace the trail you came up on. A good landmark to watch for is Colorado Mines Peak to the southeast.

Second Creek Trail is a short and fun hike that culminates in the First Creek cascades. Less than an hour and a half from metro Denver, this convenient destination offers a day filled with beautiful wildflowers.

Wildflower Hike

33

CENTURY HIKE

Grizzly Lake
(Collegiate Peaks Wilderness)

Wildflower Alert: Colonies of alpine fireweed are but one note of a rhapsody in color along this spectacular "century" trail to a high alpine lake.

Over 100 species of wildflowers line the trail that leads to lovely Grizzly Lake.

Trail Rating	moderate to strenuous
Trail Length	7.6 miles out and back
Location	Aspen
Elevation	10,560 to 12,550 feet
Bloom Season	late July through August
Peak Bloom	early to mid-August
Directions	Take State Route 82 east from Aspen for 10 miles. Go south on Lincoln Gulch Road (Forest Road 106) for approximately 6.5 rough miles to the trailhead, which is on the left, just before Portal Campground. A high-clearance vehicle is advisable.

AFTER NEGOTIATING ONE OF THE LUMPIEST access roads around, the reward is the superlative trek to sky-touching Grizzly Lake. The first and last trail segments are demanding, but the long middle portion is a delightful cruise. Crescent-shaped Grizzly Lake Trail travels up a spectacular valley just west of the Continental Divide.

Well over 100 species of eye-catching wildflowers are visible along the subalpine and alpine zones and leave no doubt that this is a "century" trail. Mother Nature went all out with the wildflowers in the scimitar-shaped valley of Grizzly Creek.

Once the initial climb through unrelenting evergreen trees is over, the majority of the trail is under open skies. Switchbacking for nearly 500 vertical feet, the trail then bursts into a seemingly endless magic meadow. This valley alone is a worthwhile hike. But the final steep approach is a law of beauty unto itself. The goal is 12,550-foot high Grizzly Lake encircled by the essence of the Rocky Mountains.

Parking is rather awkward and limited. Due to this hike's extended exposure, an early arrival is essential to avoid commonly-encountered summer afternoon thunderstorms.

Bumpy is the understated word for the access road up Lincoln Gulch. While four-wheel drive may not be necessary, a high-clearance vehicle is strongly suggested.

Grizzly Lake trailhead is directly across from the operations complex for the Twin Lakes Tunnel, which transfers West Slope water east. Step right out and up into the Collegiate Peaks Wilderness. Rocks and roots underfoot are the norm as hikers ascend nearly 500 vertical feet in short order through Engelmann spruce and subalpine fir.

The shadowy climb is forgotten as wide skies offer **scarlet paintbrush**, **many-rayed goldenrod**, and **harebells**. Youthful cream ages to salmon and finally to brick red in the full heads of **creamy buckwheat** punctuating the landscape.

Stark peaks frame a verdant valley with the onset of **pink plumes**. Adding to the tame tint of pink plumes are **pink-headed daisy** and **yarrow**. Also here is white **Coulter daisy**. Down toward the willows accompanying lilting Grizzly Creek are a profusion of **fringed gentians**.

A grassy south-facing slope, studded with rock, takes the trail into an area of **meadow rue** and the tall spires of **fireweed**. Like its cousin **creamy buckwheat**, **dwarf sulphurflower's** bright umbels age to red. Look close at hand for **stonecrop's** yellow stars, similar in color to sulphurflower. Barely yellow **western paintbrush** sings a duet with **scarlet paintbrush** in the shadow of a talus-covered peak. At just the right moment, **blue columbine** adds a cool note.

Down by the clear creek, a patch of **broadleaf** or **alpine fireweed** lends a rosy tone to the beautiful scene. **Aspen sunflowers** stand sentinel over a predominately pastel flowerscape. The edges of the slightly rising trail are trimmed with proud native **horned dandelion** in old gold and low-growing **Colorado tansy aster** in vibrant violet.

The footbed changes to scree and passes through a spruce grove. The crunchy surface reenters sunlight to introduce the bright blue goblets of **Rocky Mountain** or **Parry gentian** and midnight-blue-purple **subalpine larkspur**. A number of hot yellow **cinquefoils** contrast with the almost non-color of **tall valerian**. More east-facing **sunflowers** take the trail into another stretch of conifers. Bi-colored **whiproot clover** mats the shadows while wine-tinted **Whipple** or **dusky penstemon** grows a foot high. A pair of cousins, ferny-leaved **bracted lousewort** and entire-leaved **sickletop lousewort**, share the shade. An occasional **blue columbine** sweeps its long spurs as if conducting an orchestra.

Willows arrive with open skies, and the trail twists up to find **scarlet paintbrush** and the big, pale, rubbery leaves of yellow **blacktipped senecio**. A smattering of short **alpine fireweed** and both **rock** and **daffodil senecio** decorate a shady drainage. **Woolly** or **subalpine** and **heartleaf arnica** also put in appearances.

Where a split in the path occurs, stay on the high trail. **Ballhead** and **Fendler sandwort**, both appreciative of a xeric habitat, bring the serrated teeth of the Continental Divide into view. Two yellow members of the rose family, **blueleaf cinquefoil** and **alpine avens**, thrive in the lithic soil.

Tucked into a rockfall, sour **alpine sorrel**, tidy **rock senecio**, and early-blooming **sky pilot** call for attention. The glaucous or blue-green leaves of **alpine fireweed** act as a foil to the clear magenta flowers. Nearby and also glaucous-leaved, **dwarf chiming bells** add blue to the pretty rock garden. Down by the chatty creek, radiant **Parry primrose** and snowy **bittercress** harmonize in pink and white. On the high side, the golds of **sawleaf senecio** and **alpine avens** gild the rocky slope.

The trail rises unobtrusively, displaying wildflowers such as **blue columbine** at peak bloom. The incline increases, and if you look closely you'll find sweet **alpine violet** and the minuscule stars of **rock primrose** or **northern fairy candelabra**.

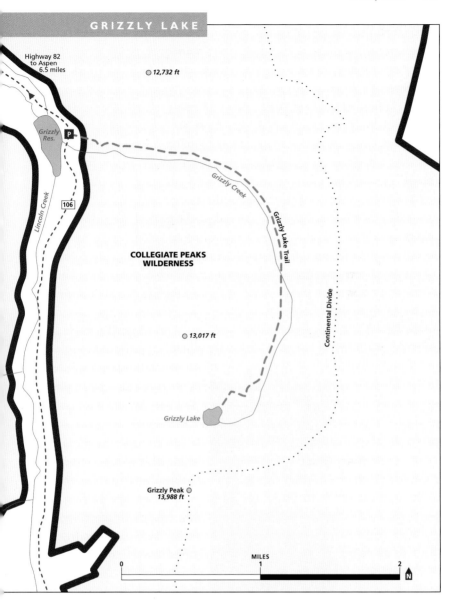

GRIZZLY LAKE

Highway 82
to Aspen
6.5 miles

12,732 ft

Grizzly
Res.

P

Lincoln Creek

106

Grizzly Creek

Grizzly Lake Trail

COLLEGIATE PEAKS
WILDERNESS

Continental Divide

13,017 ft

Grizzly Lake

Grizzly Peak
13,988 ft

MILES
0   1   2   N

The next stand of conifers has **tall chiming bells** and **daffodil senecio** along its duff-muffled path. Back out in sunshine, the trail eases, passing **silverleaf scorpionweed** uncoiling pale lavender flowerheads. **Subalpine larkspur**, **tall chiming bells**, and **arrowleaf senecio** combine as a complementary trio at the creek. You'll also likely see small but bright **yellow monkeyflower**.

Flanked by willows, the trail rises in brief spurts. **Little rose gentian** and **rosy paintbrush** are visible along an even section of the trail. Observe a golden slope across the creek. Above it rise the great peaks guarding the curving vale, and a small waterfall creases the slope across the way.

Continuing up, hikers reach the two-mile point, marked by **black-headed daisies** and an old log cabin resting on its historic laurels. A harmonious garden blooms in front of the roofless structure.

Look for the red and blue of **paintbrush** and **gentians** and, just up the trail, **king's crown.** Cross Grizzly Creek and head up a bit for another easier crossing flanked by **brook saxifrage, bittercress, cowbane, alpine fireweed** and **fringed** and **star gentians. Little pink elephants** and **yellow monkeyflower** add bright touches.

More elevation gain is ahead; however, it's tempered by the splendor of the wildflowers and majestic peaks. A newly exposed summit that resembles the signature hump of a grizzly bear appears beyond the trail. More ridge is unveiled that looks like grizzly canines. As the trail passes through more wildflowers, a pretty cascade runs off a rugged palisade up to the right. Just ahead, a glen of **rosy paintbrush** and gold **arnica** is interrupted by tailing piles—perhaps signs of the labor of the ruined cabin's occupant.

The trail is about to tackle a series of steep rocky pitches. For those who do not wish to continue the demanding climb to Grizzly Lake, the Rocky Mountain grandeur is already memorable.

Grizzly Creek, coursing through a rocky defile, lowers the pitch of its voice to imitate distant thunder. At this point, check for the sound of the real thing—skyscraping ramparts can hide building thunderheads.

Thick-leaved **purpleleaf** or **alpine senecio** emerges trailside.

ALPINE OR BROADLEAF FIREWEED

Chamerion subdentatum
(formerly *Epilobium latifolium*)

Broad-leaved willowherb and river beauty are two more names for this showy member of the evening primrose family. Racemes of four clear, rose-purple-petaled blossoms decorate reddish branch ends. A glaucous coating on the leaves contrasts well with the bright flowers. Found from the Arctic to Colorado in the subalpine and alpine zones, alpine fireweed spreads slowly by seed, rather than by rhizomes like prolific common fireweed. Both have been utilized for food. A cousin is fireweed *Camerion danielsii* formerly *Epilobium angustifolium.*

Upslope, the landscape features **fireweed** and **columbine**. Footing becomes rather precarious where **dwarf goldenrod** hugs the earth. Chest-deep willows introduce a notch where Grizzly Peak noses into the Colorado sky, a white cornice stretching along its back.

At last the rugged trail arrives atop a broad bench where a 360-degree panorama catches the soul. Granite outcrops and boulders, numerous on the grassy flat, find harmony in **rosy** and hybridized **western paintbrush**. The trail passes a craggy outcrop softened by clinging mats of **dotted saxifrage**. Little tarns reflecting bits of sky hold **marsh marigold** late into the summer. Oriental-influenced waterways behold **Parry primrose** and **narcissus-flowered anemone**, much shorter at this 12,000-foot-plus elevation. **Greenleaf chiming bells**, among a myriad of others, delight the senses.

Like a trekking route in the Himalayas, the scree-mantled trail begins a long traverse, passing rock gardens full of tranquil pastels. Rosy **Parry clover** and lovely blue-purple **sky pilot** dot the landscape before you encounter rock piles and the trail begins to climb more steeply. This is the favored habitat for **bigroot** or **alpine spring beauty**. Its succulent rosettes, stemming from a China-bound root that is extraordinarily flexible in the shifting stone, produce pink-veined white stars. Lush clumps of intensely-cobalt **greenleaf chiming bells** contrast with brick red **king's crown**.

A supporting stone wall decorated with **purple fringe** and **snowball saxifrage** reveals an escarpment so sheer that its crowning cornice almost disappears. Tall for its alpine zone environment, **subalpine valerian**, with heads of tiny blushed flowers, is charming. On the other end of the scale, **alpine parsley**'s fingernail-sized yellow umbels cling tightly to its gray-green fern-like foliage.

Perhaps it is the hoary brows of the overhead escarpment above the steep slope or merely the result

SUBALPINE VALERIAN
Valeriana capitata subspecies acutiloba

Neat hemispherical heads of delicate tubes with exerted stamens evoke an image of Victorian pincushions. Also called sharpleaf valerian, these blushed white flowers exude a pleasant scent. However, it is reported that the plant as a whole is unpleasant to the nose, even after it has dried up. Named for the Roman emperor Valerianus, valerians disperse mature seeds much the same way dandelions do—by parachute. A cousin is western valerian *Valeriana occidentalis*.

of hybridization, but the copious **paintbrush** is exceptionally brilliant. Not to be outdone, a bounty of **blue columbine** chimes in.

Looking down the sweeping mountainscape, the tenacity of those who built this heroic trail is to be admired as much as the intrepid wildflowers.

An abbreviated switchback anchored by a rock cairn raises hikers' hopes that the lake is imminent—but don't get your hopes up quite yet. **Black-headed daisies**, colonizing **sibbaldia**, waving **bistort** and an easier grade provide encouragement. Almost abruptly the long-awaited lake appears, surrounded by ferocious pewter teeth and the perpendicular prow of 13,988-foot Grizzly Peak. Brisk breezes may ruffle the deep waters of 12,550-foot-high Grizzly Lake.

An awe-inspiring hike in all ways, Grizzly Lake Trail competes for first prize. With lively wildflowers soaring in the company of Continental Divide ridges, this "century" hike is a must. Hikers find themselves feeling as if they have indeed become "men and women to match the mountains."

Wilder Gulch

Wildflower Alert: Abundant wildflowers provide a romantic setting to a magic meadow along a subalpine "century" trail just east of Vail Pass.

Wildflower Hike
34
CENTURY HIKE

Splashes of color line the tumbling waters of Wilder Gulch.

easy	**Trail Rating**
4.6 miles out and back	**Trail Length**
Vail/Copper Mountain/Frisco	**Location**
10,600 to 11,100 feet	**Elevation**
July through August	**Bloom Season**
mid-July to early August	**Peak Bloom**
Take I-70 west to Vail Pass (exit 190). Turn left onto the overpass, and then left onto the pavement to the parking lot.	**Directions**

JUST EAST, DOWN FROM VAIL PASS, a gentle stream valley filled with wildflowers and a bubbly creek awaits. A "century" hike, Wilder Gulch Trail hosts a variety of wildflowers and is an aesthetic delight.

To access Wilder Gulch, use the bike path running downhill from Vail Pass. About a half-mile down from the pass parking area, on a C-curve, a gray metal electrical box marks a right turn that travels under the eastbound freeway lanes. From there the trail proceeds genially along a reclining valley to a tree-girt meadow. The hike described here ends in a lovely meadow, although another option is to continue up to 11,765-foot Ptarmigan Pass.

The parking lot is shared by motorists taking a break at Vail Pass.

PYGMY BITTERROOT
Oreobroma pygmaea

Pygmy bitterroot's artfully-veined pink petals form stars nestled deep in bursts of basal leaves. Its succulent leaves are typical of the purslane family, although occasionally this flower will display white populations. Look for this sweet plant in open gravelly soil.

Some books designate the scientific name as *Lewisia pygmaea*. The genus part refers to Meriwether Lewis of the exploring team of Lewis and Clark. *Oreobroma* is derived from the Greek *oros* meaning "mountain" and *broma* meaning "food." Cousins are spring beauty *Claytonia rosea* and alpine or bigroot spring beauty *Claytonia megarhiza*. American Indians used the root for food.

Catch the bike path at the east end of the parking area and walk along the asphalt down to a moist place perfect for those high-country buddies, **monkshood, subalpine larkspur,** and **arrowleaf senecio. Shrubby cinquefoil** and **creamy buckwheat** are suited for the drier habitats along the path.

Down where a sign indicates a curve, a lodgepole pine shades **fireweed, little rose gentian, fringed gentian,** and clear blue **Rocky Mountain gentian** by early August.

Continue on the paved path to a warning concerning underground fibre-optic telephone cables. Turn right here at a gray metal box, and pass under the freeway to access a natural-surfaced trail on the right side of Wilder Creek.

Waltzing along the trail, **sego lilies,** decorous in their

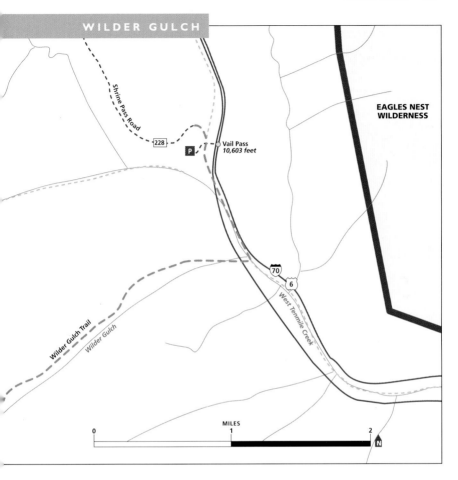

WILDER GULCH

Shrine Pass Road

228

P

Vail Pass
10,603 feet

EAGLES NEST
WILDERNESS

70

6

West Tenmile Creek

Wilder Gulch Trail

Wilder Gulch

MILES
0   1   2

N

three ample petals, are partnered by pale yellow **western paintbrush,
pink plumes**, and **Parry lousewort**. Rising along a cut bank, a whole hillside
of **sego lilies**, shaded white to lavender-blue to cool rose, may sway to a
gentle breeze.

The creek, sequestered in willows and **twinberry honeysuckle**, tunes
up to accompany **pink-headed daisies** and **meadow rue**. Nodding, burnt-red
heads of sturdy **ray-less** or **Bigelow senecio** lead to a section of rocky tread.
The hill is a vision of cream and lavender. Beaming with piquant **yellow
monkeyflower**, a rivulet borrows the trail as the path of least resistance.
Like cotillion attendees waiting for the music to begin, wildflowers in every
hue under the sun stand on tiptoe observing mossy seeps of **monkeyflower,
mountain death camas**, and prima donna **shooting stars**. Almost dainty for

its genus, **alpine milkvetch** lines the trailside. A pastel bevy of **sego lilies**, near what look like toppled maroon tombstones, appear during the third week of July accompanied by cool yellow **western paintbrush**.

Where the ground evens out and lush clumps of **mountain death camas** swing wands of green-tinged stars, a sign assures that this is indeed, Wilder Gulch. Ravaged stumps line a slope among **sego lilies** colored in soft magenta pink and lavender blue. **Pink plumes** and rebel-red **scarlet paintbrush** join in. Hues intensify, and you'll find **little pink elephants** on the grassy sidelines. Just before you come upon a dirt road, inspect a trickle for **white bog orchid** and **monkshood**.

The path grows boggy as you near a beaver pond. The trail begins to resemble a stream bed, and eventually you reach a brook pouring out of a tunnel-like channel. **Queen's crown, white bog orchids, bittercress** and lacy **cowbane** flank the dancing water.

Red sandstone precedes another damp spot where white **brook saxifrage** looks like uninhibited baby's breath. **Scarlet paintbrush** sweeps down toward scores of hot-pink **fireweed**. Under open skies, **shrubby cinquefoil** freely tosses its gold coins most of the summer. A moss-bedded brook twirls among peppery white **bittercress** and **pink willowherb**. **Whipple penstemon** joins in with dusky wine tubes.

Conifers tower over hillsides of profuse red-bracted **paintbrush, blue lupine**, and yellow **heartleaf arnica**. A rocky rill waters **subalpine larkspur, pink plumes**, and **tall valerian** in the shade of willows.

The trail ascends more steeply now toward a moss-bound seep on the right with **tall chiming bells, white geranium**, and troupes of dancing **brook saxifrage**. **White bog orchid** and bright pink **shooting stars** bloom along the trail that sweeps up beside a massive hillside seep, joined by **green bog orchids**. **Scarlet paintbrush** sweeps the hillside.

The taxing gradient smoothes out in sight of a wide mountain meadow, its curving creek providing a crystalline sound. Along its verdant banks swirl boisterous **Parry primrose** and **rosy paintbrush**, hushed by **marsh marigold** and **narcissus anemone**. Leading a herd of **little pink elephants** is a knoll of show-stopping **rosy paintbrush**.

Nestled in the emerald grasses, look for the pink stars of **pygmy bitterroot, mountain blue violet**, and sweet-scented **Parry clover**. The park-like meadow basin is a great place to spend some time.

A great high-country hike, Wilder Gulch reveals color and a chiming creek. In a good year, a late July or early August visit may offer over 110 kinds of wildflowers.

Lost Man Creek
(Hunter-Frying Pan Wilderness)

Wildflower
Hike
35

Wildflower Alert: This trail takes you on a delightful tour of wide fields filled with subalpine wildflowers.

A gentle trail filled with subalpine floral delights leads to a boxy gorge.

easy	*Trail Rating*
6.0 miles out and back	*Trail Length*
Aspen	*Location*
10,600 to 11,250 feet	*Elevation*
late June through August	*Bloom Season*
July	*Peak Bloom*
Take State Route 82, east of Aspen for 14 miles. The trailhead is directly across from Lost Man campground on the north side of the highway.	*Directions*

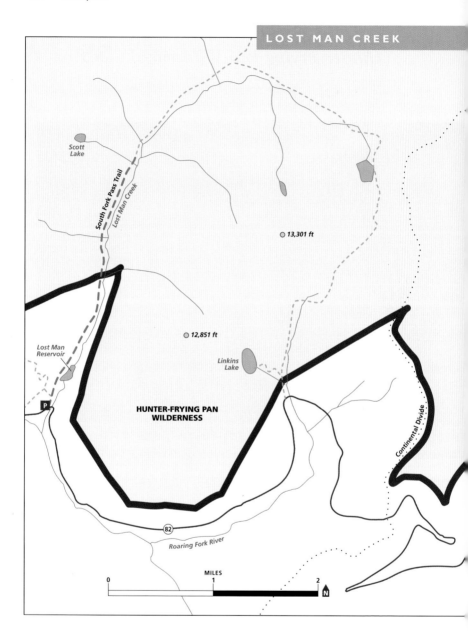

THE SOUTH FORK PASS TRAIL cruises up the Lost Man Creek drainage through vast flowery meadows, entering the roughly 83,000-acre Hunter-Frying Pan Wilderness Area. Hemmed in by a long series of connected summits over 13,000 feet, the broad valley tilts gently to the south, making the trail accessible for early hiking.

Wildflower enthusiasts will enjoy viewing about 80 species of subalpine bloomers. Much of the flowering expanses are along a gradually ascending trail. This hike begins at a roadside trailhead and winds over to a canal. You'll cross a reservoir dam and the easygoing trail travels on the west side of a creek drainage to a boxy little gorge which forms the turnaround point.

The parking lot is adequate, but an early arrival makes securing a spot easier at this popular trailhead.

A shaded trail kiosk displays maps and instructions for your perusal. Willow breaks spread across a glacier-carved valley where South Fork Pass Trail heads right along the east edge. Soon a seep on the right features both **white** and **green bog orchids** as well as **pink willowherb**. In the shadows of the spruce-fir forest, white **sickletop lousewort** and barely-blue **delicate Jacob's ladder** find a home.

The path contours and crosses a footbridge, after which the well-drained soil sustains **many-rayed goldenrod** and, just a bit farther on, native **Coulter daisy**. Rising to travel the flattened top of a levee, the pathway reveals clumps of **blacktipped senecio** with big mint-green leaves.

Walk up a lump of worn stone to a sign pointing to South Fork Pass Trail. Crossing the dam spillway brings you to the west shore of Lost Man Reservoir. Lilac **early blue daisy**, lavender **harebells**, and emphatically-violet **Colorado tansy aster** put their own spin on the color purple here. A trickle of water nurtures the dusky purple of **star gentian**.

As you leave the reservoir, willows guide the path to a creeklet flagged by succulent **queen's crown, white bog orchid, little pink elephants,** and more silky **star gentian**.

A solid concrete post announces the entry to a national forest wilderness. Spattered with bits of pigment, the fanning meadows produce strong-hued splashes including blue **Rocky Mountain gentian**, rosy-violet **Colorado tansy aster**, and **burnt-orange dandelion** or **orange agoseris**. Subtle tints are represented by pale-yellow **western paintbrush** and **Parry lousewort**.

The sound of Lost Man Creek announces damper earth, bringing on **pink plumes**. Off to the right a solid purple patch of **fringed gentian** lengthens to rise above meadow grasses. Rising another half mile above the broad valley floor is a series of summits with Geissler Mountain on the east and the Williams Mountains on the west—all in the 13,000-foot range.

Shrubby cinquefoil lines the trail as it narrows into towering conifers. A smattering of **blue columbine** and **mountain death camas** leads to a built-up causeway. Patches of rosy **Parry clover** loaf in the deepening shade while lemon-yellow **daffodil senecio** adds a bright color. Underfoot, roots take the quiet path to a log spanning crystalline Jack Creek, populated with **arrowleaf senecio, tall chiming bells,** and **cowbane.** Rosy-lavender **subalpine daisy** outlines the meadow, forest, and willows.

The trail travels along a hillside to rise above the dancing waters of Lost Man Creek. A tributary from the west, Scott Creek burbles down over a stony bed to join the main flow on its run to Aspen-bound Roaring Fork River. This is a sublime spot to view **star gentians.**

A worn "social" spur on the right sends hikers to the overlook of Lost Man Creek pounding its way through an abbreviated gorge. The stream squeezes through the water-hewn defile—a notable change in a docile journey. Take a moment to rest in the shade of an overhanging spruce and look for clumps of **blue columbine** flourishing above the creek.

The gorge is the turn-around point, but the main trail climbs on up to South Fork Pass; from there, two other trails carry on.

Almost a stroll through rapturous meadows, bits of stream, and forest, South Fork Pass Trail appeals to most every hiking ability. Not far from Aspen, it provides a choice window into the wonderful world of subalpine wild-flowering.

FRINGED GENTIAN
Gentianopsis thermalis

It is hard to believe that this elegant gentian is an annual. The pointed buds unfurl to become royal purple tubes flaring into four fringed lobes. Conserving its pollen for sunshine-oriented pollinators, this late-summer flowering gentian closes at night and on cloudy days. Also called feather gentian, this flower is partial to moist habitats from the montane through the subalpine zones. Fringed gentian is one of about 20 species of gentians found in the Rockies.

The medicinal properties of the bitter gentian family have been recorded since King Gentius of Ancient Illyria (part of the Roman Empire) proclaimed their value around 200 B.C. Cousins include Parry or Rocky Mountain gentian *Pneumonanthe parryi* and arctic gentian *Gentianodes algida.*

Milner Pass to Forest Canyon Pass
(Rocky Mountain National Park)

Wildflower Alert: This trail is a great chance to meet some of Rocky Mountain National Park's many wildflowers.

Jagged rock, craggy peaks, and spectacular scenery characterizes Milner Pass—with approximately 80 species of wildflowers hidden in ravines, seeps, and pocket meadows.

ROCKY MOUNTAIN NATIONAL PARK'S diversity is justly famous, and over three million visitors a year witness the wonder of the park's 415 square miles. Some of these folks opt for an intimate view of that diversity on some 355 miles of trail. Milner Pass to Forest Canyon Pass Trail covers

Milner Pass to Forest Canyon Pass

Trail Rating	moderate to easy
Trail Length	4.6 miles out and back
Location	Rocky Mountain National Park/Grand Lake
Elevation	10,750 to 11,320 feet
Bloom Season	July to August
Peak Bloom	late July
Directions	Take US 34 north from Grand Lake, passing the west entrance station in Rocky Mountain National Park. (The road becomes Trail Ridge Road in the park.) Continue to Milner Pass on the Continental Divide. The trailhead is located near the southwest end of Poudre Lake. Fee required.

only 2.3 miles, but offers about 80 of the roughly 1,000 wildflower species that grow in the park.

Milner Pass, on the Continental Divide, sends water west to the Pacific Ocean and east to the Gulf of Mexico. Poudre Lake, at the outset of the trailhead, sends its water down the Cache la Poudre River, which eventually ends up in the Gulf. The Arapaho called the pass Ba Ha Thoson, "Deer Pass." In damp areas, you may find not only deer tracks but also those of elk or even bighorn sheep. Almost directly above the trailhead is Sheep Rock, a jutting granite crag. And farther up the trail is a view of Specimen Mountain, a rockbound breeding ground for bighorns.

While wildlife sightings—even tracks—are iffy events, wildflowers await your viewing pleasure, blooming in the forest, glens, ravines, seeps, bogs, pocket meadows, and finally, tundra. Watch for building thunderstorms.

Though the paved parking lot at the pass is broad, it is often filled. Fortunately, many of the vehicles belong to folks taking photographs of the Continental Divide sign, staying only long enough to record their Milner Pass visit.

The trailhead is located at the south end of Poudre Lake, one of about 150 named lakes in the Park, between a buck-and-rail fence and a sign kiosk. The packed pathway is a fine way for visitors to appreciate the pretty lake and see a few wildflowers, such as **bistort**, **alpine avens**, and **scarlet paintbrush**. Numerous **black-headed daisies**, the most common fleabane or *erigeron* of the high country, fill the adjacent slope. As you look down to the lake's boggy

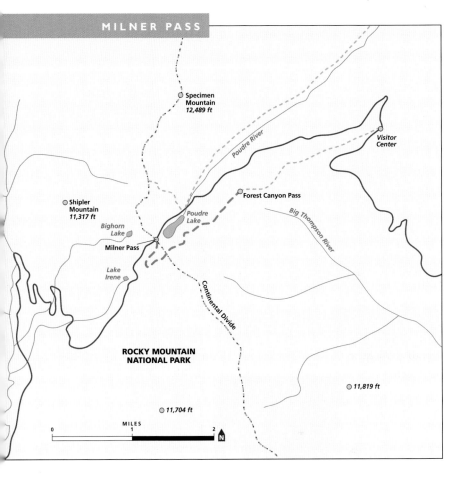

shores, a haze of pink advertises herds of **little pink elephants**. Many more of these flowers are on up the trail.

Even footing makes it easy to enjoy the subalpine wildflowers: **Whipple penstemon, one-headed daisy,** and the famous **blue columbine**. Look under the short conifers for pastel-blue **delicate Jacob's ladder**. A seep on the left reveals **rosy paintbrush**, yellow **arrowleaf senecio**, bright **white bittercress**, and airy **brook saxifrage**.

A sign announcing two miles to Forest Canyon Pass appears. Peeled logs lift the trail, passing talus slopes of both **broadleaf** and **woolly** or **subalpine arnica** and sour **alpine sorrel**. **Delicate Jacob's ladder** tucks its plush little clumps between the angular rocks.

Ahead are the jagged pinnacles of Sheep Rock, colorfully encrusted with orange lichen. At the base, **blue columbine** blooms late in the cool shadows.

Nestled in crevices of this picturesque outcropping, almost vertical in nature, are mats of **spotted** or **moss saxifrage**. Suspended on wiry stems, the pert white stars are dotted with red and orange specks. *Saxifrage,* meaning rock-breaker, is a case in point at Sheep Rock. In the debris surrounding the granite crags, **purple fringe**, with its bright exerted stamens, finds a root-hold. Later-blooming **daffodil, rock,** and **purpleleaf senecios** are also residents in the rubble.

The trail ascends along rock steps to meet colonies of rosy **Parry clover** and white **sickletop lousewort** growing under small evergreens. In the shadows of an Engelmann spruce-subalpine fir forest, S-curves begin an ascent that soon steepens on log risers.

The pathway eases as it approaches a grassy ravine spanned on a half-log bridge. **Tall chiming bells, bittercress, arrowleaf senecio,** and **brook saxifrage,** often found together in wet subalpine spots, thrive nearby.

Stone steps bring the trail up to a grand view exposing the Never Summer Range. A sign here takes the trail left. The gradient eases, and from here on up, it follows the west side route of Old Fall River Road, built in the early 1900s.

On the right is a vest-pocket meadow lush with **little pink elephants, snowball saxifrage, blueleaf cinquefoil, bistort,** and **rosy paintbrush.** A reminder of the raw power of nature is evident in a sizable chunk of unstable earth torn from the downhill slope. A nearby seep exhibits early-blooming white **marsh marigold** and creamy **globeflower,** often growing together. In various shades of pink, **Parry clover, rosy paintbrush,** and **little pink elephants** share a plush little space.

SNOWLOVER
Chionophila jamesii

This Rocky Mountain endemic looks like a poor relation of penstemons—in fact, it is. Easy to miss due to its four-inch height and off-white blossoms, snowlover deserves a tundra search. The tubular flowers emerge on one side of the short stem; lips often display brown edges as if singed by the powerful alpine sun. Look in gravelly snowbed areas in July and August where snowdrifts lingered late. The Latin genus name is quite literal: *chion* meaning "snow" and *philus* meaning "loving." The species moniker honors Dr. Edwin James who, when climbing Pike's Peak in 1821, discovered snowlover there.

With the exception of passing through stunted Engelmann spruce, the trail travels in the open. The delightful pearl-like buds of **fringed Parnassia** are tucked among fallen logs. Up on the bank, **mitrewort** calls for scrutiny with a hand lens to appreciate its green and maroon snowflake tracery.

Slumping earth precedes a rocky rill coursing down from the right, and the trail follows an easy grade to a sighting of burnt red **king's crown**. Keep an eye out for pink, ground-hugging **pygmy bitterroot** in gravelly soil. In places where snow has lingered late, watch for thready-leaved **snow buttercup**.

The trail levels and passes a lively stream and taller spruce to a fine view of 12,489-foot Specimen Mountain. Color is the order of the day as meadows parade their wildflower color guards.

The next section, flanked by peeled logs, is a stretch of hummocked moss. Diminutive waterfalls decorate this opulent miniature landscape. A close examination of this charming spot may turn up **pink bog laurel** nestled in the moss as well as the the perfect buds of **fringed Parnassia**.

The old roadbed makes walking easy as it slants up to expose Trail Ridge Road ahead. A level section reveals the creamy coiled beaks of **Parry lousewort** and a plethora of sweet little **alpine violets**.

Terraces of small ponds grace the next section of trail as it pushes toward a panoramic view. Stretching to the south like a serigraphic print, waves of mountain ranges are tinted purple, lilac, and hazy lavender blue.

With golden granite underfoot, check out the shades of native **dandelions**. In addition to the common yellow variety, ray petals of the natives range from copper to gold, sulphur to citrine. A low foreground for the rolling Mummy Range to the northeast is supplied by bony willows. *Krummholz* spruce, which roots wherever its wind-stressed branches touch the earth, signals the approach of treelimit.

Brimming with evergreens, cleft Forest Canyon falls away to the south. Look around for areas where snowdrifts protected the ridge for **snowlover**. Soon a small sign overlooking glacier-carved Forest Canyon declares that you've met your objective: Forest Canyon Pass, elevation 11,320 feet. The trail continues through tundra up to the Alpine Visitor Center. A one-way downhill hike is possible with two vehicles if you park one at each trailhead.

The variety of hikes available in beautiful Rocky Mountain National Park runs the gamut. Milner Pass to Forest Canyon Pass travels through the subalpine and into alpine zone vegetation, accompanied by brilliant wildflowers. This is a great hike for those who desire a taste of Colorado's high country and delightful blooming inhabitants.

Wildflower Hike

37

Mayflower Gulch

Wildflower Alert: A bonanza of wildflowers are everywhere in this peak-ringed amphitheater, and you'll discover a veritable goldmine of paintbrush.

Not far from Copper Mountain, Mayflower Gulch is filled not only with flowers but historic remnants of its mining past.

Trail Rating	easy to moderate
Trail Length	4.6 miles out and back
Location	Copper Mountain
Elevation	10,880 to 11,560 feet
Bloom Season	July through August
Peak Bloom	late July to early August
Directions	Take I-70 west to Highway 91 at Copper Mountain. Go south for 6.1 miles and park in the large lot to the left.

PROSPECTORS FILED MINING CLAIMS on all sides of superbly scenic Mayflower Gulch. Even today there is activity in the basin. The historic Boston Mine's log buildings, including one that recently burned, anchor the rich valley. Once, gold and other precious metals put Mayflower Gulch on every assayists' tongue. Today gold is but one of a trove of colors the wildflower treasure seeker will find on this congenial hike. Soaring mountains, including several of Colorado's numerous "thirteeners," surround the flower-strewn basin.

The trail follows an old road wide enough for side-by-side conversation. Bright pockets of subalpine flowers, including a couple of unusual ones, flourish. A prime-time visit would be around the third or fourth week of July when about six dozen wildflower species are in bloom.

Parking is generous on a paved lot adjacent to Highway 91.

Accompanied by a rushing creek, the wide flat road heads east. Along the south side of the trail, a sustained seep nurtures **bittercress** and **little pink elephants**. A spur road comes into view quickly on the left, but Mayflower Gulch Trail goes right.

Rooted by a little rill, bog birch and willow bring on **blueleaf cinquefoil**, rosy-lavender **subalpine daisy**, and "**elephants.**" On the cutbank above, sheltered under willows, is a fairly uncommon cousin—**alpine lousewort**, also pigmented in rich deep pink and sporting red-tinged ferny leaves. An arced galea (helmet) sepal protects the lower lip of the alpine lousewort, much like the headgear of a soldier of ancient Troy. These remarkable flowers, sometimes muffled in silvery wool, are perfectly designed for pollination by bumblebees.

Inclining somewhat now, the route passes a pink and white collection of elephant mimics, **brook saxifrage**, **subalpine daisy**, and **bittercress**. Ahead, looking like a crosscut sawblade, jagged peaks rise above the soft-leaved willows. Watch on the high side for the huge rosy heads of **Parry clover** and the sweet pink stars of **pygmy bitterroot**.

A forest of smooth-barked subalpine fir and rough-barked Engelmann spruce opens to the left for pale **western paintbrush**, midnight **subalpine larkspur**, and pastel **tall chiming bells**. Up on the right, creamy **narcissus-flowered anemone** leads the eye to Colorado's state flower: **blue columbine**. Nearly the size of golf balls, the round heads of fragrant **Parry clover** are exceptionally large in the mineral soil here.

Decorated with plush clumps of **tall chiming bells**, a sway-backed log cabin rests on the north edge of the road. Across from those weary wood bones, a huge tailings pile appears to be all that supports an old mining tipple.

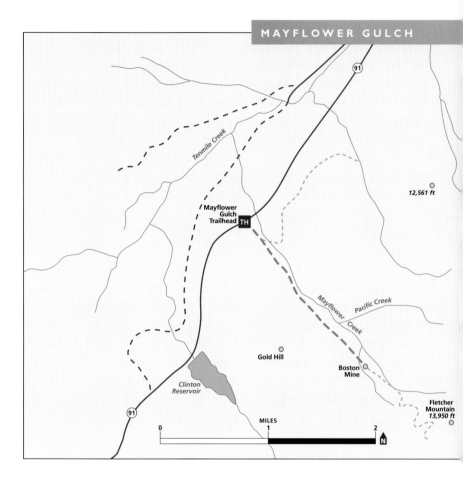

MAYFLOWER GULCH

Tenmile Creek

12,561 ft

Mayflower
Gulch
Trailhead **TH**

Mayflower Creek

Pacific Creek

Gold Hill

Boston
Mine

Clinton
Reservoir

91

Fletcher
Mountain
13,950 ft

MILES

0   1   2

N

It's dangerous to poke around these decaying wooden structures—instead, drop down to a pocket bog on the left side of the roadway to find unusual and early-blooming **side-flowered mitrewort**. Lined up like equidistant beads on a stiff string, the perfect, white-snowflake flowers best unveil their beauty through a hand lens.

Accentuated by residual snow, steep-faced Fletcher Mountain fronts the leveling trail. Tailings make scree-like habitats for sour-leaved **alpine sorrel** and fiery-bracted **scarlet paintbrush**. Paintbrushes are notorious hybridizers, explaining the many tints you'll see—a cerise hue beautifully contrasts pure white **bittercress**. **Whipple penstemon** comes along in dusky wine and **heartleaf arnica** touches the shadows with golden sun.

Water spills into the roadway from a seep on the right where old ivory **bracted lousewort** stands tall to point back toward hot-pink **Parry primrose**.

Off to the north, Pacific Creek joins Mayflower Creek. The view opens up to expose a multitude of "glory holes" from whence miners hoped fortune would come. Forest again takes the route on an ascent before easing for **Parry primrose** on the left. The right side takes in a fine grouping of refined **alplilies**, their six white tepals faintly lined with purple. A hand lens reveals their crystal-like delicacy.

Rising, the trail becomes a trickling waterway passing every warm tint that intergrading **paintbrush** can conjure up. Open skies appraise nature's blue, yellow, and cream lode of **tall chiming bells, subalpine arnica, dandelions,** and pale **western paintbrush**. The view broadens into a vista and the pastel lode evolves into a bonanza of color-charged meadowland. Burnt red **king's crown** affirms the assay, as does **daffodil senecio**. Veins of **rosy paintbrush** catch every eye.

A sign signals the arrival of panoramic splendor on every side. A multitude of 13,000-foot-plus platinum peaks ring the emerald bowl into which you've hiked. The crests of the soaring Tenmile Range are unsurpassed. On the north, Mayflower Hill's long ridge eases up to the highest of the jagged summits—13,998-foot Pacific Peak. Snow-pleated 13,950-foot Fletcher Mountain swoops up to form the graceful back wall of Mayflower Gulch.

The open foreground of the mountainscape is caught by the deteriorating remains of the old Boston Mine. In the packed scree preceding the buildings, a small infrequent sojourner of rather specific needs, **dwarf lupine,** constitutes a "find." A thumb-high

SIDE-FLOWERED MITREWORT

Mitella stauropetala v. stenopetala

Since the cruciform flowers of this less common mitrewort are white, it makes sense that it is also called white-flowered mitrewort (a mitre is a cap worn by bishops). Other names are bishop's cap and sleigh-bells. Lined up on one side of long, bare stems, the ten or more delicate flowers are shaped like intricate snowflakes. The leaves form a basal rosette. An interesting method of seed dispersal involves the spilling of ripe seed by the force of waterdrops hitting the sepaled cup. The thread-like petals complete the snowflake look.

The genus name *Mitella* is Latin for "turban." The species monikers are *stauropetala* meaning "cruciform" and *stenopetala* meaning "slender petals". A common cousin is green-flowered mitrewort or bishop's cap *Mitella pentandra.*

inflorescence of pea-type flowers sits at the hub of gray-green palmate leaves spread like spokes of a wheel.

Where the road forks, Mayflower Creek is crossed by a culvert. The sparkling water flows around stony islands of **queen's crown, king's crown, tall chiming bells, bittercress,** and lacy **cowbane.** Mother Nature is reclaiming the mine workings with lush clumps of luminous **blue columbine.** Among low willow patches, **narcissus-flowered anemone, bistort,** and purple **subalpine aster** introduce a blooming "glory hole" as far as the eye can see. Filled with mounded **tall chiming bells** complemented by great swaths of deep red **king's crown, subalpine daisies,** and posh **rosy paintbrush,** this indeed is for the wildflower lover.

Strike it rich in a motherlode of wildflowers. Treeless and gently sloping, Mayflower Gulch calls to the hiker to explore its vastness and discover the petaled treasures stored there as a priceless renewable resource—mined only by moment and memory.

Searle Gulch

Wildflower Alert: Fabulous high-country color is experienced on the way to a pass with a marvelous mountain view—and a "century" trail to boot.

A mostly gentle trail through mountain meadows surrounded by towering peaks.

easy	*Trail Rating*
4.0 miles out and back	*Trail Length*
Copper Mountain	*Location*
11,080 to 12,020 feet	*Elevation*
July through August	*Bloom Season*
mid-July to early August	*Peak Bloom*
Take I-70 west to exit 195 at Copper Mountain. Go south on State Route 91 for 4 miles, then right onto old road for 1 mile. Go right for approximately 3.5 miles to the locked gate at the trailhead.	*Directions*

FOR A SENSATIONAL TASTE OF HIGH COUNTRY SPLENDOR, both floral and scenic, reserve some time for the trek up Searle Gulch. Mining activity, historic and contemporary, is evident in the general area. Sandwiched between Elk Ridge on the south and Jacque Ridge on the north, Searle Gulch is a delectable wildflower repository. Late July summons up about 100 species.

Easygoing most of the way, the trail ascends steadily and steepens along the second half of the trip. The incidence and mass of wildflowers keeps pace with the trail as it passes into the alpine zone at 11,500 feet. Nearly the entire hike is under open skies.

A big gate stops vehicular traffic and at the same time makes the trailhead for Searle Gulch easy to find. Parking is generous. Frequently, summer afternoons are fraught with impressive thunderstorms—go prepared.

At the trailhead, get your bearings by observing 13,205-foot Jacque Peak on the north and 12,583-foot Corbett Peak to the south. An old road starts off through willows with cool yellow **western paintbrush**, white **Coulter daisy**, and lavender-rose **subalpine daisy**. In the disturbed soil of the roadway, erosion has taken a heavy toll, but vivid **Colorado tansy aster** and **silvery cinquefoil** have pushed down roots. An occasional dark spruce is enlivened by **scarlet paintbrush** and, in late summer, the sapphire chalices of **Rocky Mountain gentian**.

Wildflowers scatter bits of color along the level trail as it alternates between drier habitats that please **harebells** and **creamy buckwheat** and moist places that suit **subalpine daisy** and **rosy paintbrush**. Particularly wet (but not puddled) spots present **queen's crown**, **little pink elephants**, **cowbane**, and, in late summer, **fringed** and **star gentian**. Willows continue to be an influential element, but open fields grow wider and the wildflowers more abundant.

Footing becomes rougher, and the trail ascends through willow patches and flowery pocket meadows, each surpassing the last. Radiant barely begins to describe these jewel boxes of golden **subalpine arnica**, **aspen sunflower**, **beauty cinquefoil**, and other gems in the collection. Deep wine **Whipple penstemon**, lilac **harebells**, and **rosy** and **scarlet paintbrush** crown the effect.

Streamlets trickle down from Jacque Ridge on the right to crown willow stands with topaz **arrowleaf senecio**, opalescent **tall chiming bells**, amethyst **subalpine larkspur**, and **monkshood**.

On the right, you'll see where a miner laboriously piled up tailings right next to the log abode. The backyard is a crumbling outcrop decorated with **blue columbine** and the front yard a gentle swale which holds snow well into summer. Here, spring flowers in the form of **alpine avens, wild candytuft, blue columbine, rosy paintbrush,** and **bog** and **snowball saxifrage** luxuriate late in the growing season.

The pass appears closer than it is, an illusion not uncommon in the rarefied air of alpine elevations. The open meadows suddenly confront a rockfall. At home in such places is a sleek animal with a lively sense of curiosity, the long-tailed weasel. Though your sudden appearance may send this blond-bellied carnivore into his den, stand still awhile and usually his whiskered face will pop back up. The base of the lithic jumble sustains subtle **alpine dandelion, sorrel, speedwell,** and the greenish umbels of **Gray's angelica,** accessorized by **bistort, rosy paintbrush,** and a bit of **king's crown.** Quick-moving pikas announce their presence among the tumbled rock.

Poet Robert Frost said, "Butterflies are flowers that fly and all but sing." Perhaps we just can't hear them. But they flit among gems of cobalt **greenleaf chiming bells,** topaz **alpine parsley,** and **cinquefoils** that garland this damp domain of fallen rock. Look in the stony soil for a member of the purslane family, **pygmy bitterroot** nestling pink-quartz stars in succulent linear leaves.

Gleaming like an Australian opal in pink, yellow, and white, a jeweled meadow follows the tumbled rockpile. **Little pink elephants,** white **bistort,** and both **sulphur** and **rosy paintbrush** tint the trove. The verdancy of the vegetation here extends to the trail itself, causing it to lose definition. Breaking the ridgeline on the

ALPINE AVENS

Acomastylis rossii subspecies turbinata (Geum rossii)

Colonizing the high country in broad sweeps are brassy alpine avens, usually four to twelve inches high, which also are known as mountain avens. Blooming throughout the summer, a few of the bright five-petaled flowers may linger until fall and then the leaves that resemble ferns take on their wine-red hues. A member of the rose family, widespread alpine avens thrives from Alaska to northern Mexico as well as Asia. The Latinate genus name *acomastylis* can be broken down from the Greek: *a,* "without;" *coma,* "mane;" and *stylis,* "style"— "without a hairstyle." Unlike its cousin, the mountain dryad that sports an Albert Einstein "hairdo," alpine avens are comparatively bare-headed. The species epithet honors Sir James Ross, a nineteenth-century British explorer. Cousins include mountain dryad *Dryas octopetala* and blueleaf cinquefoil *Potentilla diversifolia.*

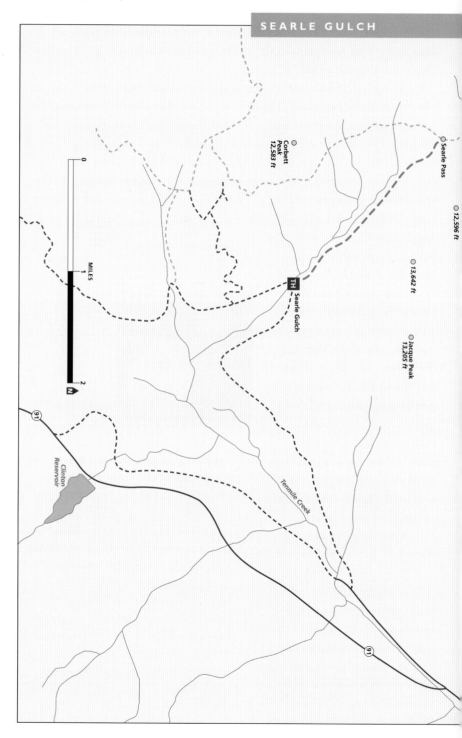

SEARLE GULCH

Searle Pass

Corbett
Peak
12,583 ft

12,596 ft

13,642 ft

TH
Searle Gulch

Jacque Peak
13,205 ft

0

MILES
1

2
N

91

Clinton
Reservoir

Tenmile Creek

91

right, a horizontal cliff of maroon sandstone and pale granite compose an interesting story in stone.

Marching up the steepening slope, masses of pastel wildflowers, including **narcissus-flowered anemone**, keep step with hikers. Look to the western skyline to see a carefully stacked cairn resembling the stone prayer walls in Nepal. **Orange agoseris** or **burnt orange dandelion**, blue **alpine speedwell**, and yellow **senecios** and **cinquefoils**—including **blueleaf**—carpet the faint trail heading for the pass.

The grade steepens, passing tundra dwellers such as **alpine sandwort, alpine violet, black-headed daisy,** and sweet-scented **Parry clover.** The pass is not much farther. Ledgy sandstone formations, mauve in color, backdrop gilt **alpine avens**, soft-purple **one-headed daisy,** and the whites of **alpine mouse-ear** and **bistort.**

Various stone cairns, including one designating the Colorado Trail, stand as sentinels. The landscape, which is more stone than soil, supports adaptable **yellow stonecrop**—at home in the alpine zone and down to the plains. The tundra character of Searle Pass manifests in early-blooming **moss campion, mountain dryad,** and **alpine sandwort. Dwarf goldenrod** and **purpleleaf** or **alpine senecio** flower a bit later on this 12,020-foot saddle.

As you reach the vista, be prepared for an unbelievable view of the dramatic, jagged peaks of the Gore Range. The more proportionate summits of the Sawatch Range to the west are highlighted by 14,005-foot Mount of the Holy Cross.

Imagine being led through wide-open fields of multicolored flowers up to a pass with a million-dollar view. The "century" trail up Searle Gulch is indeed worth a king's ransom.

Wildflower Hike
39

McCullough Gulch / Quandary Falls

Wildflower Alert: On this trail you'll experience a wildflower welcome to beautiful cascading falls beneath 14,265-foot Quandary Peak.

As the gradient of the trail gently increases, so does the variety of wildflowers—a climb well worth the effort.

Trail Rating	easy to moderate
Trail Length	2.6 miles out and back
Location	Breckenridge
Elevation	11,100 to 11,700 feet
Bloom Season	July through August
Peak Bloom	late July to early August
Directions	Go south on State Road 9 from Breckenridge for 7.5 miles and then right onto County Road 850 for 1 mile. Go right onto Forest Road 851 for 2 miles to the trailhead at the gate at road's end.

WITH THE FORMIDABLE MASS of 14,265-foot Quandary Peak dominating the skyline to the south and 13,998-foot Pacific Peak rearing west and northwest, mountains play a stirring role in the McCullough Gulch hike. One of the most beautiful cascades—a study in black rock and white water—is near the end of trek, and in between along the trail, wildflowers are tossed like festive confetti.

The trail follows an old road on a steady ascent to an off-limits mining claim and its attendant cabin. The grade increases—as do the wildflowers—on the way to kinetic Quandary Falls.

An early arrival serves two purposes: a coveted parking spot and the avoidance of infamous afternoon thunderstorms.

As soon as you step out of your vehicle, McCullough Creek introduces itself boisterously. Whitewater roars through a vertical-walled gorge toward a diversion spillway on the right. The trail begins to the left by stepping around a metal gate. Wildflowers such as **tall chiming bells**, **brook saxifrage**, and **bittercress** decorate a moist trench.

The rugged old road passes a creeklet with another helping of subalpine wet-footed inhabitants, including **scarlet paintbrush** and **arrowleaf senecio**. The base of a rugged granite outcrop on the left is garlanded with striking **Parry primrose**. The lichen-encrusted rock hides pockets of **blue columbine** and **delicate Jacob's ladder**. Creeping mats of **spotted saxifrage** soften its hard contours.

Commanding the southern landscape is a neck-craning view of Quandary Peak. The road passes fiery **paintbrush** and spires of magenta **fireweed**. A curving incline travels over a harsh roadbed to an old log mining cabin resting on a terrace. Intriguingly

COWBANE
Oxypolis fendleri

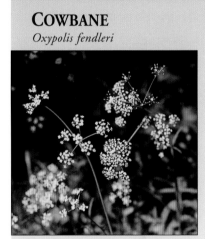

Commonly found along waterways in the subalpine zone, the white umbels of cowbane look like delicate handmade lace. Slim and fond of forest shade, this member of the parsley clan has leaves that look a bit like those of celery. In Greek *oxy* means "sharp" and alludes to the thin bracts, and *polios*, "white," refers to the petals. August Fendler was a nineteenth-century German market gardener from Texas who, with little compensation, collected extensively for Asa Gray, guiding light of the Harvard Herbarium.

named The Last Dollar Mine, the hardrock claim entertains **little pink elephants** and a **pink pyrola** or two hiding in roadside willows. The cool yellow of **western paintbrush** lines the increasingly rocky and steeper trail. Here too are **tall valerian**, **pink pussytoes**, matting **whiproot clover**, stiffly upright and starry-flowered **Fendler's sandwort**, and creeping in the roadbed itself, the minuscule stars of **Nuttall's sandwort**.

Stunted aspen tranquilize the serene, almost pooled, waters that soon will be sent thundering through a tight chasm of their own making. Before the trail enters stands of conifer, **black-tipped senecio** lifts its gray-green, foot-long rubbery leaves.

ROSY PAINTBRUSH
Castilleja rhexifolia

Typically somewhere between cool pink and hot rose, the bracts of rosy paintbrush catch every eye. Each vivid bract of this subalpine bloomer is gently lobed and defined by three obvious veins. The actual flowers, slender and green, go almost unnoticed. Fond of the spruce-fir community, this showy paintbrush is common in moist meadows and forest openings. Paintbrushes are hemiparasitic — that is, they tap into roots of other plants for sustenance while still managing to produce much of their own food. Rosy paintbrush often hybridizes with sulphur paintbrush, creating wide color variations. Domingo Castillejo, an eighteenth century Spanish botanist, is honored by the genus name. A cousin is narrowleaf paintbrush *Castilleja linariifolia*.

Leave the old road now, and head west to a sign reading: Quandary Creek Falls Trail. As an arrow points the way up, angular blocks of granite indicate the trail's upcoming composition. Just before the trail evens, hikers pass a tumble of massive logs—all that remains of an old log cabin.

Easier underfoot now, the trail comes upon aptly named **mountain death camas** carrying green-tinged white stars on bare stalks. (Native Americans called it poison onion.) On the left a puddle of a pond nestles at the base of worn rock, also the locale of a raw umber-bedded creeklet trimmed with **Parry primrose**, **bittercress**, **bistort**, **brook saxifrage**, **queen's crown**, and the alien-green umbel bursts of **Gray's angelica**. Here early season hikers will find **marsh marigold**.

As you approach a rockfall, listen for the sassy-voiced pika. It seems there is hardly a high-elevation jumble of rocks that is not occupied

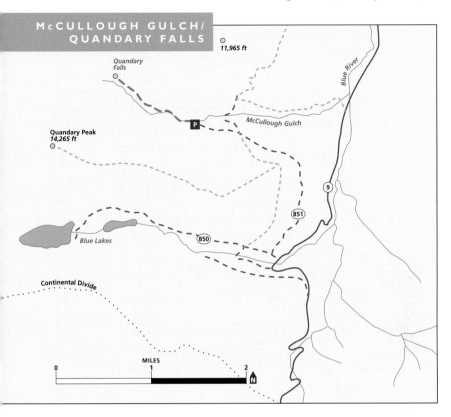

by this vocal relative of the rabbit. To continue on, edge to the left where a solid slab serves as a guide over the brief but unsteady rockpile. Stepping up, the trail brings on the blues of **tall chiming bells** and **blue columbine** and the gold of **arnica**.

Spruce and fir take the trail down over roots, passing **twistedstalk**, each kinked flowerstalk dangling a covert bell. A picturesque series of lush pocket meadows display **paintbrush**, **bistort**, **marsh marigold**, **chiming bells** and plenty of lacy white **cowbane**. Highlighting these damp delights are the bright petals of **shooting stars** and **little pink elephants**. What sounds like a great wind rushing through the trees tells you Quandary Falls is not far off.

Meanwhile, the petite meadows show off ivory **globeflowers** and **little pink elephants**. A peat bog sends the trail through evergreens so as to avoid the dubious charm of bog-slogging. Logs span a sweet-talking stream that murmurs about **queen's crown**.

Leading the trail over granite bedrock, yellowish-beaked **bracted louse-wort** finds another brook running smartly under a few logs. Up to the right, a bit of bright water serves as a prelude to magnificent cascading Quandary Falls. Like the liquid crescendo of a big-voiced canyon wren, whitewater sheets down dark stone.

At the falls, Nature admires her handiwork by tossing gold coins of **shrubby cinquefoil**. Islands of lush vegetation brave the torrent adding winsome appeal to the landscape. Great piles of raw rock lead the eye south up to the craggy majestic heights of 14,265-foot Quandary Peak.

After you've admired the beauty of the waterfall, wander up to see the ledge gardens of complementary gold **subalpine arnica** and purple **monkshood**. Tucked along the bases of worn outcrops are swatches of **rosy paintbrush, shooting stars, bistort, blueleaf cinquefoil**, and **mountain death camas**.

Climbing farther brings swaths of luminous multi-colored **paintbrush. King's crown** adds an intense hue to the flowerscape. Climb up to what imaginatively looks like elephant toes carved by the eons. This chunk of gray granite wades in kaleidoscopic color. This makes a good spot to turn around and retrace your steps through the blooming splendor of a high-country summer.

Though not long, the trek to majestic Quandary Falls is an aerobic exercise hiked to the inspiring beat of wildflower music. Easily accessed from Breckenridge, the trail is one to put you in a Rocky-Mountain-high frame of mind.

Lower Mohawk Lake

Wildflower Alert: Fabulous flowers lead to spirit-lifting
waterfalls and lakes on this delightful trail.

*Lower Mohawk
Lake is the des-
tination for this
flower-studded
trail.*

AS BEAUTIFUL AS THEY COME, Mohawk Lakes, both lower and
upper, are popular destinations. Stunning scenery, sheer-walled falls, soaring
peaks, perfectly set lakes and a "century" trail make for a wonderful hike. Over
100 species on the Mohawk Lake Trail offer wildflower lovers a trek of superb
wildflowers. This trail description begins at the upper trailhead reached via a
rough, rocky road with a couple of boulder obstacles, making the use of a high
clearance vehicle advisable.

Lower Mohawk Lake

Trail Rating	moderate to strenuous
Trail Length	3.4 miles out and back from the upper trailhead (high clearance vehicle advised); 6.8 miles out and back from Spruce Creek trailhead (2WD access)
Location	Breckenridge
Elevation	11,100 to 11,800 feet from upper trailhead 10,200 to 11,800 from Spruce Creek trailhead
Bloom Season	July to August
Peak Bloom	mid-July to early August
Directions	Highway 9 south from Breckenridge for 2.3 miles. Take a right on Spruce Creek Road (CR 800), then take the first right, then go left for 1.2 miles, following blue diamond signs on trees. 2wd cars park at Spruce Creek trailhead. High clearance vehicles continue approximately 1.5 miles, then turn left for 0.3 mile to upper trailhead and park on left.

Start by hiking up a steep, rock-bound old road before the trail becomes a single path. Ascend through forest to level out at the spur to Mayflower Lake, then head up to an emergency cabin near Continental Falls. A steep section comes out at a mining relic, and it's not far to Lower Mohawk Lake. Upper Mohawk, entirely different and not to be missed, is another 300-foot vertical climb. (The next chapter covers this hike.)

An early arrival secures the best parking and the best chance to avoid powerful fast-moving thunderstorms, common here on summer afternoons.

Shaded by Engelmann spruce and subalpine fir, the Spruce Creek Trail arrives at the upper trailhead in time to tackle an erratically cobbled and deeply eroded passage leading up to a diversion dam. Along the roadside are rosy-lavender **subalpine daisies** and **whipple penstemon**. Down in the forest, the rayed suns of **heartleaf arnica** beam.

Where the road ends, the route goes right. 13,164-foot Mount Helen rises to the north as the trail dips into the forest. Crossing a creeklet reveals **tall chiming bells**, **fireweed**, **yarrow**, **pink-headed daisies**, and **pearly everlasting** by the trailhead sign.

As the trail begins to ascend, you'll pass a granite outcrop embellished by **scarlet paintbrush**. Just ahead a minor "glory hole" sparkling with mica was probably dug by some hopeful prospector. Nearby, look for the bright blue goblets of **Parry** or **Rocky Mountain gentian** in late summer.

Continue up to an overlook off to the right where the first whitewater of Continental Falls can be seen. Here, look for **bracted lousewort** and pretty **narcissus-flowered anemone** as well as **beauty cinquefoil, many-rayed golden-rod**, and the poor relation of the gold representatives, **rayless arnica**. Up ahead, a vest-pocket meadow provides moisture for **monkshood, arrowleaf senecio, bistort, subalpine** or **woolly arnica. Marsh marigold** and **globeflower** will greet early season hikers.

The trail arrives at a junction where the short spur to Mayflower Lake goes straight ahead to pass several tumbled-down miners' cabins. Head over to them to access this sweet little lake tucked up against the talus flank of Mount Helen. On the way, the white streamers of Continental Falls can be viewed between dark conifers. The meadowed area along the lake's outlet and shores nurtures ever-faithful **subalpine daisy, bistort**, and **little pink elephants. Orange agoseris** and **mountain death camas** grow in slightly drier areas. Later in the season, this is a good place to compare the diversity in the gentian family by examining velvety purple **fringed**, silky mauve **star,** and true blue **Rocky Mountain gentians** blooming here.

Returning to the Mohawk Lakes Trail, curve around to cross a brook on rustic logs. Another derelict log cabin rests in the shadow of spruces with **delicate Jacob's ladder** at their feet.

The trail pitches up now through angular rock and exposed tree roots. The easier route up is to the left, over a big log.

AMERICAN BISTORT
Bistorta bistortoides

Generally called simply bistort, this member of the knotweed family seems to be at home anywhere in the high country where there is sufficient moisture. It carries other common names alluding to its growth characteristics, such as snakeweed (roots), knotweed (stems), smartweed (astringent leaves), bottlebrush (inflorescence), and—of uncertain reference — miner's sock. Up to two feet tall, bistort stems terminate in a cylindrical head crowded with myriad white to blush five-sepaled flowers, each bearing eight stamens. Bistort is an important food source for wildlife: pika, ptarmigan, elk, and deer relish the plant, and bears dig the contorted roots. Native Americans found bistort's astringency useful for healing. The scientific name *Bistorta bistortoides* translates, redundantly, as "twice twisted." Yes, both the genus and the species name mean the same thing.

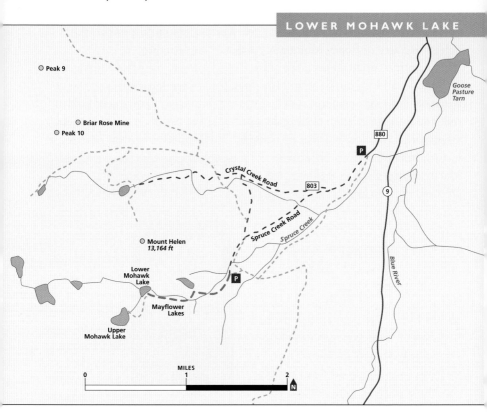

At the top of the incline are the remains of a mill. A bit of stone foundation and scattered bricks are all that is left.

Resume the trail over natural stone by heading south around the mill remnants to approach an intact cabin. A sign there heads hikers left one half mile to Lower Mohawk Lake. To the right, a "social" trail ends at a rather precipitous spot overlooking Lower Continental Falls. Crashing through a water-hewn chasm, the spray nurses vivid **Parry primrose** and sweet clumps of **blue columbine**, while below **tall chiming bells**, **subalpine larkspur**, **arrowleaf senecio**, and **bittercress** thrive. Up where the water has cut itself a vertical channel, the American dipper or water ouzel may be dashing through the spray or bobbing underwater to find a meal. Waterfalls are favorite nesting places for this slate-gray bird.

Back on the main trail, hikers enter a confetti-showered garden of **Parry clover**, **subalpine larkspur**, and both **rosy** and **scarlet paintbrush**. The big somber umbels of **Gray's angelica**, **cinquefoils**, **arnicas**, **senecios**, and **columbine** round out the swirling party.

The trail ascends a rocky bed and curves around to face massive Mount Helen. **Fireweed** may ignite later in the season. **Narcissus-flowered anemone**, demure in pale cream, waits with blushing **pink-headed daisy**.

There is no doubt that this trail is in the Rocky Mountains, as the route crosses raw rock. Clinging mats of **spotted saxifrage** soften the outcrop edges. Soon the roar of Upper Continental Falls directs you past a low stacked stone wall and an S-curve to a confusion of "social" spurs. Choose the acute-angled one, a bit up the trail, to switch back to access the base of Upper Continental Falls. Find a steady place to stand as you behold the thunderous creek.

Turn back to the main trail, and pass a standing snag on the right. The footbed is rugged as it proceeds south to overlook an ancillary gorge lined with wildflowers. Switchbacks take the hiker quickly up a very steep face. Pause to look back toward Breckenridge and Bald Mountain's triple summits. Then turn southeast to 13,229-foot Red Mountain, another of Colorado's 740-some "thirteeners."

While still zigzagging, the trail smoothes somewhat before resuming its rough character. Off to the left, a cascading rivulet endears itself with lovely **blue columbine**, **bittercress**, **tall chiming bells**, **senecio**, and a host of others.

You'll traverse a section of bedrock and arrive at a timbered structure with rusting cables. These hefty cables, which likely delivered ore to the mill below, must be crossed to reach the right side of the bull-wheel frame.

Golden bedrock leads along the edge of a shallow cleft where the trail passes through a gap and drops to a plush area where **marsh marigold**, **bistort**, **senecio**, **arnica**, **tall chiming bells**, and **brook saxifrage** flourish. Willows flank the way to pool-and-drop cascades, forming an uncommonly beautiful grand staircase with wide landings.

Willows form tussocked coves studded by rich pink **alpine lousewort**. Looking straight down on one of these less frequently encountered louseworts reminds one of a child's pinwheel. Sharing kinship and fern-like leaves with **little pink elephants** and the nearby creamy **Parry's lousewort**, the satiny rose galeas (helmet-shaped sepal) of **alpine lousewort** often issue from a mass of silvery "wool."

Now lovely Lower Mohawk Lake comes into view. The west shore, anchored by a warm-hued log structure, showcases a silvery inlet cascade. The north shore's granitic skirts belong to the titanic bulk of that formidable lady, Mount Helen. This is a great place to sit and enjoy the cool depths of Lower Mohawk Lake and its splendid setting.

Though not a particularly long hike from the upper trailhead, reaching Lower Mohawk Lake makes you feel you have really arrived somewhere. Not only is the trail a good workout, but its incredible floral arrays are worth every step —as well as the glory of Continental Falls, the mountainscapes, and the lake.

Upper Mohawk Lake

Wildflower Alert: This hike is the crowning glory in a gloriously floristic area.

Continuing on to Upper Mohawk Lake brings you into the pristine alpine zone—but beware of afternoon thunderstorms.

Trail Rating	moderate to strenuous
Trail Length	4.0 miles out and back
Location	Breckenridge
Elevation	11,100 to 12,120 feet from upper trailhead
Bloom Season	July through August
Peak Bloom	mid- to late July
Directions	Highway 9 south from Breckenridge for 2.3 miles. Take a right on Spruce Creek Road (CR 800), then take the first right, then go left for 1.2 miles, following blue diamond signs on trees. 2wd cars park at Spruce Creek trailhead. High clearance vehicles continue approximately 1.5 miles, then turn left for 0.3 mile to upper trailhead and park on left.

UPPER AND LOWER MOHAWK LAKES are very different from each other. Despite its alpine zone elevation, Lower Mohawk Lake, covered in the preceding chapter, is more subalpine in character. So much diversity is offered by continuing on to the higher lake that it is served separately in this description. This chapter treats Upper Mohawk Lake as worthy of standing on its own.

Upper Mohawk Trail begins from the south shore of Lower Mohawk Lake and is an awesome goal. The wildflower extravaganza begun on Lower Mohawk Lake Trail continues with more beautiful floral specimens, including the gems of the alpine zone. As the upper lake is located above treelimit, it's wise to plan an early start to avoid afternoon thunderstorms.

Traveling around the south shore of Lower Mohawk Lake is a beautiful way to access the trail to Upper Mohawk Lake. The biggest problem is locating the route, which overall is well-defined with the exception of the first few feet that climb over trail-less boulders.

The trail curves around a little slope, heading away from the lower lake into a gentle ravine with willows on the right. Look for a big granite outcrop, as well as a three-foot-high rock cairn of the same mineral make-up as the surrounding boulders. This cairn is a number of feet to the right or west of the trail spur you want. A second point of reference is another rock cairn up on the left side of the desired trail. Hop up on the confusion of boulders and the trail materializes within feet, headed south.

Once on the trodden trail, you'll take in a multi-ribboned cascade where the snow melts late. Passing flagged spruce—their windward sides stripped of branches—take the rocky route in a southeasterly direction. A sizable boulder pockets a little garden of its own with a great variety of wildflowers, **Parry clover** among them.

Like an antique lace collar on a black dress, the cascade drapes its white tracery over dark rock. The trail evens out, allowing you to enjoy snowy curtains of falling water. Whipped by wind-driven debris, the spruces shrink to *krummholz* size, branches rooting as they touch the ground. A good stand of cheerful pink **alpine lousewort** introduces a wee tarn on the right. Thick tundra grasses move the trail past the humming cascade to a point where the serrated incisors of a 13,000-foot ridge appear.

A steeper pitch pushes the trail up to a great granite wall. At its base, pale **delicate Jacob's ladder** accents **tall chiming bells**—a mauvy-pink here instead of the usual blue (although even the blue flowers begin as pink buds). Another stone wall sites the round, rosy heads of **Parry clover** and the inflated tubes of **Whipple** or **dusky penstemon**. A fine view of Lower Mohawk Lake pooled at the hem of 13,164-foot Mount Helen's skirts can be enjoyed from a leveling trail now.

A paint-box pocket meadow is stuffed with white **bistort, rosy paintbrush**, cobalt blue **greenleaf chiming bells** and chrome-yellow **cinquefoil**. Burnt-red **king's crown** and the subtly green umbels of **Gray's angelica** accompanies the trail to a section of bedrock. You'll find more sweet-smelling **Parry clover** where willows flank the trail. Here also is another stand of deep pink **alpine lousewort**. This bright lousewort is common in Alaska, but confines itself to selected alpine locales in the Rocky Mountains.

Traversing above the cascades brings a spur into view, while the main trail heads left to be embraced by low willows. Continue on to a rock garden offering **narcissus-flowered anemone** and vivid **Parry primrose** tucked in at the feet of a friendly wall. A wide open vista swings full circle, with dramatic mountains all around.

Snow lingers far into the summer on this northern exposure, allowing spring bloomers to flourish. Hardly waiting for the high-country earth to thaw, white-sepaled **marsh marigold** loves cold, even frigid feet —imaginatively alluded to by steel blue sepal reverses. It is joined at the cascade by **bittercress** and showy **Parry primrose**.

Sometimes, stubborn snowbanks in the vicinity are the color and, it is said, the smell of watermelon. A taste of the red algae is not worth the effort—your digestive system will pay the awful price.

Rocky and steepening, the trail passes lovely, pink, white, and blue gardens, including one with lots of **Parry primrose**. The trail eases up to wide mats of **whiproot clover**, whose important roots knit together eroding soil. Up a bit

PARRY PRIMROSE
Primula parryi

Widespread and very showy, Parry primrose is a star of high-country summer. Enjoying wet or marshy ground, this attention-getting wildflower has pink five-lobed corollas with yellow centers. The leaves, which may grow a foot long as the season progresses, and the notch-petaled flowers tend to have an unpleasant odor. All the perfume went to a diminutive tundra cousin, fairy or alpine primrose *Primula angustifolia. Primula parryi* commemorates an ardent collector of eastern slope plants, Dr. Charles Parry of Iowa. A physician and botanist, he lived from 1823-1890.

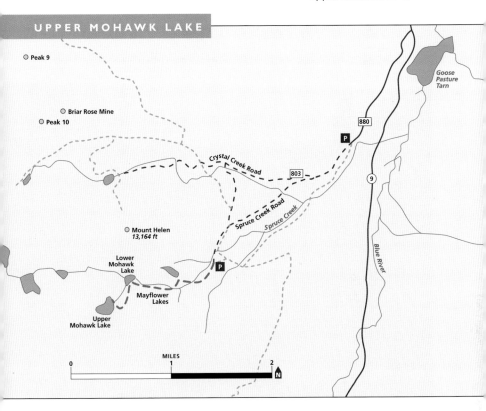

UPPER MOHAWK LAKE

where the outlet creek roams, look among the tussocks of grasses for two tiny but charming tundra dwellers—light purple **moss** or **compass gentian** and deep purple **one-flowered** or **alpine harebell**.

Wade through willows to reach a low manmade wall sheltering **alpine sorrel** and **queen's crown**. Edge around them and you get an odd perspective of Upper Mohawk Lake—water at eye level without getting wet.

Wildflowers, such as **alpine** and **Fendler sandwort** in white, as well as **alpine avens**, **thick-leaved draba** and silver-bunned **alpine cinquefoil** in yellow, color the lumpy shores of the lake. Nooks and crannies in the rugged outcrops tuck bouquets of **blue columbine** in their rough folds. Looking up across the wine-bottle green lake, you'll see a toothed ridge of 13,000-plus feet biting into the south skyline.

The half-mile trail up to Upper Mohawk Lake offers a splendid addition to the mile already hiked to Lower Mohawk Lake. Far fewer visitors experience the stark beauty of this alpine lake and the charming way wildflowers are arrayed along the way. Beat the summer afternoon thunderstorms and enjoy the grand trek to Upper Mohawk Lake.

Wildflower Hike
42

Shrine Ridge

Wildflower Alert: Where shattered rainbows come to rest.

Waves of flowers greet you on this pleasant hike which explodes with color in late June and again in late July.

Trail Rating	easy to moderate
Trail Length	3.0 miles out and back
Location	Vail Pass/Vail/Copper Mountain
Elevation	10,080 to 11,760 feet
Bloom Season	late June to August
Peak Bloom	late June for tundra; mid- to late July, lower
Directions	Take I-70 west to Vail Pass exit 190. Go left over the overpass and straight onto a dirt road (Shrine Pass Road) to the turnoff for Shrine Mountain Inn. Park, go left (adjacent to the turnoff) at the signed parking area. Walk 0.3 mile to the trailhead on the left.

NOT FAR WEST OF VAIL PASS and up the flower-lined dirt road leading toward Redcliff is the start of a wonderfully florescent trek. Shrine Ridge
Trail should actually be hiked twice during the summer: once in late June to
catch some of the region's largest patches of hot blue alpine forget-me-nots
and other tundra flowers (even if it means encountering some late snowbanks),
and a month later, when a riot of about six dozen wildflower species erupts.
Inspiring views are present in all seasons.

The trail begins as a boardwalk where once a bog had to be crossed. It
traverses easy slopes, then turns up through evergreens to reach open meadows
before rising more vigorously to gain the tundra, along the Tenth Mountain Trail.

Though a road accesses Shrine Mountain Inn (a memorable place for
a stay or a meal), hikers are requested to park at the designated national forest
lot on the south side of Shrine Pass Road. From here, the trail is one-third
mile down the Inn's approach road.

From the generous parking area, follow the wide road through dark conifers,
and find more than a dozen kinds of wildflowers along the way. Log-built
Shrine Mountain Inn comes into view at a bend in the roadway, where both sides
display a patriotic patchwork of intensely-tinted blue **lupine**, **scarlet paintbrush**,
and white **daisies**.

Soon you'll reach a gap in the split-rail fence on the left, posted as
Shrine Ridge. Turn here and you'll pass evergreens and a moist spot where
little pink elephants wave their trunks. The boardwalk reaches out across
an extensive bog. Firm footing allows the luxury of looking for pink **queen's
crown** and dusky-purple **star gentian** in mid-summer. June hikers headed for
tundra exploration will find bog buddies **marsh marigold** and **globeflower**
enjoying the cold conditions. By August, plenty of **fringed gentian** freshens
the waning flowerscape.

The boardwalk section ends with a white flourish of native **Coulter
daisies**. Continue on a natural surface. The trail then begins rising slightly
through flowery meadows dominated by fiery **scarlet paintbrush**. As the
incline eases, look north to the jagged peaks of the Gore Range in the distance. A bit farther on, check out an interesting red rock formation anchoring
the west end of Shrine Ridge.

Heavily logged in the past, the next trail segment marches through
fields of **subalpine arnica**, red **paintbrush**, and lavender **daisies**. In damp places
along this north-facing slope, **little rose gentian** appears demurely in the company of showier **rosy paintbrush** and **fringed gentian** swirled in purple velvet.

In drier areas, **pink-headed daisies** with their fuzzy buds and prostrate **Colorado tansy aster** with its luminous violet rays join in. Unfettered air makes colors 25 percent more intense in the high country.

The trail crosses a seep where light-hearted **brook saxifrage**, **white bog orchid**, and **little pink elephants** flourish. Another seep on the right supports more water-loving species such as lacy-bloomed **cowbane** and sturdy **bog saxifrage**.

As the gently ascending path approaches the forest, June hikers may discover the occasional **Calypso orchid** hidden by rotting logs. The early summer period is also celebrated by power-pink **Parry primrose** and white **marsh marigold** partnered at a creeklet dancing across the trail. Up on the far bank, look for bi-colored **whiproot clover** colonizing under big conifers.

The route enters an area of willow shrubs where spires of rich purple-blue **subalpine larkspur** peek out. Not much farther on, Mother Nature has carved an artistic waterway, cuing a scenic pause ahead. A huge worn log presents an opportunity to leisurely admire the grand view of the Gore Range.

SNOW BUTTERCUP

Ranunculus adoneus

Named partly for the Greek god Adonis, snow buttercup sports halos of five lacquered yellow petals. Another common name is alpine buttercup. This brave wildflower pops up in the wake of retreating snowbanks, sometimes even right up through their icy edges. The leaves are thready and the sepals underlying the petals are slightly purplish. Pika, casual in their "haying" choices, add snow buttercup to their stockpiles. Native Americans used the petals for a dye and reportedly made flour from the roasted seeds, although today the plant is considered toxic. *Ranunculus,* meaning "little frog," is an indicator of buttercups' favored habitat. Cousins include narcissus anemone *Anemonastrum narcissiflorum subspecies zehyrum* and Pasqueflower *Pulsatilla patens subspecies hirsutissima.*

Heading steadily uphill, the path enters evergreens where patches of low-growing **black-headed daisies** make their home. You'll emerge at a broad meadow featuring **yellow paintbrush**, **dandelionleaf groundsel**, and **alpine avens**. Snowmelt in this meadow brings out bunches of **globeflowers**.

Outcrops of striated-red sandstone counterpoint smatterings of **white geranium**. A ravine on the left unrolls **groundsels**, **arnica**, **larkspur**, and **blue columbine**. A big maroon boulder on the right signals the advent of a hillside of noble **narcissus-flowered anemone**, surrounded by a rainbow retinue.

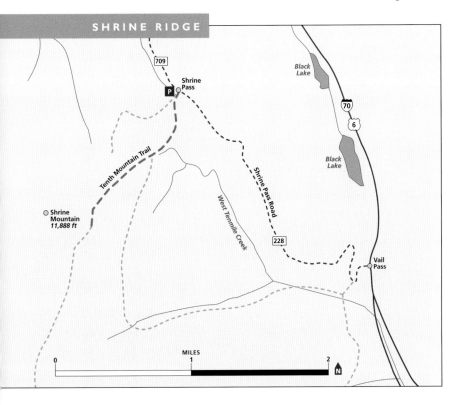

Climbing steeply now, the trail passes a waterway where **blueleaf cinquefoil**, **alpine parsley**, and round-headed rosy **Parry clover** thrive. Receding snowbanks are footnoted by fine-foliaged **snow buttercup**.

Keep right of divergent "social" trails at the last pitch to gain the saddle where the trail forks. Heading right passes widely spaced **lupine** and **paintbrush** on the way to sculpted red-rock formations. Early-season hikers will want to head left on the treeless tundra to discover mat after mat of incredibly blue and fragrant **alpine forget-me-nots** (with a few white ones sprinkled in). Add to that cushions of sassy pink **moss campion**, cool purple trumpets of lush **sky pilot**, and the big disc heads of **old man of the mountains**. This landscape filled with surprises makes it worthwhile to tromp through late snowbanks.

Shrine Ridge performs all season long, and this pleasant trail rates as one of the great wildflower destinations of the Colorado Rockies. Outstanding not only for its floral displays and expansive views but also for its accessibility, Shrine Ridge deserves a place high on a wildflower aficionado's summer-hike list.

Straight Creek

Wildflower alert: A memorable "century" hike to the top of the tundra world on the Continental Divide.

Watch for afternoon thunderstorms on this oft-overlooked subalpine–alpine hike—a spectacular color display in late July.

Trail Rating	moderate to strenuous
Trail Length	4.0 miles out and back
Location	Eisenhower Tunnel/Dillon
Elevation	11,150 to 12,500 feet
Bloom Season	July to August
Peak Bloom	mid-July to early August
Directions	Take I-70 west through the Eisenhower Tunnel. Park on the north side of the west portal. The main trail begins on the road next to the tunnel air intakes.

EVERY YEAR, hundreds of thousands of motorists pass the unmarked trail-head of a floral treasure chest as they exit the Eisenhower Tunnel's west portal. Over 100 species of wildflowers accompany the hikers' climb of 1,350 vertical feet along Straight Creek, then up to an old wagon road that tops out on the Continental Divide.

The first mile more or less follows the Straight Creek drainage north, and the second mile traverses an old abandoned wagon road on an east axis. The third week in July seems to be a magic time for catching peak bloom in the high country. It is also a time of afternoon thunderstorms. Plan to be back down by noon to avoid dangerous lightning activity, especially since this hike is above treelimit. A huge parking area on the north side of the west portal accommodates any number of vehicles.

Immediately adjacent to the decomposed edges of the parking area, dozens of subalpine wildflowers await discovery. Look on the lush south-facing slope to find **subalpine larkspur, queen's crown, cowbane,** and **daffodil senecio** rejoicing on the moist hillside. In drier habitats, sheltered by spruce trees, look for **delicate Jacob's ladder, heartleaf arnica,** and **Whipple** or **dusky penstemon,** in both wine and white. Bushwhack through the dense vegetation in an easterly direction to discover **little pink elephants,** lilac-pink **subalpine daisy,** and the no-nonsense spheres of **Gray's angelica.** All this and more is within yards of the parking area.

Drop back down to access a paved side road that heads up to pass gargantuan tunnel air-intake ducts. Carefully circumvent an area with a warning sign stating Danger: Explosives. A hillside to the left explodes in red flames in the form of **scarlet paintbrush.** Farther up the road, cool tones arrive with prime specimens of **blue columbine.**

Follow the wide road up and watch on the left for sunny spots of **yellow monkeyflower** wading in spreading seeps. Beyond and down a bit where Straight Creek rushes off to the Continental Divide, vivid pink **Parry primrose** flirts with whitewater as does white-flowered **brook** or **bittercress** and **brook saxifrage.**

Return to the road to pass clump after clump of picture-perfect **blue columbine.** Soon, it's time to head up in an easterly direction to connect with the old wagon road. Lacking true definition at this point, the trail veers to the right, passing both **Parry** and **bracted lousewort** with their creamy yellow-beaked blooms. **Snowball saxifrage** and its homely cousin, **bog saxifrage,** dwell here as well.

Rising steadily now, the trail pokes through a drier grassy neighborhood populated by brassy **alpine avens** and its color complement, warm-blue **sky pilot**. The disturbed edges of the trail are favored by white **mountain candytuft** and **purple fringe**, whose crowded column of amethyst trumpets boldly display gold stamens.

Fed by a swift rivulet on the right, the boggy environs are home to **Parry primrose**, **king's crown**, and **marsh marigold**—a rich palette of pink, burnt red, and white.

A fairly hard turn to the right keeps the trail underfoot. Up ahead, at the feet of lingering snowbanks, bare zones are just right for brilliant yellow **snow buttercups**. These brave bloomers sometimes assert themselves by popping right up through persistent snow.

Gaining altitude and beauty, the trail wanders a bit vaguely. Keep traversing toward a natural chute of tumbled rock spilling forth a bounty of yellow **paintbrush**, **cinquefoil**, ultramarine **greenleaf chiming bells**, **sky pilot**, and **purple fringe**. Straining wood wheels once traveled this route, so the gradient is not excessive. It evens out for a bit, flanked by more purple and yellow wildflowers before resuming its upward course.

Here, far above treelimit, descriptively named **woolly** or **frosty ball thistle** sports misleading-looking fuzzy bent heads and is the tallest flowering plant around. Ascend a slope of scattered boulders and take time to pause and admire the expansive view and locate Mount of the Holy Cross to the west. At the foot of the rocks, look for little wildflowers which often go unnoticed such as **alpine speedwell**, **pygmy bitterroot**, and **alpine violet**. Here too is tiny **moss gentian**, whose blue corolla resembles the compass emblem found on antique mariners' maps, earning it the moniker **compass gentian**. The Siberian gentian genus, in which moss or compass gentian occurs, can indeed be found at all points of the compass from the

MOSS CAMPION
Silene acaulis subspecies *subacaulescens*

A large mounded cushion of bright pink moss campion might be a century old. Notched at the tip, each five-petaled fragrant flower has its own stem. Conservative in growth, this member of the pink family may be a decade old before it starts blooming and is anchored by a long taproot. This pioneer plant of windy, gravelly, exposed tundra migrated ahead of the ice—a glacial relict.

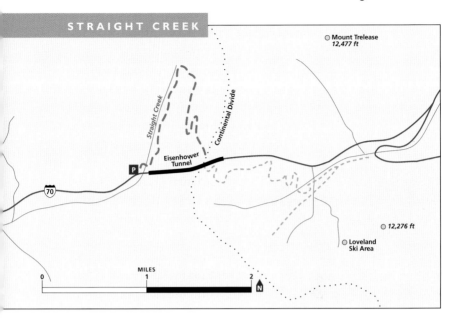

STRAIGHT CREEK

Mount Trelease
12,477 ft

Straight Creek

Continental Divide

Eisenhower
Tunnel

P

70

12,276 ft

Loveland
Ski Area

MILES

0   1   2

N

Alps to the Andes, the Himalaya to the Siberian Atlai, and from Australia's mountains to those on which you stand.

Continuing up toward the crest, **rosy paintbrush**, bi-colored **whiproot clover**, and **old man of the mountains** encourage hikers on. In moist swales, creamy **globeflower** partners white **marsh marigold** in sizable colonies. Well-drained soil is the place to look for subtle flowers such as **alplily**, **snowlover**, **black-headed daisy**, and **Smelowskia**, which looks like a cross between dwarf yarrow and mountain candytuft, earning it the common name **fernleaf candytuft**.

Along the next segment, ravines embrace remarkable rock gardens where buns of pink **moss campion**, succulent rosettes of **alpine spring beauty**, and tight mats of **alpine sandwort** stabilize the hard-won soil. Also be on the lookout for **one-flowered** or **alpine harebell** and the fragrant **fairy primrose**.

Keep the cutbanks of the overgrown road in sight as the pathway dims and switchbacks before leveling somewhat. Along the gravelly edges, uncommon **purpleleaf groundsel** or **senecio** forms thick clumps to present its yellow composite flowers.

The trail wanders gently now, passing a blue and yellow palette of **greenleaf chiming bells** and **alpine wallflower**. A keen eye may find an occasional golden **whiplash saxifrage**.

At last the broad saddle of the Continental Divide broaches the skyline. Within a six-week window of summer, flowers must emerge, bloom, get pollinated, and set seed on this windswept ridge. Sweet-scented ground-huggers

alpine forget-me-not and **alpine phlox** are worth a search, as their bloom time is quite early.

From the top of the tundra world here, you are worlds away from I-70's whizzing traffic passing less than 1,400 feet directly below your feet. Just down from where you stand is Loveland Ski Basin; in the distance is 13,234-foot Mount Sniktau and to the southeast, another "thirteener," Grizzly Peak. Beyond it, Gray's and Torrey's Peaks stand at 14,270 and 14,267 feet respectively. To the west is the rugged Gore Range.

A "century" hike, Straight Creek and the trail to the Continental Divide is nothing short of sensational, both floristically and scenically. Easy access and exhilarating exercise are bonuses which should put this high-country trail up near the top of the summer wild-flowering agenda.

ALPINE WALLFLOWER
Erysimum capitatum

The clear, yellow inflorescences of alpine wallflower stand out on the tundra. This fragrant mustard family member's flowers consist of four opposing petals in a cross shape. Blistercress is an old-fashioned name stemming from the mustard's blister-healing qualities. Its genus name *Erysimum* derives from the Greek *eryomai*, meaning "help" or "save" and *capitatum*, which is Latin for "headed." Cousin wallflower *Erysimum asperum* is a species generally of the eastern plains.

Old Ute Trail/ Tombstone Ridge
(Rocky Mountain National Park)

Wildflower Alert: Enjoy early summer tundra jewels on an easy trail in Rocky Mountain National Park.

Follow the footsteps of early Native Americans as you enjoy the delicate wildflower gems in the high tundra.

easy	**Trail Rating**
2.0 miles out and back	**Trail Length**
Grand Lake/Rocky Mountain National Park	**Location**
11,510 to 11,620 feet	**Elevation**
late June to mid-July	**Bloom Season**
early to mid-July	**Peak Bloom**
Take US 36 and go past the west entrance station. Travel approximately 13 miles (less than 1 mile east of Forest Canyon Overlook parking area) to a small pullout on the right. Fee required.	**Directions**

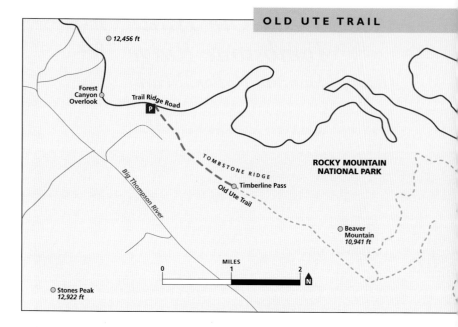

OF THE MORE THAN 350 MILES OF HIKING TRAILS in Rocky Mountain National Park, Old Ute Trail is the most historic. The segment encompassing Tombstone Ridge is also one of the best to view the inspiring subtleties of tundra plants while following in the footsteps of Native Americans who trod here above treelimit for thousands of years.

Only 240 feet of elevation gain is accumulated in the mile walk, making the fact that there is one-third less oxygen at this elevation a little easier. Walk slowly to enjoy the tiny wildflower gems at your feet. A narrow trail wends its way through a veritable rock garden of flowering mats, buns, and cushions. Views of Forest Canyon and Longs Peak are bonuses.

Parking is limited in the extreme, and thunderstorms are always an afternoon possibility. Be especially alert on the exposed ridge.

Direct access to the wonderful wildflowers of early-blooming tundra is limited south of the Arctic Circle. But here on an intimate segment of Old Ute Trail, the magic exists for those who want to walk the same path as the ancients. Here is an opportunity to examine and appreciate the lengths to which nature goes to adapt and indeed flourish in a harsh environment.

From the first step along this narrow ribbon of crushed rock trail, the earth spangles the rocky landscape with tiny treasures beginning in late June.

At the trailhead sign, brassy **alpine avens**, rose-pink **dwarf clover**, and **golden draba** claim a bit of protection provided by the posts. Later, drumsticks of **bistort** will add their waving white heads.

Fragrance is a plus for flowers trying to attract pollinators, ensuring survival of the species in a few compressed weeks. Adapting astonishingly well in the harsh limits of its home is the unforgettable electric blue of **alpine forget-me-not**—a shining example in the first week of July (white specimens may be found here and there). Sharing that same attribute are sweet-scented **alpine phlox**, which has starry light flowers facing the sky, and **dwarf clover**, which tends to produce its pea-type blossoms singly while tenacious roots expand its mats. A single plant may measure a handspan wide and be a half-century old.

Standing bravely is clear-yellow **alpine wallflower**, which offers its perfume to passing insects. This is a mustard family member as is nearby **golden draba**. But the bravest of all is **old man of the mountains** or **Rydbergia**, which flowers a bit later in the season. Its sunflower head is nearly as wide as the plant is tall. After years of gathering energy to put forth the notable bloom, it dies, having accomplished its reproductive mission.

As the rock-studded trail pulls up, boot soles look huge placed carefully alongside the tight mounds of **moss campion**. Its cheery pink flowers sprinkle the ground like spilled sequins. The crowded foliage of this pioneer plant may have been photosynthesizing for a decade before producing its first blooms. Some mats, such as the almost stemless white **alpine sandwort**, find a root-hold at the base of boulders, and proceed to stretch their aerodynamic foliage over the stone in artistic contours. Others, such as sturdy **sky pilot** and delicate **alplily**, lift their

FAIRY PRIMROSE
Primula angustifolia

Alpine primrose is another common name for this delightfully fragrant denizen of the high country. Though small in stature, the five vivid pink, notched petals and star-shaped yellow eye combine to attract attention, especially on the tundra. It is worth the time for inhaling the sweet scent of this delicate treasure. The Latin species name *angustifolia,* meaning "narrow leaves," adds a clue to the physical appearance of fairy primrose. Though its much bigger and unpleasant-smelling cousin, Parry primrose *Primula parryi,* flourishes in wet habitats, fairy or alpine primrose prefers a drier environment.

blooms on longer stems. Each plant has carved out a niche in nature's carefully orchestrated rock garden along Old Ute Trail.

Views to a dished spur, pegged with upright liths and rugged Forest Canyon beyond, are breathtaking. Rivers of ice, thousands of feet thick, gouged out the river valley below—the glaciers themselves not quite reaching this high tundra area. Peaks fronting the Continental Divide sweep the horizon beyond the conifer-lined canyon.

A sign soon appears telling the hiker Upper Beaver Meadows is 6.5 miles away. In the vicinity are wonderfully fragrant **alpine phlox** and a few—perhaps even more fragrant—hot pink **fairy primroses**. Cobalt-blue **greenleaf chiming bells**, bright yellow **alpine avens**, and pink **dwarf clover** add to the colorful scene.

ALPINE PHLOX
Phlox condensata

Both the Latin genus and common names for this showy wildflower are the same. In this case *Phlox* translates to "flame." The wide, starry blossoms of perfumed alpine phlox can virtually cover the compact cushions that stem from a woody taproot, allowing it to survive the harsh conditions of the tundra. Each delectable flower, a study in purity of color from white to hints of lavender or pink, is accented by a yellow stigma in the throat of the flower tube. In partial to well-drained soil, spreading cushions of this tundra dweller may be seen at their finest during peak bloom, typically late June to early July.

The trail ascends among boulders. On the left rises the ragged jumble of Tombstone Ridge, its pale granite piles sometimes dotted with dark, furry animals. Yellow-bellied marmots can be sizable and may whistle shrilly when alarmed. Hikers most often see the big rodents draped on rocks in the strong rays of high-country summer sun. At ground level, **yellow stonecrop** pokes up red-striped teardrop buds that open to sunny stars in its favored gravelly habitat. At home from the plains to the tundra, stonecrop's waxy succulent leaves fend off the elements. It is said to have been a food source for Native Americans, perhaps those who wore this intriguing trail into immortality.

Pale granite lifts the trail to capture the arête of the Keyboard of the Winds to the southeast. Next to it, from this vantage point, the summit of 14,255-foot-high Longs Peak appears to have been sheared off.

Continuing the panorama south and west is a wider view of Forest Canyon, which is still being carved by the Big Thompson River and calls for an appreciative pause.

Hereabouts, a little later in the bloom season, lavender **single-headed daisies**, buttery **alpine paintbrush**, and burnt-red **king's crown** put in appearances. It takes a keen eye to spot the occasional deep-purple **alpine or one-flowered harebell** among the tufts of grasses. This tiny contender for space in the competitive tundra world sports a crinkled funnel facing out across its domain.

The trail of the Utes and Arapahos stretches out more evenly as it approaches a three-potholed flat rock. All around, in their season, mats of profusely blossomed **alpine phlox** look like puddles of early morning sky fallen to earth. This makes a good turnaround point for the Old Ute Trail tundra walk. From here, Old Ute Trail continues down six more miles and nearly three thousand vertical feet.

Retracing your footsteps offers the opportunity to once again marvel at the secret alpine garden all around you. Not only is Old Ute Trail a portal into the jeweled world of wide-skied tundra, but it is a privilege to walk where ancient footsteps trod.

Wildflower Hike

45

Linkins Lake
(Hunter-Fryingpan Wilderness)

Wildflower Alert: Climb to see springtime blooming far into summer at this high, picturesque lake.

A steep but short climb leads to a pristine mountain lake revealing over seventy types of wildflowers.

Trail Rating	strenuous, but short
Trail Length	1.25 miles out and back
Location	Aspen/Independence Pass
Elevation	11,515 to 12,008 feet
Bloom Season	late July to late August
Peak Bloom	early to mid-August
Directions	Take Highway 82 for 2 miles west of Independence Pass near milepost 59 (18.5 miles east of Aspen). Park on the north side of the highway.

THE SPECTACULAR DRIVE along Independence Pass is a high-country classic. Grand scenery, mining town sites, and the 12,095-foot pass itself are popular objectives. Between Aspen and the pass, a trailhead serving a number of hikes—including the one to Linkins Lake—is situated in a curve at State Road 82, not quite 20 miles east of Aspen. Here Roaring Fork River pelts under the highway on its way to Aspen.

Though the climb to beautiful Linkins Lake is steep, it is over quickly. Start through willows by Roaring Fork River and enter the Hunter-Fryingpan Wilderness Area before ascending the aggressive incline that lands you at the lake in short order. Over 70 wildflower species are showcased along this three-quarter-mile hike. For the best floral collection, head for the south end of treeless Linkins Lake.

Keep a weather eye peeled for threatening thunderstorms when hiking, especially above treelimit. An early start helps avoid these summer afternoon phenomena and also makes securing a parking spot easier.

Linkins Lake's outlet waters join Roaring Fork River not far from the beginning of the hike. The trail starts on the north edge of the parking area where the rock-confined river piles into a culvert. Here, on the right, the hiker encounters thick-leaved **rock senecio** and **alpine sorrel**. On the left is a seep which sports **yellow monkeyflower**.

As you step up from the carpark to peruse the trailhead kiosk sign, note a dozen different kinds of wildflowers on the way. Among them are rosy-lavender **subalpine daisy** and yellow **woolly** or **subalpine arnica**. Nearby **little pink elephants** keep in step with the **gentians** of August. **Fringed, Rocky Mountain,** and **little rose gentians** have a starring role in late summer.

The trail continues to rise and expresses its intimate willowy character. White **Coulter daisies** and upright native **horned dandelions** grow along the path. A rivulet weaving through the willows introduces yet another gentian: **star gentian** in dusky purple. The moist environment also encourages stately **monkshood** and **arrowleaf senecio**. Early-season hikers will observe **marsh marigold** and **globeflower**. Common here, but undistinguished in dingy-white bloom, is **bog saxifrage**, which ages well, becoming wine red.

Where the trail eases on this splendid peak-wrapped stage, pocket meadows feature the rounded, pink inflorescences of **queen's crown** and the maroon-stemmed spikes of **little pink elephants** with their perfectly-formed pachyderm heads. Both **rosy** and **scarlet paintbrush** daub the backdrop. The trail curves right to span a crystalline creek decorated with showy **Parry Primrose**.

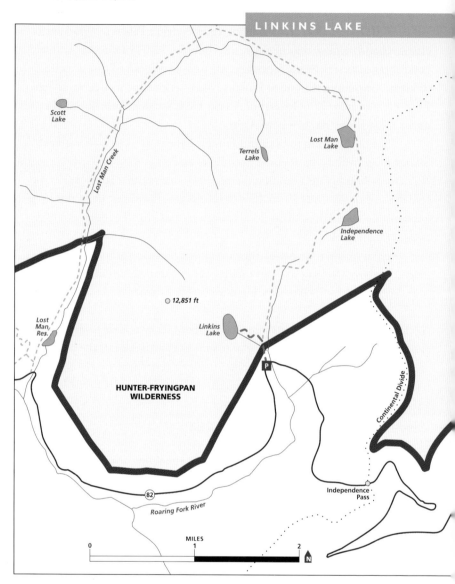

Scott
Lake

Lost Man Creek

Terrels
Lake

Lost Man
Lake

Independence
Lake

○ *12,851 ft*

Lost
Man
Res.

Linkins
Lake

P

**HUNTER-FRYINGPAN
WILDERNESS**

Continental Divide

82

Independence
Pass

Roaring Fork River

MILES

0   1   2

N

A sign which sends hikers left up toward Linkins Lake appears as the
trail reaches the Hunter-Fryingpan Wilderness boundary. The ascent ahead looks
almost perpendicular. Concentrate instead on the pretty combination at your
feet — royal blue **Rocky Mountain gentian**, yellow **blueleaf cinquefoil**, and
hot violet **Colorado tansy aster**. **Fireweed** waits in the wings. The trail is
flanked by mounds of long-blooming **golden aster** and **dwarf goldenrod**
nudging treeline-defying spruces.

A south-facing slope warms up early to accommodate **ballhead sandwort** and **bracted lousewort**. When you reach a flat spot, pause to enjoy a long, braided waterfall trimmed in yellow, pink, and white. The incline lessens on a sparsely vegetated ridge before crossing a bit of bright water and again resumes the upward trend in view of a golden sheet of **sawleaf senecio**. Willows protect yellow **mountain parsley** and **white geranium**.

Rocks lead to the next steep pitch. Growing almost prostrate from a woody rootstock, **Colorado tansy aster's** lustrous violet heads divert attention from the climb and shaggy-rayed **horned dandelions** and snowy **Coulter daisy** assist. Zigzagging, the trail passes outcrops encrusted with many-colored lichens, tough pioneers that are a combination of algae and fungus.

Stay left when a "social" trail veers off. Cross an inclined slope to arrive at a gentle segment to peruse the view back down the valley. Far below, the highway snakes up toward 12,095-foot Independence Pass on the Continental Divide. Over the pass to the southeast soars 14,361-foot La Plata Peak. To the south is 12,703-foot Independence Mountain. At its base, the ruins of the Independence townsite show evidence of bygone mining days. Far to the northeast, the tips of Deer Mountain at 13,761 feet and Mount Oklahoma at 13,845 feet are visible along the Continental Divide. Due east of Mount Oklahoma is Colorado's second highest summit, 14,421-foot Mount Massive, and just a few miles farther south, starring as the state's highest point, is 14,433-foot Mount Elbert. After visually "bagging" a plethora of peaks, glance back down at your feet to find two of the 20 Rocky Mountain

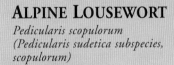

ALPINE LOUSEWORT
Pedicularis scopulorum
(Pedicularis sudetica subspecies, scopulorum)

When viewed from directly above, rich rose-pink alpine lousewort looks like a child's pinwheel. Shaped like a helmet (galea), the upper lip protrudes to protect two pairs of stamens and the pouting lower lip. These interesting blossoms are generally nestled in silvery wool of the terminal spike. The size and strength of the industrious bumblebee, necessary for pollination, suit the flower's structure. Rocky Mountain lousewort is another name. Quite common in arctic Alaska, alpine lousewort is alpine-specific in Colorado. Cousins include little pink elephants or elephantella *Pedicularis groenlandica* and sickletop lousewort *Pedicularis racemosa*.

gentian species: velvety **fringed gentian** and satiny **star gentian**, each with its own interpretation of purple.

Damper ground supports ankle-high willows, which in turn promote plush specimens of cool yellow **western paintbrush** and more spirited "**elephants.**" The terrain and habitat are conducive to the needs of bright pink **alpine louse-wort**. **Narcissus-flowered anemone** presents bouquets of creamy blossoms that develop into clusters of flat black seeds called achenes. Waving white wands over the showy anemones and curved-bracted **sulphur paintbrush** is **American bistort**.

A flattened area, enlivened by a meandering creeklet, is home to **Whipple** or **dusky penstemon**. Catch your breath here because the emerald waters of Linkins Lake in its breathtaking setting are just ahead. Arriving along its level shores in August, hikers are treated to **fringed gentians** everywhere.

To revisit spring, head left around to the south side of the scenic lake, crossing the outlet stream on stones. A trickle, cuing **tall chiming bells** and the whites of light-hearted **brook saxifrage** and peppery **bittercress**, joins the lake's sparkling waters. Pretty by sight if not by name, **alpine lousewort** gleams beside a stony-bedded inlet. Its cousin, **little pink elephants**, is here too. On this north-facing exposure, wildflowers of spring and early summer greet the hiker like remnants of a double rainbow. A wandering seep obscures the last vestiges of trail, making it a good turnaround point. Vibrant-pink **Parry primrose** and white **marsh marigold** revel in the emerald moss. Golden **alpine avens**, ivory **narcissus-flowered anemone**, and cobalt-tubed **greenleaf chiming bells** clothe the slope above. Where rough-textured rocks stud the verdant slope, white **black-headed daisy**, lilac **alpine violet**, and pink **pygmy bitterroot** audition for supporting roles.

Set in a peak-encircled bowl of rugged rock, Linkins Lake is an alpine gem. Add to that the colored jewels blooming around it, and this hike rates a standing ovation.

Hoosier Pass West

Wildflower Alert: In the latter half of July, narcissus anemone and six dozen other wildflower species grace this scenic hike.

This gentle trail halfway between Breckenridge and Fairplay leads to an old mine.

easy	*Trail Rating*
3.4 miles out and back	*Trail Length*
Breckenridge/Fairplay	*Location*
11,542 to 11,720 feet	*Elevation*
July to August	*Bloom Season*
mid- to late July	*Peak Bloom*
Go south from Breckenridge on Highway 9 to Hoosier Pass. Park on the west side of the road.	*Directions*

LOCATED MIDWAY between Breckenridge and Fairplay, Hoosier Pass straddles the Continental Divide at 11,542 feet above sea level. Around the time of the Civil War, prospectors from Indiana filed many claims in the vicinity of the pass—the west side in particular. This hike travels to one of these mines.

For wildflower aficionados, a number of uncommon species (early alpines in particular) may be found in the pass area. The latter half of June is the time for alpine forget-me-nots and alpine or fairy primrose. Hikers can expect to find about 75 species of flora on the mile-and-a-half-long route around the third week of July.

From the parking area, the trail follows a seriously eroded old road up through conifers and then turns north along a generally level road. At its end is little Crystal Lake and the old Crystal Mine. The parking area at the signed pass is huge.

MOUNTAIN CANDYTUFT

Noccaea montana (Thlaspi montanum)

Also called wild candy-tuft, this member of the mustard clan is one of the earliest spring bloomers. From the foothills to treelimit and above, its four-petaled white flowers are configured in the shape of a cross. Though blooming close to its leaf rosette at first, the flower stalk elongates with the season as the notch-tipped seedpods form. Widespread in the Rockies, mountain candytuft commemorates an eighteenth-century Italian botanist, Domenico Nocca. The species name *montana* explains the first half of its common name. Though related to familiar garden vegetables such as raddish and cauliflower as well as the domesticated border flower, mountain candytuft's wild cousins include western wallflower *Erysimum capitatum* and alpine or fernleaf candytuft *Smelowskia calycina*.

Striking out to the west where big spruces line the deeply rutted road, look for dusky **Whipple penstemon** and creamy **narcissus-flowered anemone**. The old conifers shelter bright **heartleaf arnica** and pale **delicate Jacob's ladder**. Perky **subalpine daisy's** rosy-lavender heads and the coiled ivory beaks of **Parry lousewort** appear intermittently. The entrenched furrows require an eye on your feet as well as the flowers, even when **scarlet paintbrush** kindles interest. In open spots, late summer calls to the deep-throated blue goblets of striking **Rocky Mountain** or **Parry gentian**.

A turn to the left introduces a willow-hung seep chiming in with ground-hugging pink **pygmy bitterroot** and **little pink**

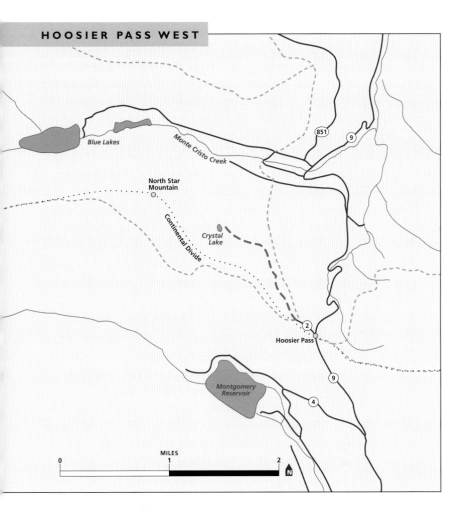

HOOSIER PASS WEST

Blue Lakes

Monte Cristo Creek

851

9

North Star
Mountain

Continental Divide

Crystal
Lake

2

Hoosier Pass

9

Montgomery
Reservoir

4

MILES
0   1   2

N

elephants. Hikers may even view a white "elephant," which is a mutant of the common coloration.

The trail makes its way up to a junctioned switchback. To the southwest are side by side "fourteeners," Mount Lincoln at 14,286 feet and Mount Bross at 14,172 feet. After taking in the vista, head north toward the old Crystal Mine and its attendant pond.

After turning right, the roadway ascends slowly. Where the spruce trees towered below, they now shrink to "flagged" *krummholz* size on the ridge above. Willows cloak the uphill slope, interspersed with the lovely **narcissus-flowered anemone.** Moist spots among road-flanking willows encourage pink-budded, blue-tubed **tall chiming bells** and **little pink elephants.** Rose family members, **alpine avens** and **blueleaf cinquefoil,** add yellow touches to sweet gardens.

Level now, the route travels past cutbanks scattered with **alpine blue violet**, **snowball saxifrage**, and **pygmy bitterroot**. Sometimes called **pygmy lewisia**, this succulent-leaved purslane family member keeps its rosy stars cozy. In the same vicinity, the mustard clan is represented by white **mountain candytuft**.

Quandary Peak's 14,265-foot summit peers around the corner to the northwest where a seep requires some choosy boot work to evade the resulting morass. Rosy **milkvetch** contrasts with somber **Gray's angelica** as the road itself starts sprouting **single-headed daisy**, **whiproot clover**, and **cinquefoil**. Speaking in tongues of high-country color, **subalpine larkspur**, **anemone**, **elephants**, and **chiming bells** are music to the eye.

A lingering snowbank feeds a tinkling creeklet where **chiming bells** chant with **western paintbrush** and **alpine avens**. An extensive seep where **mountain death camas**, **mountain parsley**, and **little pink elephants** sound a clarion call emerges along the trail. As the snowbank recedes, white **marsh marigold** and sunny **snow buttercup** are followed closely by **globeflower** and **mountain candytuft**.

Willows continue to march along as the roadway curves up gently. Bounteous **tall chiming bells** ring in rosy **Parry** and bi-colored **whiproot clover**. The Continental Divide ridge accompanying the trail on the west leads up to North Star Mountain, almost two thousand feet above your head. To the north are the colorful tailing piles of an old mine.

To keep vehicles at bay, earthen berms are slowly making themselves into mini gardens. A short distance up a spur to the left are graceful **blue columbine**, clear-yellow **alpine wallflower**, and rosy **Geyer onion**. The beaming broad face of **old man of the mountains** appears also. More alpine dwellers, such as **fernleaf** or **alpine candytuft**, **pinnate-leaved daisy**, **sky pilot**, and if your timing is right, the quiet **alplily** and fuchsia-pink **fairy primrose**, add their colorful blend.

Back along the willow-flanked main road where the berms decree foot traffic only, the wildflowers continue to pop up. Crossing the outlet of Crystal Lake leads to the site of the Crystal Mine.

Ringed by mountains of talus and scree with mine-pocked North Star Mountain marking the Continental Divide due west, little Crystal Lake reflects the long-gone dreams of hopeful prospectors and laboring miners. Above the mine tunnel, bristlecone pines watched that era come and go. (In Colorado, bristlecone pines may be well over a thousand years old.)

For a genial look into the beauties of high-country Colorado, try the trail to Crystal Mine and Crystal Lake from Hoosier Pass. The colorful subalpine and alpine flora on this hike will delight you.

Corona Lake

Wildflower Alert: Showy subalpine daisies dance along the trail on the way to this pretty alpine lake.

An easy-going trail that heads mostly downhill to serene Corona Lake.

easy	**Trail Rating**
2.0 miles out and back	**Trail Length**
Winter Park	**Location**
11,660 to 11,270 feet	**Elevation**
July through August	**Bloom Season**
mid- to late July	**Peak Bloom**
Take I-70 west to US 40 and to the Winter Park Ski Area. Turn right on Forest Road 149/Rollins Pass Road, which is half-way between mileposts 231 and 232. Proceed for 14 miles to the unmarked trailhead that is across from the pullout on the right overlooking Pumphouse Lake, 1.0 mile this side of Corona Pass parking area.	**Directions**

TUCKED IN A BOWL of talus-covered slopes, attractive Corona Lake is a short easy downhill hike. Along the way, alpine wildflowers bask in the generous light above treelimit. When Corona Lake Trail dips back into the subalpine zone, even more and different flowers appear.

From a start at 11,600 feet, the trail journeys down before rising a short distance to lake level at 11,206 feet. A few water hazards add pizzazz to the hike.

The historically risky Moffatt Hill railroad route makes it easy for today's driver to reach Rollins/Corona Pass on the Continental Divide. Graded to locomotive requirements, the 15-mile road, though bumpy in places, is accessible to passenger vehicles. One mile from the parking area on Rollins Pass, at approximately the 14-mile mark, a series of boulders and stakes on the west side of the road mark the start of Corona Lake Trail. Directly below is Pumphouse Lake, backed by Mount Epworth.

Parking is limited at the two pullouts across from the trailhead. On most summer afternoons, rolling thunderstorms move with amazing speed across the high country. Keep a weather eye peeled and act accordingly.

Wide open tundra greets the hiker immediately with **alpine avens'** brassy flowers and ferny leaves. Autumn turns the colonizing foliage wine red, accounting for much of the alpine zone's fall color. Cutbanks at the pullout harbor snowdrifts that melt late in the season. This is a good place to find spring still in bloom with flowers such as rosy **Parry clover** and tiny but pert **golden draba**.

Across the dirt road, granite boulders block all but foot travel. When the main road is clear of snow, early season hikers catch tundra habitués, such as **moss campion** and **one-headed daisy**. Even in late summer, those two may linger in sheltered spots. Dense-matted **alpine sandwort** is one of the last of the alpine buns, mats, and cushions to quit blooming.

Growing a little taller along the descending route are pale **western paintbrush** and **old man of the mountains,** with its yellow head almost as wide as the plant is high. Another name is **alpine sunflower.**

The trail veers left, leaving the one-time road to head down a single trail toward Pumphouse Lake. Descending more quickly through cool-rose pools of showy **subalpine daisies,** the trail meets the first of treelimit spruce trees. A few steps puts **sky pilot** on either hand. Harbored by granite chunks and tufts of tundra grasses by a lone spruce, this early bloomer shows off orange-gold stamens popping from purple-blue trumpets. This plant has arresting inflorescences, but beware the foliage's skunky aroma.

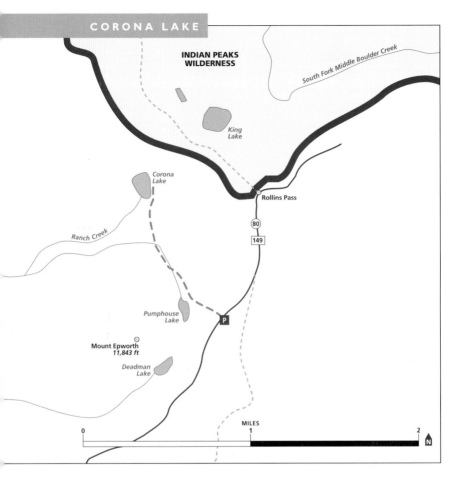

Continue curving down above Pumphouse Lake towards its bubbly outlet. The outlet stream emerges from willows where both **king's** and **queen's crown**, the former in burnt red and the latter in warm pink, enjoy varying degrees of moisture according to their needs, the queen being the thirstier of the two. **Little pink elephants, marsh marigold,** and **Parry primrose** also thrive here. Crossing the clear stream is not difficult as the trail follows on the far side, but it soon becomes apparent that the trail itself is the stream bed. After this water-covered stair-step section, the creek must again be crossed to resume the trail. Haphazard stepping stones are the answer. On the other side, look among the willows for **delicate Jacob's ladder** and **purple fringe. Little pink elephants** and **star gentian** point the way to drier ground. **Rosy paintbrush** increases in number as well as in shades from shell pink to vivid cerise.

Contrasting with a swath of hot-red **scarlet paintbrush**, a marshy seep area brings on **caltha-flowered buttercup**, the whites of breezy **brook saxifrage,** and peppery **bittercress**. The leaves of bittercress (sometimes called brookcress) can be a tasty addition to a backcountry salad. Their "bite" is similar to that of its cousin, watercress. **Tall chiming bells** point up to the right where "flagged" spruces shelter little rock gardens. Pink, red, and yellow dominate the palette along the lower side of the trail with **paintbrushes** and **arrowleaf senecio**— the latter in great patches.

Tumbled rockfalls usher in **bistort**, **Parry clover**, **greenleaf chiming bells**, and beautiful **blue columbine**. These lichen-encrusted boulder slopes are headquarters for the penetrating vocalizations of the pipsqueak pika. This busy charmer may take a moment from his "haying" operations to see who's invading his territory.

While trying to spot the ventriloquist pika, a member of the order of rabbits and hares, the eye may pick out the bent heads of **woolly** or **frosty ball thistle**. **Shrubby cinquefoil** scatters gold coins farther up the slope.

Down to the left, a seep area of **pink willow-herb** and **alpine speedwell** asks that the small wildflowers be noticed too. The ensuing mud requires agility, but inducts **woolly** or **subalpine arnica** into the ongoing floral procession. Studded with angular rock, the trail passes lush-leaved mounds of **rock senecio**. To the left, a willow bog supports **bog saxifrage**; its dingy white heads are more noticeable when they age to a reddish tone.

Back on the right, a boulder-strewn swale is a bright wildflower treasure box jampacked with red **paintbrush**, rosy-lavender **subalpine daisy**, and **golden arnica**. Big spruces,

SKY PILOT
Polemonium viscosum

This flower exhibits lush heads of lavender-blue trumpets with fluorescent gold stamens—bees sometimes sport neon legs from repeated visits. Though the blossoms themselves are reportedly pleasantly scented, it is the sticky foliage that gives this member of the phlox family its stinky reputation. A crushed leaf is said to smell like skunk. A favored habitat of open-sky-loving sky pilot is the churned-up soil of subalpine and alpine gopher gardens. Talus areas rate high, too. Occasionally a white flowered mutant will show up. Also called sticky Jacob's ladder, the species epithet *viscosum* refers to its tacky leaves. Cousin delicate or subalpine Jacob's ladder *Polemonium pulcherrimum* subspecies *delicatum* likes the shelter of conifers.

with pale blue **delicate Jacob's ladder** and white **sickletop lousewort** at their feet, tone down the landscape as the trail rises.

At the top of this stony segment, take a moment to turn around and look south over conifers and willow to 11,843-foot Mount Epworth covered in blisters of stone and tundra. If you continue hiking north past a flower-bedecked hillside (worthy of a Monet canvas), you'll reach the lip of beautiful Corona Lake.

Like an uncut emerald placed in an old-fashioned setting, the lake reposes in a circle of slopes rising 400 feet above the water. Heading right, you'll find the perfect place for high-country contemplation: a multitude of granite chunks right on the shore. Among them, lovely **blue columbine** urges hikers to relax. Late summer incites a riot of magenta **fireweed**, and August's waning days present **arctic gentian**. Look at the grass carpeting the spaces between the lakeside boulders, and you'll find subtle **white gentian**, purple-streaked on the outside. Last-to-bloom **arctic gentian** tells a sad tale of summer's end—snow is only six weeks away.

Delightful Corona Lake offers a far-away feeling, but it is surprisingly easy to get to. About a mile of casual hiking through tundra and subalpine wildflowers—at least five dozen species—delivers you to the shores of a classic alpine lake. The drive up the old railroad grade includes a big timber trestle and a top-'o-the-world feeling with vast tundra and vistas near the top. This is a fine hike for those just discovering the wonderful high country. Those who hike long trails but want a quick jaunt to remind them of the treelimit glories of a Colorado summer might want to give Corona Lake a try.

Wildflower Hike
48

Monte Cristo Gulch

Wildflower Alert: Climb through wildflowers to a hanging valley fortified by mining relics.

Although somewhat arduous, this trail leads to remnants of stone mining structures from the late 1800s—but today's Monte Cristo gold is in petals and pollen.

Trail Rating	strenuous, but short
Trail Length	2.5 miles out and back
Location	Breckenridge
Elevation	11,700 to 12,300 feet
Bloom Season	July through August
Peak Bloom	Late July to early August
Directions	Go south for 7.9 miles on State Road 9. Turn right onto Blue Lakes Road 850 to the sign that reads: Blue Lakes 2 miles. At the road's end, park at the north edge of the dam.

'MONTE CRISTO' has a ring of riches to it, which is why hopeful miners were prospecting the hanging valley at the head of Monte Cristo Gulch. Far above treelimit, the obvious building material was rock. Ruined stone structures of the late 1800s languish in the unforgiving elements that patiently reclaim the efforts of man, but riches did come to the hopeful when gold was found here in 1860. Today's Monte Cristo gold is in petals and pollen.

Mother Nature regales humankind with large and small doses of beauty. Monte Cristo has both. The sweeping landscape of the hike encompasses wide skies, high peaks, and clear waters. The intimate beauty is one of color, shape, texture, and intriguing design.

The beginning of this hike is the most difficult. Even the starting cairn, which is the second one from the dam, is not easy to find. The trail generally ascends strongly with intermittent level sections. There are also a number of water hazards, but none are insurmountable. This trail is a lovely adventure inspired by wildflowers all the way.

Like marauding renegades, great heaps of thunderheads can surprise unwary hikers with their speed. Being above treeline calls for increased wariness.

A huge parking area accommodates all—quite possibly including a couple of smiling marmots draped over nearby boulders.

On the northwest periphery of the parking area, the wildflowers begin their appeal with **bistort, cinquefoil, king's crown, harebell, star gentian,** and **stonecrop.** Over twenty species ask to be noted.

Work your way right, up the dam's rock face next to granite bedrock to the top. From there, a well-trod trail traverses shaly stone punctuated with robust clumps of **black-tipped senecio.** Jumbled rock invests in **blue columbine, whiproot clover, purple fringe,** and buns of **moss campion.**

With the depths of Blue Lake on the south, the 14,265-foot height of Quandary Peak rises to the north. Soaring about half a vertical mile above your head, this fourteener ranks 13th among Colorado's 54 fourteeners.

Look for a rock cairn appearing on the right about a hundred yards west from the paved dam top. Continue on about 50 feet past the first cairn to a second. Turn up here to the north to access Monte Cristo Gulch Trail. Finding the starting point is worth the effort, and once found, the trail stays obvious for most of its adventurous length.

Clamber up to a moist swale harboring **marsh marigold** and **Parry primrose.** A small rockfall cues hikers to watch for the succulent rosettes and pink-lined white stars of **alpine** or **bigroot spring beauty. Blue columbine, whiproot clover, purple fringe,** and buns of **moss campion** share the domain. In the tundra vegetation, a keen eye may spot tiny **compass** or **moss gentian;** its up-facing blue flowers close on cloudy days or even from the shadow of a patient hand.

After the initial steep pitch, the trail contours with the terrain for a stretch before ascending again. Waterproof boots are beneficial as the trail merges with a bouncy little creek leading up to bedrock and stunted spruce. Already big Blue Lake is receding below. At your feet, soil-binding buns, mats, and cushions greet early season hikers. The delight of cascading waters is repeated in the flow of **narcissus-flowered anemones** as the trail passes them. Nearby, **bistort** and both **rosy** and cool yellow **western paintbrush** wave in the winds of summer.

Willow and square-needled spruces close in as the trail approaches a cascade to be crossed. Golden **shrubby cinquefoil** and burnt-red **king's crown** vie for attention with **tall chiming bells** and **little pink elephants**. Pushing through the encroaching willows is like a jungle experience at 12,000 feet. Huffing and puffing can be expected here as there is one-third less oxygen than at sea level.

PURPLE FRINGE
Phacelia sericea

Crowded with purple funnels spewing a mouthful of pistils and yellow-tipped purple stamens, purple fringe's spike-like racemes are memorable. Covered with fine fuzzy hairs, the plant earns its species name *sericea* meaning "silky"—which, in turn, brings on the common name silky phacelia. Despite the hairs, elk eat purple fringe in spring and bumblebees crave the flowers' zesty nectar. Not pleasant smelling, this member of the waterleaf family finds gravelly soil, especially if it is disturbed, to their liking. One of about 100 phacelias in North America, perennial purple fringe generally grows in the subalpine and alpine zones. A cousin is silverleaf scorpion weed *Phacelia hastata*.

Along a leveling segment, **whiproot clover** knits the mineral soil where jagged 13,950-foot Fletcher Mountain summits northwest while 13,694-foot Wheeler Mountain peaks southwest.

Crossing a talus slope, watch for low, woody, light violet-blue **Harbour alpine penstemon**. Partial to great heights and loose scree, this creeping penstemon's tubes are downy, and its thick matte leaves a gray-green. Sweep the slope for **frosty ball** or **woolly thistle** and at the same time, you may discover plump, golden-brown marmots.

Lichen encrusts the angular stone of the rockfall, softened by aristocratic clumps of **blue columbine**. Take a moment to enjoy Monte Cristo Creek flowing into Blue Lake from the west end of the vale below. Then listen to the inlet beside you as it bursts into watersong from under a lingering snowbank.

On the far side of the tumbled rocks, the crystalline creek joins company with the trail. Handy willows

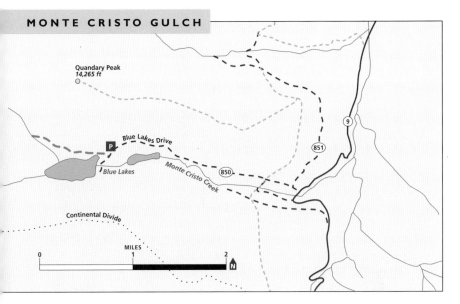

MONTE CRISTO GULCH

help pull hikers up along the watery trail. Crossing the stream above treelimit, the trail enters a tundra realm. While **whiproot clover** forms stabilizing mats up here, it is the unique **one-flowered** or **alpine harebell** that captivates the wildflower enthusiasts. Tucked into the tufted grasses and sedges, the little crepe-paper purple corollas are shaped like coronets sounding notes in an alpine band.

Farther on, mats of white-funneled **alpine sandwort** patiently cover bare soil with dark foliage so dense that it feels solid to the touch. Gold comes in the form of **alpine avens**. Stark beauty beckons—look up to the gilded rawness of Quandary Peak's south flank. Wild and watchful from its rugged heights, the mountain peers down on the insignificant efforts of humankind. Even though miners borrowed stone from the mountain, their buildings are already in ruins. Having extracted the gold, miners left their stone structures to fall into the relics seen today in Monte Cristo Gulch.

The intimate basin is hemmed in by rock on all sides. The basin floor is grassy right up to the lithic skirts of Quandary Peak where **rock senecio, alpine sorrel**, and **purple fringe** swish along its granite hem. Beside the crumbling building, the burbling brook's grassy marshes call to the wildflower lover to note **bittercress, alpine paintbrush, Parry lousewort**, and **Parry primrose**. **Greenleaf chiming bells** and **star gentian** turn up, courting attention as do both **king's** and **queen's crown**.

For a hike that is anything but ordinary, not to mention short, Monte Cristo Gulch is a great choice. Wildflowers abound along a trail that lifts you into the extraordinary.

Wildflower Hike
49

Dauntless Mine Loop

Wildflower Alert: This trail features an alpine rill high above treelimit, flanked by a flower baron's wealth of concentrated color.

A relatively short hike featuring a tumbling brook, an old mining road, and a treasure trove of wildflower color.

Trail Rating	moderate because of elevation, but short
Trail Length	1.4 mile key-hole loop
Location	Fairplay
Elevation	11,840 to 12,200 feet
Bloom Season	July through August
Peak Bloom	mid-August
Directions	Take US 285 south of Fairplay 1.5 miles. Turn right onto Fourmile Creek Road (County Road 18) for 1.2 miles. Stay to the left and go approximately 10.8 miles. Park on the right before arriving near the steep, rough section and the metal gate. Parking is about 12 miles from US 285.

FULL OF HISTORY AND DREAMS OF WEALTH, the Dauntless Mine area today claims one of the region's most concentrated theaters of wealth: wildflowers. The ore of yesteryear's silver barons is long gone.

Tucked into a couple of short but flowery ravines, run-off waters nurture some six dozen species of wildflowers—a concentrated alpine flower-scape without parallel in the region. A path has been blazed by those seeking the best of the floral displays. Changes in blooming sequence may be apparent in successive visits made just two weeks apart, with 60 species during the last of July and 80 species by mid-August.

Park at a wide cobbled area on the right, well before a swinging metal gate. The next rocky incline of the mining road is extremely rough.

From the parking area, Mount Sherman's summit is 14,306 feet to the northwest, while 13,748-foot Mount Sheridan and its long ridge rises west. The ridge's highly visible Hilltop Mine structures once boasted nearly two miles of cable transporting silver ore to the Leavick Mill (passed on the right back down the road). To the southwest, aptly named Horseshoe Mountain curves around a world-class glacial cirque, once an encircling womb of moving ice.

Fireweed and **angelica** stand at attention by the carpark. Follow the right side of the ascending road to a willow-sheltered creeklet assembling **bittercress**, **arrowleaf senecio**, and both **western** and **scarlet paintbrush**. Draining through rugged limestone on the north, a rill entertains **alpine golden aster**, **redstem cinquefoil**, and **alpine yarrow**. Nearby, **purpleleaf senecio** and **whiproot clover** guard ground-hugging, limestone-loving **Leadville milkvetch**, a rare endemic of the region.

While wildflowers are rooted to the spot, watch for the quick-moving pika in the big rockpile up from the roadway. With rabbits and hares in his ancient lineage, the busy little pika possesses a voice bigger than he is. Sharing the lithic tumble is **old man of the mountains** and **shrubby cinquefoil**. Additional willows introduce a talkative cascade lined with **paintbrush**. Close by in late summer, **Colorado tansy aster** spreads low foliage to frame its radiant violet, daisy-like flowers. Though not exactly common, the hiker cannot miss this aster; showy is the word. Also popping up are fringed-throated stars of **little rose gentian**.

A culvert cues the appearance of **yellow monkeyflower** and sends hikers to the right of a rivulet on an ascending path through willows. It must be tough being a gopher in the stony soil here, but the trail is flanked with gopher gardens displaying pale **western paintbrush** and striking **Hall's**

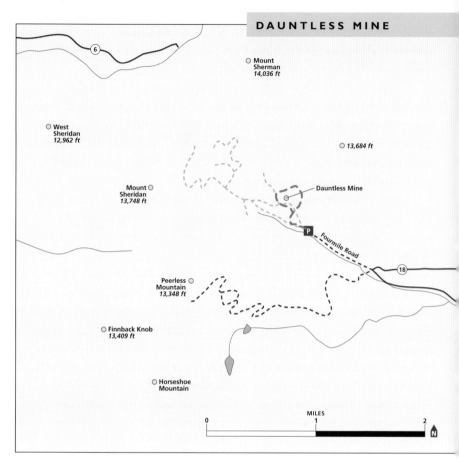

penstemon. The glowing violet-rose, blue-tinged tubes of this paintbrush relation are big in comparison to the overall size of the plant. Up a bit, a clear waterway is glimpsed through **queen's crown, bistort, scarlet paintbrush,** and **tall chiming bells.** About midway up the slope is a prismatic meadow brimming with wildflowers clear up to a jumble of rocks. Mosses accent vivid **Parry primrose, arrowleaf senecio, marsh marigold, little pink elephants,** and more **monkeyflower** among a battalion of others.

Head right toward the base of a hill to meet a partial trail through rocks. Look for the pink-veined stars of rosetted **bigroot** or **alpine spring beauty** and more of that eye-catching **Hall's penstemon.** Also at home here are **alpine avens, whiproot clover,** and **purpleleaf senecio,** an endemic often known as **alpine groundsel.**

As you climb up the right edge of the rockfall, your carefully chosen footfalls will likely sound metallic on the limestone. Mount Sherman rears it hoary head above the draw where **snowball saxifrage** stands erect above its leathery-leaved rosette. With a root that is likely as long as hikers are tall, the succulent, often red-margined leaves of **bigroot spring beauty** protect porcelain-looking flowers. The white and yellow theme of **bistort, mouse-ear, avens,** and **cinquefoil** is repeated in the rocks underfoot.

Up here, at over 12,000 feet, breath is as short as the sky is high. Take time to pause, appreciating the compact window of growth. Both spring and summer-blooming flowers emerge, bloom, lure pollinators, set seed, and disperse it according to nature's plan—all in a few brief weeks.

A brief pitch tops out on a flat, where **greenleaf chiming bells** dangle matte-blue tubes and **sky pilot** lifts full heads of purple-blue trumpets, each bearing neon gold stamens. Well-watered, this level willowy area guides the hiker through a beguiling alpine garden of many colors. Light purple **subalpine aster** lifts its orange-centered head a foot above **black-headed daisy.**

For all practical purposes the trail disappears about here, signaling a crossing of the drainage just below the willows to the west. The hillside is pigmented by the plump heads of **Parry clover, Parry primrose, senecios, greenleaf chiming bells, mountain candytuft,** and **alpine pussytoes.** Traversing the left side of the intimate draw reveals **monkeyflower** and, in churned-up gopher gardens, **Whipple penstemon, burnt orange dandelion, pinnate-leaved daisy,** and **single-headed daisy.** The last two are lavender-purple fleabanes.

Rusting cables tell of miners' efforts to move extracted minerals, in this case, silver, from the tram tower of the Hilltop and Dauntless Mines to the Leavick Mill. In the distance, tiny figures trudge up Mount Sherman's south flank.

HALL'S PENSTEMON
Penstemon hallii

Favoring places near the Continental Divide, often in the rocky ground of the alpine zone, short but stunning Hall's penstemon shows well. Several luminescent corolla tubes, tinged warm violet to purple blue, congregate loosely on sturdy stems. Marked with white in their inflated throats, the two-lipped sticky flowers bloom in mid summer. Soil stabilizing Hall's penstemon is one of about 60 species in Colorado. Taller cousins include Rocky Mountain penstemon *Penstemon strictus* and mountain or alpine penstemon *Penstemon glaber.* Elihu Hall, a Civil-War-era plant collector and botanist from Illinois, botanized in South Park in 1862.

Note that from here you can choose to climb the taxing slope to the tram tower and even farther to a little lake confined in a steep-sided dip to the north, but this description does not include it.

At this point, make your way southwest, cresting a ridge overlooking a curvy drainage, and follow the ridge down to where the parking area is in sight.

About halfway down the ridge crest, head into a grassy glen lined with **black-headed daisy**, **mountain candytuft**, **purple fringe**, and sweet-smelling **Parry clover**. Tundra dwellers **moss campion** and **alpine sandwort** may be blooming in the vicinity. At its end, turn north to access a barren drainage. Descending it welcomes hikers to a concentrated Garden of Eden where a crystalline waterway issues from deep beneath the talus. Water changes the character from rockscape to flowerscape. Late-melting snowbanks allow **snow buttercup**, **greenleaf chiming bells**, **pygmy bitterroot**, **snowball saxifrage**, **Gray's angelica**, and **little pink elephants** to bloom—to name a few. **Yellow monkeyflower** all but smothers the flanks of the tinkling brook. Flirting with the water are **queen's crown**, **tall chiming bells**, **bistort**, and delicate **pink willowherb**.

As you step down beside a golden staircase of clear water, notice how the gravelly south bank is dotted with myriad **purpleleaf senecio** or **alpine groundsel**. Each free-spirited yellow head complements the maroonish leaves. The scree offers the possibility of more sprightly **Hall's penstemon**. As the delightful rill prepares to meet the road, turn to take in the majesty of colorful surround-sight mountains.

Monumental peaks, classic cirques, wide-eyed skies, historic relics, and wonderful wildflowers make the Dauntless Mine Loop jaunt a memorable one.

Loveland Pass, West Ridge

Wildflower Alert: Wildflower gems of the tundra
begin from the first step at the Continental Divide
to a far-horizon view.

*An hour's drive from Denver, this hike is a
delightful adventure in the tundra.*

moderate (due to elevation)	*Trail Rating*
2.6 miles out and back	*Trail Length*
Loveland Pass/Keystone	*Location*
11,990 to 12,479 feet	*Elevation*
late June to August	*Bloom Season*
early to late July	*Peak Bloom*
From Denver take I-70 west. Go south on US 6 to Loveland Pass. Park on the east side of the pass.	*Directions*

ONE OF THE MOST DIRECT ACCESSES to alpine wildflower viewing is just an hour from Denver. Sitting astride the Continental Divide, Loveland Pass reaches 11,990 feet into the Colorado sky. This is the land of tundra, of high country above treelimit, and a place of wide skies where snow leaves late and returns early. During this short time, this land of tundra emerges, blooms, and sets seed—all in great beauty.

While most visitors head up the well-worn east trail toward 13,234-foot Mount Sniktau, a lesser-used trail begins across the highway. This one follows the west ridge of the pass, a good portion of it along the spine of the Continental Divide. While much of the west "bowl" can be snowbound well into summer, the exposed ridge itself may be snow-free reasonably early. Whether the alpine wildflower seeker aims for early tundra flowers or waits until later in the bloom season for different species, the alpine floristics are amazing. July's first week count may be about 40, and during July's third week, the count may be as high as 60.

Hikers along the Loveland Pass West Ridge Trail ascend through rainbows of color along a rocky trail and then traverse a lusher slope up to a saddle with splendid views. An easygoing segment continues out to another wonderful vista point. There, circles of stone have been erected for protection from the cold wind that sometimes sweeps the Continental Divide.

The unpredictable elements of tundra exploration can be surprising. Go prepared for cold, wind, sudden afternoon thunderstorms, and sometimes snow. Be prepared for great beauty as well.

Plenty of parking is available on the east side of US Highway 6.

A gravelled pathway leads past a sign conveying the importance of staying on established trails to protect the fragile and slow-to-heal tundra. Right away exhilaration sets in.

A stone-walled overlook gives visitors a clear view of the west bowl, Loveland Ski Basin, and Interstate 70 traffic whizzing through the Eisenhower Tunnel. West Ridge Trail hikers should continue past the wall in a southerly direction.

Yellow comes in many shades and shapes here, starting with **paintbrush**, **rock senecio**, **stonecrop**, and **alpine avens**. Like many in the rose family, brassy yellow alpine avens have five petals. Color is this flower's forte even when its flowers are gone. Fall-tinted foliage turns extensive avens patches into giant spills of wine red. The biggest bloom on the tundra is **old man of the mountains** or **alpine sunflower**. With its fuzzy back to the prevailing winds, this species gathers energy for years to put forth a head that can be four inches across—the grand finale.

Passing a gap revealing the south side of the pass, the trail lifts on chunks of angular rock embedded in the path. Clinging to their sheltering edges are tight mats of **alpine sandwort**, also called **sandywinks**, and **dwarf** or **deer clover**; its pinkish blossoms are shaped like the tiny hoofprint of a fawn. Slightly looser mats of bi-colored **whiproot clover** nestle by their stone mentors.

At such a popular stop as Loveland Pass, it is not surprising that many "social" trails have been worn into the earth. Stay on the apex of the ridge through an ascending rock garden of buns, mats, and cushions, some of which are early blooming **moss campion**, fragrant **alpine forget-me-not**, and **alpine phlox**.

Spruce *krummholz* (German for "crooked wood") mitigates the harsh elements for **purple fringe** and **rock senecio** to attain a longer bloom time. Knee-high willows lead the path into an area where expanding colonies of **mountain dryad** or **white mountain-avens**

stabilize the gravelly soil. A member of the rose family like cousin alpine avens, this creamy wildflower typically sports about eight petals instead of the usual five. The distinctive seedheads twist into glistening plumes.

Collections of common **mouse-ear** and **alpine mouse-ear**, both starry white, precede a steeper climb. The trail rises on a rocky footbed to show hikers the important role that matting vegetation plays in holding this complex habitat together. Soil-gathering cushions, taprooted buns, and expanding mats such as **whiproot clover** weave a stronghold, both above and below ground.

Where the route eases a bit, low willows protect burnt-red **king's crown**. Gaining footholds between tufts of thick grass, saturated cobalt **greenleaf chiming bells**, rosy, round-headed **Parry clover**, and sunny **alpine avens** combine in a pleasing medley.

MOUNTAIN DRYAD
Dryas octopetala subspecies hookeriana

The Latin genus name *Dryas* comes from Greek mythology. A dryad was a wood nymph. Though at first it is not apparent, mountain dryad is a woody sub-shrub, rooting as its prostrate stems touch the soil. Other common names are white mountain avens and alpine rose. The showy creamy-white flowers generally have 8 petals, which is what the Latin species name *octopetala* means. Feathery seed plumes keep mountain dryad showy as they await dispersal by the obliging wind. Its veined and scalloped lance-shaped leaves are evergreen. Ptarmigan, those feathered alpine masters of seasonal disguise, relish them.

Favoring dry, limestone-infused tundra around the world in arctic and alpine regions, mountain dryad not only stabilizes the soil, but, just as importantly, serves as a nitrogen fixer. Cousin alpine avens *acomastylis rossii subspecies turbinata* is prolific in the high country.

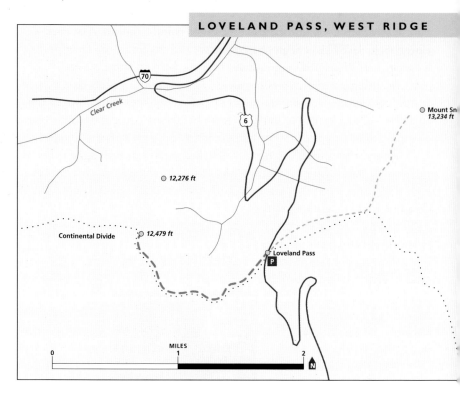

Resuming its ascent along the ridge's backbone, the trail is flanked by sheets of scalloped-leafed **mountain dryad**. Like alpine avens, it too will take on warm hues in autumn. A breather comes as the trail becomes level where pikas perform their ventriloquist illusion. Their busy little bodies can be seen dashing about in their rocky homes.

At a break in the ridge, the view expands to full circle. As you continue along, hummocky grasses become more prevalent when the trail begins descending. Sharing the locale is white **Fendler sandwort**, with leaves that look like stiff grass. This flower is found from the foothills to the fourteeners. **Alpine sandwort**, mainly a tundra resident, hugs its white blossoms close to mats so dense they feel hard.

At the base of a rockfall, look for bright pink **moss campion**. A hand-span-wide cushion of this member of the pink family may be a century old. Its long tap root and aerodynamic shape help make it a pioneer plant on the tundra. Along this eased grade, keep a sharp eye out for the solitary blooms of **alpine** or **single harebell**, with its small purple-blue trumpets facing out. Here too is more soil-binding **mountain dryad**, which is at home in rock crevices and on open ground.

Passing momentarily between sheltering banks, the trail starts dropping toward a herd of **little pink elephants**, which are quite short at this elevation and are gathered in a moist spot. Not far away, **paintbrush** and **alpine avens** are showy in yellow. Not showy by nature but still interesting is **snowlover**. Growing where snowdrifts accumulate, the brown-edged ivory flowers of this penstemon relation emerge on one side of the short sturdy stalk. Another lover of this snowbank habitat is lacquer-yellow **snow buttercup**. On the left, a bib of spring flowers decorates a swale, indicating more late-lying snow. Here **bigroot** or **alpine spring beauty, mountain candytuft, snowball saxifrage**, and **greenleaf chiming bells** are accented with bits of **marsh marigold**. Spring, revisited here, also presents **blueleaf cinquefoil** and **Parry primrose**.

The trail rises to a substantial rock cairn at 12,414 feet, pointing the view west to distant Mount of the Holy Cross. Quandary Peak anchors the south end of the Tenmile Range, home to Breckenridge Ski area. Keystone's carved slopes dominate the foreground.

The trail turns north now to follow the Divide. Shining knight of the wind-lashed tundra, **mountain dryad** armors the gravelly soil with its leathery, dark leaves, large creamy flowers, and invaluable creeping woody stems.

Continue to another pocket bowl, this one replete with woolly-chinned **black-headed daisies**. Ahead, Pettingill Peak at 13,553 feet and Hagar Mountain at 13,195 feet form part of the Continental Divide.

Follow the cairns and you'll pass tundra dwellers such as **old man of the mountains, moss campion** and stubby, but beautiful **blue columbine**, whose blossoms tend toward washed pastels at this elevation. The way is level until an initial pitch brings it up to a spa-sized ring of rocks. Surrounding it are **bistort, snowlover**, and **Parry clover**. Another pitch takes hikers up to a 360-degree panorama. A change arrives with a drop that evens out coming into a patch of spruce *krummholz* and willow. Hot-yellow **alpine sulphurflower**, its gray-green leaves and bright flowerheads not more than a couple of inches high, forms a wide patch on the right.

The exposed ridge is often windy, but this doesn't deter electric blue cushions of **alpine forget-me-not** nor star-struck **alpine phlox**; they just keep wafting their wonderful perfume.

Trail-flanking, knee-high willows signal the last climb, this one reaching the goal. The best way appears to be around to the left. Tackle it by picking your way up through jumbled rock on an almost nonexistent trail. On top, the view overlooks Loveland Ski Basin—which you can enjoy from a stone wind shelter. Lovely **sky pilot** welcomes you. The high point of the hike is here at 12,479 feet above sea level.

The tundra character of Loveland Pass and the hike along its ridge to the west offer a convenient window on the world of flowering gems and their ability to survive. Awesome vistas of any number of proud Colorado peaks make this hike a special one.

Index

NOTE: Citations followed by the letter "p" denote photos, citations followed by bold page numbers denote maps.

Pamela Dearborn Irwin and David Harlan Irwin

Pamela has been a volunteer naturalist at Roxborough State Park southwest of Denver since the early 1980s and was introduced to wildflower identification as a volunteer at the Denver Botanic Alpine Gardens. She has participated in many wildflower identification hikes from the plains to the tundra with such experts as Andrew Pierce, formerly senior horticulture advisor at the Denver Botanic Gardens and now executive director of the Hudson Gardens.

Pamela is a member of the Rocky Mountain Nature Association, the Rocky Mountain Chapter of the American Rock Garden Society, the Windflowers Garden Club, the Colorado Mountain Club, and the Audubon Society.

David purchased his first 35mm SLR camera as a teenager and has been behind a lens ever since. His favorite subjects are people of foreign lands, the remnants of past civilizations, and the textures of western terrain.

The two maintain an extensive slide library and have given slide-illustrated talks for various organizations. Additionally, many of David's photographs and Pamela's watercolors are now in private collections.

The Irwins' first best-selling volume, *Colorado's Best Wildflower Hikes: The Front Range,* is available through Westcliffe Publishers.